A New History of Cromwell's Irish Campaign

[with maps, plans, and illustrations]

Philip G. McKeiver M.A. Hons.

ADVANCE
PRESS

ISBN 978-0-9554663-0-4

Printed and bound in Great Britain by
William Clowes Ltd., Beccles, Suffolk

First published in the UK in 2007 by

Advance Press
Suite 191, 792 Wilmslow Road, Didsbury, Manchester, M20 6UG

For my parents, Edward and Marie McKeiver,
and my grandmother, Dorothy Jones

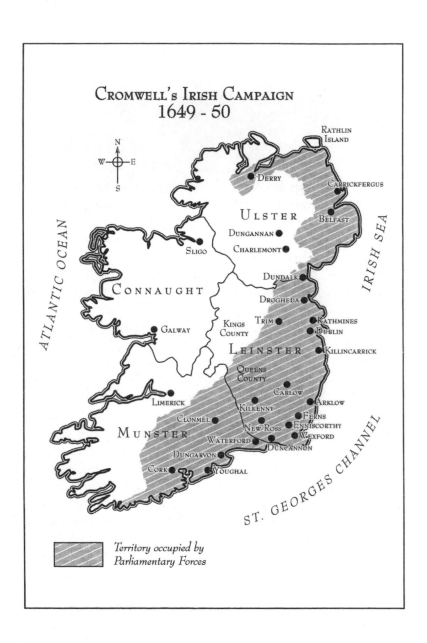

CROMWELL'S IRISH CAMPAIGN
1649 - 50

RATHLIN ISLAND

ATLANTIC OCEAN

DERRY

CARRICKFERGUS

ULSTER

BELFAST

IRISH SEA

DUNGANNON

SLIGO

CHARLEMONT

DUNDALK

CONNAUGHT

DROGHEDA

TRIM

RATHMINES

GALWAY

KINGS COUNTY

DUBLIN

LEINSTER

KILLINCARRICK

QUEENS COUNTY

CARLOW

ARKLOW

LIMERICK

KILKENNY

FERNS

CLONMEL

ENNISCORTHY

MUNSTER

NEW ROSS

WEXFORD

WATERFORD

DUNCANNON

DUNGARVON

CORK

YOUGHAL

ST. GEORGES CHANNEL

Territory occupied by
Parliamentary Forces

Preface

The purpose of this Book, is to show through an analysis of the relevant historiography, that the major myths, associated, with Cromwell and Ireland, are not necessarily the most plausible, or reasonable, explanation of the events they purport to explain. Created as propaganda, and given mythic status, by constant re-assertion as popular opinion, such myths have muddied the historical picture. 'In demythologising Cromwell, it is hoped that a more accurate historical picture will be discovered.'

As Peter Gaunt, Chairman of the Cromwell Association, emphasised in his book *Oliver Cromwell* (1996), 'From his own lifetime to the present day, Cromwell's standing and reputation have always aroused great passions; and provoked heated debate. Even people, whose interest in history is minimal, seem to have strong opinions about him.' Nevertheless, this book is a serious attempt to deal with a very controversial historical topic.

Although this Book is essentially, a historiographical study, and solidly based on the historiographical evidence, I have used relevant primary sources and have preferred Thomas Carlyle's collection, *Oliver Cromwell's Letters and Speeches with Elucidations* (second revised edition), (3 Vols. in One), London, 1846, to the collection compiled by W.C. Abbott, the weakness of which I detail in the text. I have also presented, many of the primary documents, relating to the Irish Civil War, which have been reprinted in J.T. Gilbert (ed.), *A Contemporary History of Affairs in Ireland (1641-52), containing the narrative, entitled, 'An Amphorismal discovery of a treasonable faction,'* 3 vols., Irish Archaeological Society, Dublin, (1879-80.)

7

Acknowledgements

This Book would not have been possible without the support of my supervisors, Associate Professors Geoff Quaife and David Kent, at the University of New England, New South Wales. In particular I am grateful for their advice, criticism, and encouragement, which was, at all times, most necessary. My thanks also to the staff of the University of Manchester, Trinity College, Dublin; and my own library at the University of New England, who have responded to my requests with great efficiency. I am especially grateful to my good friends, Professor Patrick Gallagher, and Anthony Goulding, B.Sc (Econ.), University College, Cardiff, for their advice and input, especially in the final planning stages of this book. My thanks also to Dr Peter Gaunt, University College, Chester, for reading one of my early drafts and for making numerous, helpful suggestions. I am also grateful to Alyson Belski of RAH Advertising Ltd for the valuable assistance with maps and plans, and, finally, to Roger Wickham of Amherst Publishing for the overall pre-press production of this book.

As far as possible, modern spelling has been used throughout, although printed primary documents appear in their original form.

Contents

List of Maps

List of Illustrations

Chronology of Events and Major Military Encounters in Ireland 1639-1653[1]

1639 Proclamation of the 'Black Oath.'

June   First Bishop's War ended by Treaty of Berwick, 18 June.

1640

April 13 Short Parliament in England dissolved on 5th May.

July.   Wentworth's 'New Irish Army' assembles at Carrickfergus.

Aug.   Scottish army crosses the Tweed. Beginning of Second Bishop's War ended by Treaty of Ripon, 21 Oct.

Nov. 3   Meeting of the Long Parliament.

Nov. 11 Wentworth impeached.

May 12   Wentworth, executed for his plans to use force against Parliament.

1641

Oct.22   Outbreak of the Irish rebellion.

Oct.22   Attempt to seize Dublin Castle fails.

Oct.26   Sir Phelim O'Neill captures Armagh.

Oct.28   Scottish Parliament offers to send an army of 10,000 to put down the rebellion in Ireland.

---

[1] This chronology is based on the relevant sections of Thomas Carlyle *Oliver Cromwell Letters and Speeches with Elucidations*, 2nd revised edition, (3 Volumes in One), London, (1846); Jane H. Ohlmeyer, (ed.), *Ireland from Independence to Occupation 1641-1660*, Cambridge, (1995), pp. xv-xli; John Kenyon and Jane Ohlmeyer, (ed.), *The Civil Wars: A Military History of England, Scotland and Ireland 1638-1660*, Oxford, (1998), pp. 355-81, and on research material in the subsequent chapters.

Nov.4	Sir Phelim O'Neill issues commission, purporting to be from the King.
Nov.11	Ormond, appointed Lieutenant-General of the King's army in Ireland.
Nov.21	'Rebels' begin the siege of Drogheda raised in March 1642.
Nov.28	'Rebel' attack on Lisburn repulsed.
Nov.29	Irish insurgents open negotiations with Old English.
Nov.30	Sir Charles Coote, garrisons Newcastle, County Wicklow and relieves Wicklow Castle.
Dec.1	Charles I, presented with Grand Remonstrance by the English Parliament.
Dec 3	Lords of the Pale, summoned to a conference in Dublin on 8th Dec., but they refuse to attend.
Dec 30	Sir Simon Harcourt and 1,100 foot arrive in Dublin from England.
Dec.	Alliance, between Old English, and Ulster insurgents Counties Roscommon, Mayo, Sligo, Kilkenny, and Tipperary, join the Rising.

1642

Jan.	Catholics in Counties Antrim, Limerick, and Clare, join the Rising.
	Coote routs 'rebel' forces at Swords.
Jan.11	O'Neill's attempt to take Drogheda, fails.
Feb.1-3	Ormond burns Newcastle, and takes Naas, County Kildare
Feb 12	Lord Lambert, defeats Wicklow 'rebels,' and clears Dublin of insurgents.
Feb.	Viscount Muskerry, and County Cork Catholics, join the rising; a further assault on Drogheda fails.
Mar.	Siege of Drogheda raised.
Mar.19	Adventurers Act, introduced.
Mar.19	Town of Galway declares for the 'rebels,' and besieges Galway fort to June 1643.
Mar.	Henry Tichborne retakes Ardee and Dundalk.
Apr.2	Ormond campaigns in County Kildare, and relieves Borris, Birr, and Knocknanuss.

Apr.	Gates of Hull shut against the King.
May	Government offensive almost grinds to a halt, due to shortage of arms, men and money.
	Two English regiments arrive in Munster.
June	Confederate Oath of Association drawn up, and provisional Supreme Council nominated.
Aug.22	King raises his standard at Nottingham, the start of the 'First English Civil War.'

1643

Apr.23	King orders Ormond to treat with the Confederates.
Sept.15	Royalist and Confederates agree on a ceasefire.
	Troops from Ireland recruited to King's army.
Sept.25	The Solemn League and Covenant, is signed.

1644

June 27	Earl of Antrim, dispatches 2,000 Irish soldiers to Scotland, to fight for the King under Montrose.

1645

June 25	Preston invests, Duncannon Fort captured 19th. Mar.

1646

June 5	Confederate victory over the Scots Battle of Benburb.

1647

Aug. 8	Jones defeats Preston at Dungan's Hill.

1648

Apr.3	Lord Inchiquin declares for the King.
May	The start of the 'Second English Civil War.'

1649

Mar 13	Council of State meet, to organise the mobilisation of forces to go to Ireland.
Mar 15	Cromwell was asked to go to Ireland.
Apr 20	Cromwell nominated to go.

1649

July 10	Cromwell left Windsor, to travel to Bristol.
July 19	Cromwell at Bristol, to Board ship 'John,' for Ireland.
Aug.12	Received news from Lieutenant General Jones, stating Ormond, had besieged Dublin (Rathmines), with 19,000 men, or thereabouts, 7,000 Scots, and 3,000 men, who were coming to join him in that work. Jones,

routed this whole army.

Aug. 13   Cromwell at Milford Haven, waiting for wind to change, funds, and provisions.

Aug. 15   Cromwell arrives in Dublin, – Speech to the people of Dublin.

Aug. 30   Rendezvous, with 8 regiments of foot, 6 of horse, and some troops of Dragoons, 3 miles north of Dublin.

Sept. 2   Cromwell, and the New Model Army arrive before Drogheda.

Sept. 8   2000 troops from the Drogheda attack Cromwell's army at St. John's Hill.
Protestants thrust out of Church of St.Peter's by the defenders.

Sept. 9   Cromwell's 'batteries began to play'. Summons, to Sir Arthur Aston. No satisfactory answer received.
Refused summons. Cromwell, proceeds to beat down steeple of St.Mary's church, on the South side of town.

Sept.10   Storm of Drogheda, began at 5.00p.m.

Sept.11   Fall of Drogheda.

Sept.12   Cromwell sends summons to the Commander-in-Chief of Dundalk.

Sept. 23   Army marched to Arklow, (Wicklow), Cromwell, remained in Dublin. Army captured Killcarick, and Ormond family seat, Castle of Arklow. Cromwell left Dublin, rejoined army. Marched towards Limerick. Limerick Castle already fired by enemy, who had quit. Marched towards Ferns, summonsed it, town surrendered. March to Enniscorthy. Castle yielded.

Oct. 1   Cromwell, and army, before Wexford.

Oct. 3   Summonsed Wexford, – Col. David Sinnot
Sinnot refused summons.
2nd summons to Wexford – Sinnot.

Oct. 4   Received reply from Sinnot, – trying to negotiate terms.
Reply from Cromwell, – giving Sinnot, 1 hour to respond.
Response from Sinnot – asking for terms.

Oct. 5   Offer from Sinnot – to send agents to talk.
Letter from Sinnot, beseeching Cromwell, and telling of arrival of relief troops.
Ormond, offered Wexford 1,800 horse and foot, Wexford refused.

Oct. 6   Letter to Sinnot from Cromwell, – revoking all offers of safe passage.
Cromwell, sets artillery upon castle at Wexford.

Oct.11   Cromwell spent 100 shot on castle.
Letter from Sinnot, requesting, safe passage for four persons, – carrying a Proposition.
Letter from Cromwell, – disdaining, to accept Proposition
Cromwell, offers quarter to soldiers, and non-commissioned officers, – to leave and go to their homes, – but, not take up arms. Commissioned officers, were also offered, quarter for lives.
Inhabitants, – offered peace, – no violence, or plunder.
While waiting for Answer from Sinnot, one of Sinnot's Captains, yielded the Castle, to Cromwell's men, – the enemy, quit the walls. Cromwell's men stormed walls with ladders. Met with stiff resistance. Two boats, put out with approx. 300 persons, on board. All, were drowned when boat sank. Approx. 2,000 enemy killed in all. Cromwell lost 20 men.

Oct. 17   Army before Ross, – Barrow.
Summons to Ross (Taaff). Summons refused, – 1,000 foot, in town. Cromwell prepared batteries making ready to storm. Ormond/Ardes/Castlehaven were on the other side of the river. Batteries played.

Oct. 19   Taaff, replies to summons, – wants to negotiate.
Letter from Cromwell, to Taaff, – offering inhabitants peace, and enemy army, opportunity to march away.
Batteries continued to play – making a breach. Letter from Taaff to Cromwell, – proposing that towns people, be permitted to leave in peace, and he (Taaff) and his army leave with their guns, shot, etc.

Cromwell replies – stands by first offer – denies leave, for enemy to leave with guns,etc. Taaff, accepts conditions offered. Cromwell replies to Taaff – honouring offer, and offers safe passage to four agents.

Nov. 10 Coleraine taken by storm, and Venables besieges Carrickfergus.

Nov.13 Cork, and Youghal, had submitted. Lord Broghill, in Munster, with army who came over from Inchiquin.

Nov. 14 Cromwell and troops, lying at Ross. Building bridge over Barrow river.
Owen Roe O'Neill, with 6,000 foot and horse, waiting on Nore River, ready to attack-Cromwell retreats.

Nov.15: Army marched on Nore (Cromwell was not there – he was sick) towards Inistogue (which the enemy left the night before his troops arrived.)
Cromwell's troops, attempted to cross Nore, but it was impassable.
Army marched north of Nore toward Thomastown, but enemy had destroyed bridge. Army, marched towards Kilkenny.
Split the army into two – Col. Reynolds marched towards Carrick where he surprised enemy, by attacking a town gate and entering by another. Took Ormond's castle, approx. 100 enemy escaped by boat. Remainder of army returned towards Ross.

Nov. 21/22 All army sped towards Carrick. Given access to Suir, they could now look at storming Waterford. Cromwell rejoined troops.

Nov. 23 Troops having rested, crossed River Suir, leaving Reynolds at Carrick.
Cromwell and troops, marched towards Waterford. Summoned Waterford. Mayor of Waterford refused summons.

Nov. 24 2nd summons of Waterford.
Summons refused by Mayor of Waterford.

Summonsed Waterford again. Agreed to a cessation of hostilities for 4-5 days, so long as no more enemy troops were allowed in city. Decided to take Fort Passage, which gave access to rations by water and prevented enemy from receiving supplies.

Dec. 2 Left Waterford to find winter quarters, via Kilmore and Thymes

Enemy tried unsuccessfully to regain Fort Passage.

Dec. 4 Bishops met at Clanmacnoise.

Dec.17 Cromwell at Youghal, with Lord Broghill, and Ireton.

1650

Jan. 8 English government sent letter of recall to Cromwell to address issues of Scotland.

Jan.15/29 Cromwell replies to Clanmacnoise Manifesto with his Declaration.

Jan. 29 Cromwell leaves winter quarters at Youghal.

Jan. 31 Cromwell takes Kilkenny Castle. Summons Roghill Castle successfully.

Crosses Suir.

Before Fethard. Summons, no shots fired, taken successfully.

Feb. 2 Before Cashel. Takes it successfully.

At Callan, all three castles taken, including Butler's Army marches back to Fehard and Cashel.

Feb. 15 Cromwell requests more money for troops, supplies, etc.

Feb. 25 Letter from Cromwell (15/2) reaches Commons, recounting successes.

Commons resolve to reward Cromwell with London property.

Feb. 27 Before Cahir, summoned it. Successfully.

Mar. 5 At Cashel. Writes to Council informing them of success. Previously Earl of Essex' castle.

Mar. 22 Cromwell finally receives letter from Commons (8/1) requesting his presence in London re Scotland.

Marches on Kilkenny.

Mar. 25 Opens batteries.

Mar. 28 Terms agreed at Kilkenny.

Apr. 2 Letter from Cromwell to Lenthall, recounting above and requesting army to be paid (owed five months pay).

May 9 Storm of Clonmel - New Model Soldiers caught in a trap set by O'Neill – over 2000 killed.
That night; the inhabitants sent to parley. Cromwell agreed to terms, including no hardships or death. Signs terms then finds out enemy have gone.

May 29 Cromwell left Ireland on 'President Frigate'. Leaving Ireton in charge. Waterford, still not taken.

May 30/31 Lands at Bristol.

May 31 Arrives in London, cheered by crowds, lining streets.

JUNE Start of 'Third English Civil War.'

June 21 Parliamentary victory, at battle of Scarrifhollis, County Donegal, Army of Ulster wiped out.

July 24 Carlow surrenders.

Aug: 6 Waterford surrenders.

Aug:14 Charlemont Fort surrenders.

Sept:15 Catholic bishops excommunicate Ormond's supporters.

Dec: 6 Ormond appoints Clanricarde as his deputy in Ireland.

Dec:11 Ormond leaves for France.

1651

June 4 Limerick invested, surrenders 27 October.

Aug.12 Parliamentarians blockade Galway until April.

Sept: 3 Cromwell defeats Charles II at the battle of Worcester, ends 'Wars of the Three Kingdoms.' War in Ireland drags on miserably.

Nov:26 Ireton dies of plague, replaced by Edmund Ludlow.

1652 Parliamentary soldiers stationed in Ireland exceeds 34,000.

April 12 Galway surrenders to Coote.
Majority of His Majesties forces in Ireland and the Irish, begin signing articles of agreement of surrender. Irish soldiers allowed to serve in Foreign armies not at war with the Parliament of England.

Sept. Fleetwood succeeds Ludlow as Commander-in-Chief in Ireland.

1653

April 27 Last formal capitulation, of Irish forces when, Colonel
Phillip O'Reilly, finally surrenders, with regiments of
both horse and foot to Parliamentary Commanders
Colonel Jones, and Lord General Fleetwood, at the
Castle of Cloughwater. Completes the Parliamentary
re-conquest of Ireland.

James Butler, Earl of Ormond,
The Commander of the Royalist Forces in Ireland.
(National Portrait Gallery)

Introduction

Of all the mid-seventeenth century revolutions in Europe, the one that took place in England, was the most complex and fascinating. It involved, no fewer, than three civil wars: the first, was fought from 1642 to 1646; the second, began early in 1648 and resulted in the trial, by some of his own subjects, of King Charles I, a traumatic event which was followed by his execution; and finally, there was the premature attempt, during 1649-51 by Charles's eldest surviving son, to regain his father's throne, with the aid of, Irish Roman Catholics, and Scottish Presbyterians, which collapsed completely after the destruction of his army, at the battle of Worcester. [Maurice Ashley][1]

These wars, took place in the three sparsely populated Stuart Kingdoms. The initial conflict in England, was triggered by events in Scotland, and Ireland. Charles I, failed to suppress, uprising by his Scottish subjects in 1639-40 and was forced to recall Parliament, which wanted to settle grievances, rather than grant the financial aid, the King required. The outbreak of the Irish rebellion, in October 1641, raised the question of who was to control an army recruited to suppress it. Whilst the English Parliament, was not willing to allow the King, to command an army in Ireland, fearing it might be used against themselves, they were also determined to restore

---

[1] Maurice Ashley, *The English Civil War – A Concise History*, London, (1974), p. 9.

security, and supremacy, in the British Isles.[2] Throughout the time frame of these years, the English Parliament, played its cards slowly, firstly, dealing with the security of England, then, the security of Ireland, and finally with Scotland. 'In the intervening years of civil war, Parliament's military victories over the King and his party owed more to Cromwell than anyone else.'[3]

> The terms, 'Royalist Party,' 'Cavalier Party,' and 'King's Party,' were commonly used by all shades of opinion. Without much subtlety they identified those, as a group, who had supported Charles I in the first civil war, or who, after the war were in favour of restoring the crown's original powers, without binding limitations.[4]

However, this Book is largely restricted, to the civil wars in Ireland. To place the period in historical context, by February 1649, the three traditional British kingdoms, had changed dramatically. England, became a republic, with a Presbyterian-inclined national church, which also tolerated the more radical Protestant religious sects. Scotland, was a kingdom, with a Presbyterian kirk, which would not tolerate dissent of any kind. Ireland, on the other hand was largely controlled by Royalists, who were prepared to agree to religious toleration of Roman Catholics, and Episcopalian Protestants, in return for their military support.[5] It must be remembered of course, by the beginning of the 1640s Ireland was inhabited by a mixture of 'Anglican English, Anglican Anglo-Irish, Catholic Irish, and Presbyterian Scots,' whose families had lived there, for generations.[6]

---

[2] *Ibid.*

[3] David L. Smith, *Oliver Cromwell, Politics and Religion in the English Revolution, 1640-1658*, [documents and commentary], Cambridge, (1991), p. 11.

[4] David Underdown, *Royalist Conspiracy in England*, Yale, (1971), p. 2.

[5] Ronald Hutton, *The British Republic 1649-1660*, London, (1990), p. 1.

[6] Antonia Fraser, *Cromwell, Our Chief of Men*, London, (1973), Paperback edition reprinted, (2004). p. 90. The complex religious situation, in mid-seventeenth century Britain, is summarised briefly in Ivan Roots, *Cromwell-A Profile*, London, (1973), pp. 5-6.; also see Phil Kilroy, 'Radical Religion in Ireland,1641-1660,' in Jane H Ohlmeyer, (ed), *Ireland from Independence to Occupation 1641-1660*, Cambridge, (1995), pp. 201-217.

Although, England, Scotland and Ireland, were at this stage independently; economically viable. The major difficulty was, of course, that they were not prepared, to recognize and accept, the separate existence of the others. This situation was resolved by the wars of 'The Three Kingdoms,' with the conquest of Scotland, and Ireland, by the English republicans, which led to the union of all three states, administered by the Long Parliament, sitting at Westminster.[7] 'This creation, of a 'British moment' through the conquest of Ireland and Scotland, owed much to Cromwell's campaigning, vigour, and ruthlessness.'[8] However, with the Restoration of Charles II; the situation, reverted back to three independent Kingdoms. Therefore, the history of the Commonwealth; shows how a small group of Englishmen, 'gained, and lost control, of the whole British archipelago.'[9]

Historians, including myself, believe that British history, should not; just be an expansion of English history, focusing on Westminster, and only using events, in Scotland and Ireland, to interpret events in England. 'The traditional labels, used to describe the conflict, that engulfed Britain and Ireland, throughout the 1640s, which include the 'Puritan Revolution,' 'English Revolution,' and the 'British Civil Wars,' tend to perpetuate this Anglo centrism.' The difficulty, of course, is the fact, that the conflict first began in Scotland and Ireland and throughout the 1640s encompassed England, Ireland and Scotland. Moreover, whilst sharing a 'pan-British,' and 'Irish dimension,' each of the individual Stuart kingdoms experienced their own economic, and social civil wars. The new term, 'Wars of the Three Kingdoms,' acknowledges the effects and 'centrality,' of the various civil, wars fought within the Stuart Kingdoms, as well as the dynamics, and interaction between them.[10] There is no doubt, Charles I; viewed the conflict of the 1640s, as the same war, and used the resources in each of his

---

[7] Hutton, *op.cit.*, p. 1.
[8] J.C. Davis, *Oliver Cromwell*, [Reputations series], London, (2001), p. 196.
[9] Hutton, *op.cit.*, p. 1.
[10] Jane H. Ohlmeyer, 'The wars of the three kingdoms,' *History Today*, November, (1998), p. 16.

kingdoms, to combat his opposition, wherever it arose.[11] In this way Ireland, was dragged into the conflict, between King and Parliament, and with the onset of the 'Second English Civil War,' in 1648, simply became an integral part of it. The king; seeking to raise an Irish army, to use against his 'rebellious British subjects.'[12]

During the Irish Rebellion, a Catholic Confederacy, at Kilkenny, had been established intent on returning the Church to its pre-Reformation position and secure legislative independence, for the Irish parliament. From Kilkenny, it virtually ruled Ireland for almost a decade. James Butler, Earl of Ormond, who in 1644 was appointed the king's Lieutenant in Ireland, did not fight these Irish insurgents, beyond the opening years of the rebellion, but tried on the contrary, to persuade them to furnish the King, with military support against the English Parliamentarians, in return for promises of benefits, when the civil wars were over. Although the Irish, were divided on the issue, after negotiations at the start of 1649, a treaty was drawn up, to which the Old Irish and the Anglo-Irish, agreed to support the Royalist cause, in return for religious toleration. 'Nine Irish bishops, urged their followers to fight fiercely, against sectaries, and rebels, for God and Caesar, since under those banners you may well hope for victories.' The alliance, was strengthened, by the news of Charles I's execution, and during 1649, Ormond, succeeded in gaining military control, of most of Ireland, apart from Londonderry and Dublin. He declared for King Charles II, and invited him to come to Ireland, to prepare for the invasion of England.[13] From the Parliamentary perspective Gardiner summarises that:

> with Ormond planning an invasion, and with the Royalist gentry ready, from Lancashire to Cornwall, to welcome him and his Irish followers, the army – or at least its commanders – could have no other thought

---

[11] John Kenyon and Jane Ohlmeyer, (eds.), *The Civil Wars – A Military History of England, Scotland and Ireland 1638-1660*, Oxford University Press, (1998), p. 31.
[12] Jane H. Ohlmeyer, 'The wars of religion 1603-1660,' in Thomas Bartlett and Keith Jeffrey, (eds.), *A Military History of Ireland*, Cambridge, (1996), p. 164.
[13] Maurice Ashley, *The Greatness of Oliver Cromwell*, London, (1957), p. 230.

than to tear up the mischief by the roots in its own soil. It is easy to say that England could never have been conquered by an Irish Army, or that the party, which endeavoured to profit by such aid, would have been condemned to lasting obloquy. It was Cromwell's duty to take care that the danger should never arise. Ormond had without difficulty thrown English regiments from Ireland on the Western coast of England in 1643; and if he now succeeded in mastering Dublin it would be hard to prevent a repetition of the same operation with Irish regiments in 1649.

Cromwell's acceptance, of the command in Ireland, was but one step more; in the evolution of the original quarrel. For some time, it had been becoming clear that the conflict between King, and Parliament, for supremacy, at Westminster, was widening; into a conflict for the supremacy of England, in the British Isles. That it was so, was owing to the eagerness of Royalists, to enlist the forces, of Scotland and Ireland, in their own behalf, and it is no wonder, that Cromwell and his officers, had made up their minds that rather than Scotland, or Ireland, interfering in the political development of England, an English army, should interfere, in the political development; of Scotland and Ireland.[14]

On 15th August 1649, Cromwell, landed near Dublin with his army, to begin his campaign in Ireland, which only lasted for a period of nine months. On 29th May 1650, Cromwell left Ireland never to return there again.[15]

It will be demonstrated, that far too much of the re-conquest of Ireland, in 1649-1650, has been attributed to Cromwell. It should be remembered that Michael Jones, had already saved Dublin,

---

[14] Samuel Rawson Gardiner, *History of the Commonwealth and Protectorate 1649-1651*, London, (1894), Vol. I, pp. 29-30.
[15] Toby Barnard, 'Irish images of Cromwell,' in R.C. Richardson, (ed.), *Images of Oliver Cromwell: Essays for and by Roger Howell Jnr.*, p. 182.

from being captured, with his victory, over a combined Royalist and Confederate Army, before Cromwell arrived in Ireland. Cromwell's severity at Drogheda, is mainly justified in terms of his intention to demoralize, other enemy garrisons to promote a widespread surrender. Initially, this may have been the case, in regions close to Drogheda, but in the more remote areas hearsay reports had no impact whatsoever.[16]

Of great importance, of course, is that far from, 'Cromwell passing like lightening through the land' he 'restricted his campaign to only some of those areas where English rule, had been previously fully established and where deserters, from the Royalist armies, made his work easier.'[17] It must be noted, that Cromwell, did not travel with his forces to Ulster,[18] and when he returned to England, much of Ireland was still unsubdued. The final re-conquest of Ireland, was achieved by other parliamentary commanders; including Henry Ireton, Edmund Ludlow, Lord Broghill, Sir Charles Coote; and Charles Fleetwood.[19] In fact, organized Irish resistance, continued until 27th April 1653, when, Colonel Phillip O'Reilly, finally surrendered, with his regiments of both horse, and foot, to Parliamentary Commanders Colonel Jones, and Lord General Fleetwood, at the Castle of Cloughwater.[20]

It seems clear, that even from some of his own accounts; of the campaign in Ireland, Cromwell was creating an image as a conquering hero. At the same time, ignoring his setback at Clonmel, and glorifying, in what he and his soldiers had achieved. This self-promotion, was backed by propaganda, from the Parliamentary Government, in England, which created conflicting images. Nevertheless, as Toby Barnard emphasises, 'his contemporary detractors, whether dejected Royalists or Irish refugees, neither

---

[16] *Ibid.,* p. 181; Barry M. Taylor, 'Siege and slaughter at Drogheda,' *Military History*, October, (1999), 16 (4), p. 62.

[17] Barnard, *op.*cit., p. 181.

[18] Tom Reilly, *Cromwell - An Honourable Enemy, The Untold Story of the Cromwellian Invasion of Ireland*, London, (1999), p. 50.

[19] Barnard, *op.cit.*, p. 181.

[20] John T. Gilbert, (eds), *Contemporary History of Affairs in Ireland from 1641 to 1652,* Vol. III, Part II, pp. 374-375.

regretted the brutalities nor emphasised his mistakes,' although there was a certain brutality, not previously seen during his military career.[21]

This Book, will focus, on the 'Civil Wars in Ireland' to assess the Irish aspects of Cromwell's image. It must be emphasised, however, that Oliver Cromwell, has been 'both praised and reviled, in other centuries and in other countries, than his own.' This complex historiography, has created conflicting images, of Cromwell; as a man, a general and a statesman. It is clearly demonstrated in Chapter One, how these conflicting images formed part of a systematic myth- making process.

The myths, that have been developed, surrounding Cromwell's Irish campaign of 1649-50, cannot be fully understood, in isolation, but must be placed in a wider context; of the period. A major contributory factor, was the Irish Rebellion, which, broke out on the 22nd October 1641.[22] However, the years between the close of the rebellion, in 1643, which preceded, Cromwell's arrival in Ireland, in 1649, was also a critical factor. Therefore, in Chapter Two, I have attempted to clarify the political manoeuvring, and hitherto, confusing, military campaigns, which, took place in Ireland during these years. Although, the main focus of this book, will be on Cromwell's Storm of Drogheda, and Wexford, and other aspects, of his military campaign.[23]

The myths that have grown around Cromwell's storm of Drogheda, are that he obtained possession of the town by treachery; and broke his word, directly, after all had surrendered; that he ordered an indiscriminate massacre, not only the whole of the garrison of the town, but the bulk of the civilians as well, sparing neither women nor children; that the garrison consisted of mostly Irishmen, who were nearly all Catholics; that only one Royalist officer escaped from the garrison with his life. Similar myths, surround Cromwell's storm of Wexford, namely that, the majority

---

[21] Barnard, *op.cit.*, p. 182.
[22] Keith Lindley, 'The impact of the 1641 rebellion upon England and Wales 1641-5,' *Irish Historical Studies*, Vol. XVIII, No 70, September, (1972) pp.143-76
[23] Barnard, *op.cit.*, p. 182.

of the unarmed inhabitants, were indiscriminately killed and that two or three hundred women, were put to death, in the market cross and, finally, Cromwell exterminated the citizens of Wexford by the sword.

Other significant myths, associated with aspects of Cromwell's military campaign in Ireland, are that it was a war fought on the basis of English Protestant against Irish Catholic, and that Cromwell ordered, the wholesale and indiscriminate massacre, of ordinary unarmed Catholic citizens, in the towns that he besieged. In Chapter Five, it will be argued that these myths when compared with other explanations, and the evidence from secondary works, used to support the latter, appear more fiction than fact.

The major myths, that emerged, regarding Cromwell's storm of Clonmel, are that Cromwell; conspired with a Major Fennell, to betray this garrison, for the sum of five hundred pounds. It will also be shown that in reality, the death of 2,500, of Cromwell's soldiers, at Clonmel occurred in circumstances, no less severe than the alleged massacre of enemies, at Drogheda and Wexford. Furthermore, in marked contrast, 'while the events at Drogheda and Wexford have been magnified and well publicized, the storm of Clonmel has been quietly passed over, by Cromwell's enemies.'[24]

A major popular historical belief concerning Cromwell and Ireland, is that Cromwell during his Irish campaign, accomplished the final re-conquest of the country.

This Book provides argument and documentary evidence, which suggest, that there are more believable explanations and assessments, than those manifest in the myths.

Philip McKeiver
January 2007

---

[24] *Ibid.*

CHAPTER ONE

Demythologising Cromwell

Oliver Cromwell, (1599-1658), ranks as one of the most frequently discussed and most hotly debated figures, in the whole of English history. A key figure, in the creation of the New Model Army and in the Parliamentarian victory in the Civil Wars, in the conquest of Scotland, and Ireland and as Lord Protector in England's only republic.
[R.C. Richardson][1]

Recently, J.C. Davis emphasised that, 'the vigour of Cromwell's reputation has given it a life and force, of its own, at both popular and academic levels and since it can arouse extremes, both of anger and devotion, we do well to keep it under observation.'[2] There is, of course, no doubt that widely differing historical opinions about Cromwell's character and achievements, have evolved with the passage of 400 years. Few other statesmen in history have had so many conflicting judgements made about them. I agree with Maurice Ashley, that 'historians are accustomed, when they declare their moral convictions, to act as avengers, who lift up the fallen and beat down the proud, and on no figure in modern times has the historian exercised that prerogative, more industriously than upon Oliver Cromwell.' This was originally stimulated, by the anger

---

[1] R.C. Richardson (ed.), *Images of Oliver Cromwell: Essays for and by Roger Howell Jnr.*, Manchester, (1993), p. 1.
[2] J.C. Davis, *Oliver Cromwell*, [Reputations Series], London, (2001), p. 1.

of the returned Royalists after 1660 and, for close on 200 years; little of note was written in his defence.[3]

It will be demonstrated in this Book, that the conflicting interpretation of Cromwell's role in the re-conquest of Ireland after 1649 is a manifestation of a far more fundamental debate. The contrasting images of him, both as a soldier, and as a politician, beg the basic question, was he a 'champion of liberty' or an 'oppressive tyrant?' The first view, 'celebrated each year by the Cromwell Association, is of a man who destroyed Stuart tyranny, the promoter of civil and religious liberty and the opponent of dogma, privilege and injustice.' By marked contrast, the second popular image, 'portrays an autocratic tyrant, a military dictator, who imprisoned his enemies at will, who gratuitously wrecked castles and churches, who *butchered the Irish*, and who ruled as arbitrarily as the Stuarts.'[4] As one historian said, 'Cromwell, appears to one set of writers as guilty of common treason and horrible murder' and, to the other of course, as always – 'he is a bronze and marble hero.'[5] In the words of Blair Worden:

> From the Restoration of the monarchy in 1660 until around the accession of Queen Victoria in 1837, historians and politicians mostly portrayed him not as a hero but as a villain. They condemned his seditious deeds: the regicide, the establishment of a republic, the imposition of military and sectarian rule. They assailed his character, which was generally held to have been one of ruthless ambitions and cunning dissimulation.[6]

Members of Parliament, were outraged at the end of the nineteenth

---

[3] Maurice Ashley, *The Greatness of Oliver Cromwell*, London, (1957), p. 12.
[4] David L. Smith, *Oliver Cromwell: Politics and Religion in the English Revolution, 1640-1658*, Cambridge, (1991), p. 6.
[5] Hillaire Belloc, *Cromwell*, (second edition), London, (1934), p. 284.
[6] Blair Worden, *Roundhead Reputations, The English Civil Wars and the Passions of Posterity*, London, (2001), p. 215.

century, when the Prime Minister, Lord Rosebery, planned to put up Cromwell's statue within Westminster Palace. The statue, was subsequently placed outside the palace, when Rosebery paid for the statue, mostly from his own funds and attempted to do so anonymously. In marked contrast in '1902, Huntingdon's MP, successfully opposed plans to erect a statue of Cromwell, in the town of his birth.' Since then, Cromwell has remained a controversial figure, for example 'during the 1960s, the reigning monarch, vetoed proposals by a Labour government to include Cromwell's image on a postage stamp.'[7]

Books and articles on Cromwell, have been prolific. 'Biographies of Cromwell, far outnumber those of any English, or British, monarch.' 'Whilst some are scholarly and judicious, most of them are irredeemably biased,'[8] particularly in regards to Cromwell's role in the re-conquest of Ireland.[9] W.C. Abbott's essay in *Conflict with Oblivion*, (1924), made a short survey of the historians of Cromwell, while his bibliography of Oliver Cromwell appeared in 1929, and listed 3,500, items including over a hundred biographies. Since then the spate of publications, for and against Cromwell, has increased rather than subsided. The last few years, have seen the appearance of new biographical, and other studies of Cromwell.[10] For example, John Morrill's, collection of essays, *Oliver Cromwell and the English Revolution*, (1990), Barry Coward's, *Cromwell*, (1991), David Smith's, *Oliver Cromwell, Politics and Religion in the English Revolution; 1640-1658*, (1991), R.C. Richardson's, (ed.), *Images of Oliver Cromwell, Essays for and by Roger Howell Jnr.*, (1993), Peter Gaunt's, *Oliver Cromwell*, (1996), Tom Reilly's, *Cromwell: an Honourable Enemy*, (1998), James Scott Wheeler's, *Cromwell- in- Ireland*, (1999), J.C. Davis's, *Oliver Cromwell*, (2001), Blair Worden's, *Roundhead*

---

[7] Peter Gaunt, *Oliver Cromwell*, Oxford, (1996), p. 8.

[8] *Ibid.*

[9] Toby Barnard, 'Irish images of Cromwell,' in R.C. Richardson (ed.), *Images of Cromwell: Essays for and by Roger Howell Jnr.*, Manchester, (1993), pp. 180-206.

[10] Richardson, *op.cit.*, p. 1.

Reputations, the English Civil Wars and the Passions of Posterity, (2001). Peter Gaunt's *Oliver Cromwell,* (2004), and Keith Roberts, *Cromwell's War Machine, The New Model Army 1645-1660,* (2005).

After Cromwell's death, the *'Exact Character or Narrative of the Late Noble and Magnificent Oliver Cromwell,* (London, 1658)'*, argued, that Cromwell 'constantly stood firm and trusty in upholding,' the 'liberties of his country.' This belief was more recently expressed by, the late "Roger Howell, who described Cromwell as; "a major contributor to the growth of English liberty."[11] There is a great deal of evidence, in support of this argument, 'because; Cromwell fought to defend the rights of Parliament against Charles I.' He was also; an 'instrument in the king's defeat and in the abolition of the monarchy.' Furthermore, as Lord Protector, he remained committed to both, civil and religious, liberty. He also showed more tolerance towards, religious diversity, than most of his contemporaries and proposed changes to the legal system, to make it fairer and more available to the general public. The nineteenth century statue on the front cover actually; 'symbolises the idea, of him as a champion of popular liberties.'[12]

In marked contrast, as David Smith emphasises, 'the opposite view also has a long history. Within Cromwell's own lifetime, he was attacked as a 'usurper and an oppressor. A good example; was, *A Declaration of the Freeborne People of England Now in Arms Against the Tyranny and Oppression of Oliver Cromwell,* (London, 1655).' Soon after this appeared, 'Cromwell established, the military rule of the Major Generals, 'to root out opposition,' and to enforce a 'reformation of manners." Moreover, he "claimed to rule for the peoples good, not what pleases them."

---

[11] Smith, *op.cit.*, p. 7.

[12] *Ibid.* The photograph on the front cover depicts the bronze statue of Oliver Cromwell, sculpted by Sir Hamo Thorneycroft, completed in 1899, to mark the tercentenary of Cromwell's birth, stands on a plinth in front of the Palace of Westminster (photograph by Dr. Maxine Forshaw), as it appears on the front cover of Peter Gaunt, (ed,), *Cromwell 400* published by the Cromwell Association, Brentwood, (1999).

'Blair Worden, has more recently argued, that 'even Cromwell's religious toleration, was limited because papists and prelatists,' were always excluded.' Finally, Cromwell's anti-Catholicism, was highlighted during his Irish campaign of 1649-50. Even though Cromwell remained, at all times, within seventeenth century rules of war, he also showed a brutality not seen elsewhere in his military career. The two, conflicting images of Cromwell are of course incompatible, and as always the truth probably lies somewhere in between,[13] although historical truth is not a question of the 'average.'

Most of the myths, surrounding Cromwell, do not derive from historiography written during his own lifetime, but derive mostly from reflections of his contemporaries, written much later, 'through the distorting glass of the Restoration,' when both 'prudence and experience,' prevented accurate disclosure.[14]

Without doubt, this is why the historiography of Oliver Cromwell, is of such importance, as it reveals why common perceptions are tainted in origin. During the seventeenth and eighteenth centuries, history was mostly written in the form of chronicles, which were understood to be records of actual events. In reality, 'Royalist propaganda swept the board.'[15] Without accusing Edmund Ludlow, Richard Baxter and Bulstrode Whitelock, of 'deliberate distortion,' it is not safe to depend on their accounts when attempting to establish how, Cromwell, was viewed in his own lifetime.[16] Furthermore it is also obvious, that the remaining records of his letters and speeches have been to a large extent 'compressed, paraphrased or deliberately distorted.'[17]

Immediately after Cromwell's death; his detractors, far outweighed his supporters, and he was, 'portrayed as the very devil incarnate.' The fact that Cromwell, had bad press, following the Restoration is not surprising. 'A regime that exhumed, hanged,

---

[13] Smith, *op.cit.*, p. 7.
[14] John Morrill, 'Cromwell and his contemporaries,' in John Morrill, (ed.), *Oliver Cromwell and the English Revolution*, London, (1990), p. 259.
[15] Ashley, *op.cit.*, p. 21.
[16] Morrill, *op.cit.*, pp. 259-60.
[17] Gaunt, *op.cit.*, p. 17.

and then beheaded his body, was unlikely to miss any opportunity to blacken his reputation.'[18] In addition, the Restoration, was accompanied by the 'inevitable flood of vituperation' with such works as; *Cromwell's Bloody Slaughterhouse*, *The English Devil*, and *Hell's Higher Court of Justice*, in which the popular theme, frequently copied, was the discussion among the regicides in hell. Further, and more substantially, Walker's *History of Independency,* and the many works of Pryne, provided a mixture of wit and fact, with which to discredit all the Cromwellian Side. Royalist propagandist, James Heath's *Flagellum: The Life and Death of O. Cromwell the Late Usurper*, (1663), which Carlyle calls, 'the chief fountain of lies about Cromwell,' achieved six editions under Charles II.[19] More recently Blair Worden; has described Heath's vituperative biography as; 'a sensationalist caricature embellished by a wealth of slanderous invention.'[20] The popular historians of the century, either followed the fabrications of Heath or the Royalist Party line, in the First Earl of Clarendon's *History*, (1702).[21]

> In most publications throughout the reigns of Charles II and James II, Cromwell was portrayed as an ambitious and hypocritical king-killer, a cruel and cowardly tyrant, not above greed, villainy and immorality who had been in league with the devil. To the Tories, Cromwell was a wicked and godless usurper who had unforgivably killed Gods anointed. To the Whigs he was a hypocrite, a man who had betrayed the cause of liberty in favour of his own ambition.[22]

---

[18] Roger Howell, Jnr., 'The imp of Satan: The Restoration image of Cromwell,' in R.C. Richardson, (ed.), *Images of Oliver Cromwell*, Manchester, (1993), p. 33.

[19] D.H. Pennington, 'Cromwell and the historians,' *History Today*, Vol. 8, No. 9, September, (1958), p. 598.

[20] Worden, *op.cit.*, p. 218.

[21] Thomas Carlyle, *Oliver Cromwell's Letters and Speeches with Elucidations*, second revised edition, (3 volumes in one), London, (1846), p. 12.

[22] Gaunt, *op.cit.*, p. 10.

Eighteenth century historians, such as David Hume, in his *History of England,* (1757), tended to write 'philosophical' works, which subjugated, historical evidence, to accepted opinion and the prevailing morality. In the words of Maurice Ashley, 'there is hardly a statement about Oliver Cromwell's character, or policy, which is not false. This is because Hume, was content to follow the accounts of Cromwell's enemies.'[23] Furthermore, Hume described Cromwell, as; 'a most frantic enthusiast... the most dangerous of hypocrites... who was enabled after multiplied deceits to cover under a tempest of passion; all his crooked schemes and profound artifices.'[24] The negative image, of Cromwell, remained pretty much the same, until non-conformist historiography, found more positive things to say about him. 'For the vast majority of Englishmen, there was no fundamental re-interpretation of Cromwell until Carlyle; proclaimed him a hero in the nineteenth century.'[25]

There's little doubt Cromwell's reputation, was blackened, by an active propaganda campaign, during the Restoration, and this remained unchallenged until the 1840s, when 'Carlyle found in him the active and decisive force which England needed.' In 1845, the appearance of Carlyle's collection of, *The Letters and Speeches of Oliver Cromwell*; 'transformed scholarly knowledge and understanding of England's greatest commoner.'[26] A second edition, appeared in 1846. This was followed by a second revised edition, which also appeared in 1846, (three volumes in one), designated by Carlyle, as 'the final one,'[27] although there was a third edition in 1849. All three editions of Carlyle's work, found

---

[23]Ashley, *op.cit.*, p. 10.

[24]Roger Howell, Jnr., 'Cromwell, the English Revolution and political symbolism in eighteenth century England,' in R.C. Richardson, (ed.), *Oliver Cromwell: Essays for and by Roger Howell, Jnr.*, Manchester, (1993), pp. 64-5.

[25]Howell, *op.cit.*, pp. 33-4, 'The imp of Satan.'

[26]John Morrill, 'Textualising and contextualising Cromwell,' *The Historical Journal*, (1990), Vol. 33, September, No. 3, p. 629.

[27]Ivan Roots, 'Carlyle's Cromwell,' in R.C. Richardson, (ed.), *Images of Oliver Cromwell*, Manchester, (1993), p. 74.

their way on to the bookshelves, in many Whig and Liberal homes.[28] Carlyle's achievement, was to make Cromwell, exciting again; 'as a man and part of a superman, not as a monster.'[29] Although not everybody, admired Cromwell, from then on and of course, many did not, but, except for his alleged treatment of the Irish, it was difficult to hate him like before.[30] It is easy to agree with Blair Worden, who convincingly argues, that, 'the cult of Cromwell was not only the product of political, social and religious movements. It was the achievement of Carlyle's collection of, *The Letters and Speeches of Oliver Cromwell*, which spoke to Victorians with extraordinary power.'[31]

In marked contrast to Carlyle's work, the children's classic, *The Children of the New Forest*, first published in 1847, was to influence many generations, with its image of Cromwell and the evil Roundheads, battling against the heroic King Charles, with his dashing Cavaliers.[32] Only a year later Lord Macaulay's *History of England,* was also influential in creating a perception of Cromwell. Most English readers, had their view, of the origins of the Civil War formed, directly or indirectly, by the first chapter of Macaulay's *History*. This is partly because, from the vantage point, of modern constitutional history, the Parliamentarians were seen to be on the winning side. Moreover, the lasting popularity of Macaulay, stems also from his forceful style, and sweeping interpretations. 'The natural enemy of Royalist claims, he thinks, was Puritanism, inside and outside Parliament.'[33] Describing Cromwell in Ireland, Macaulay says, 'Cromwell waged a war, resembling that which Israel waged on the Canaanites, smote the

---

[28] Morrill, *op.cit.*, p. 629.

[29] Pennington, *op.cit.*, p. 598.

[30] Howell, *op.cit.*, pp. 63-4, 'Political symbolism in eighteenth century England.'

[31] Worden, *op.cit.*, p. 263.

[32] Capt. Frederick Marryat, *The Children of the New Forest*, London, (1847), (this edition 1968).

[33] Philip A.M. Taylor, (ed.), *The Origins of the New English Civil War, Conspiracy, Crusade or Class Conflict?* Boston, (1960), p. XII.

idolaters, with the edge of the sword, so that great cities were left without inhabitants.'[34]

More recently, it has been argued, that Cromwell's Irish image, was more a construct of nineteenth century historians; than a contemporary perception. It appears that, 'Irish demonisation,' began in 1865, when John Prendergast, published *The Cromwellian Settlement of Ireland*. This is when Prendergast diverted attention away from the Irish rebellion of 1641; to Cromwellian Ireland. Interestingly enough, partial Irish independence in 1922, was marked by a new edition of Prendergast's book. In the words of Toby Barnard, 'as a tract for the times.'[35] Within a few years James Anthony Froude, published his riposte, *The English in Ireland in the Eighteenth* Century, (1872), in which he stated:

> I cannot pass over this part of my narrative without making my acknowledgements to Mr Prendergast, to whose personal courtesy I am deeply indebted, and to whose impartiality and candour in his volume on the Cromwellian settlement I can offer no higher praise than by saying, the perusal of it has left on my mind an impression precisely opposite to that of Mr Prendergast himself. He writes as an Irish patriot – I as an Englishman; but the difference between us is, not on the facts, but on the opinion to be formed about them.[36]

Most recently, Irish historian Roy Foster, describes Froude, as a 'Carlylean Chronicler of Protestant heroism, and Catholic villainy,'

---

[34] Lord Macaulay, *The History of England – to Death of William III*, Vol. 1, London, (1976), p. 102.

[35] Barnard, *op.cit.*, pp. 193-9; John Prendergast, *The Cromwellian Settlement of Ireland*, Dublin, (1865).

[36] James Anthony Froude, *The English in Ireland in the Eighteenth Century*, London, (1887), Vol. 1, pp. 148-9. Originally published in three volumes between 1872-74.

and believes the chief value of Froude's work; was that it prompted W.D.H. Lecky, to write his riposte *A History of Ireland in the Eighteenth Century*, (1878).[37] Lecky, was probably the best of Ireland's nineteenth-century historians, who was outraged, by Froude's forceful style, and interpretations. Although Lecky, did in fact recognise, much of Irish history, writing amounted to, polemical myth making, he attempted to counter Froude's offensive and racist assessment of the Irish character. Nevertheless, Lecky agreed with Prendergast's conclusion that; 'the root of the Irish problem was the land question', giving added weight to his nineteenth century assessment. In fact, Lecky, only included a survey of the Cromwellian conquest, as a tedious but necessary introduction, to his main topic, Ireland, in the eighteenth century. However Lecky's 'analysis, often silently followed, but seldom bettered, may stand here, as the essence of Cromwell's Irish image.' According to Lecky the ' sieges of Drogheda and Wexford, and the massacres that accompanied them deserve to rank in horror with the most atrocious exploits of Tilly and Wallenstein, and they made the name of Cromwell eternally hated in Ireland.'[38] Lecky also recognised, 'the name of Cromwell, even now acts as a spell upon the Irish mind, and has a powerful and living influence in sustaining, the hatred both of England and Protestantism.'[39]

Irish historian Tom Reilly in *Cromwell – An Honourable Enemy – the Untold Story of the Cromwellian Invasion of Ireland*, (1998), has emphasised that this nineteenth century construct, was further developed, by the appearance of, Denis Murphy's *Cromwell in Ireland, a History of Cromwell's Irish Campaign*, published in 1883. According to Reilly, 'as a Jesuit priest Murphy's evaluation of Cromwell's Irish campaign is far from complimentary. Murphy, consistently argues from secondary sources; rarely using the reports of actual eye witnesses, since they do not corroborate his

---

[37] R.F. Foster, *Modern Ireland, 1600-1972*, London, (1988), p. 103.
[38] Barnard, *op.cit.*, p. 181.
[39] W.D.H. Lecky, *A History of Ireland in the Eighteenth Century*, 5 Vols., London, (1913), Vol. 1, pp. 101-3. This work was originally published between 1878 and 1890.

allegations.' Moreover in modern Ireland, understanding of the battles of Drogheda and Wexford, are sadly clouded with 'historical inaccuracies,' due to the misconceptions of nineteenth century historians, exacerbated by the prejudiced teachings of the twentieth century.[40] Many of the recent Irish authors cited in this Book, are part of the historiographical movement known as 'revisionism.' This 'new history; is often identified, with efforts by some historians to propagate a different political agenda.'[41]

There is simply no doubt, that the accounts of Cromwell's role; in the re- conquest of Ireland, have been 'politicized' for centuries. This is clearly reflected, in the words of Murphy, and Samuel Rawson Gardiner. Murphy's account of, Cromwell's Irish campaign, appeared in 1883. Later the same year, Gardiner, published his volumes, on the *History of the Great Civil War, 1642-1649*, this was followed by, his *History of the Commonwealth and Protectorate 1649-1656*. Gardiner's, 'Whiggish interpretation of British history,' attempted to 'rationalize the English conquest of Ireland' and magnify, Cromwell's role in it.[42] In 1885, a contrasting view appeared, when Patrick Francis Moran, published his *Historical Sketch of the Persecutions Suffered by the Catholics of Ireland Under the Rule of Cromwell and the Puritans.*[43]

Cromwell however, was rescued from a largely critical press in the middle of the nineteenth century. This began, with the publication of Carlyle's collection, of *Oliver Cromwell's Letters and Speeches with Elucidations* (1845). Moreover, for 'many Victorian and early twentieth-century historians, most notably S.R. Gardiner and C.H. Firth, Cromwell was the acceptable face of reform, a man possessed of a character, which was highly complex

---

[40] Tom Reilly, *Cromwell – An Honourable Enemy. The Untold Story of the Cromwellian Invasion of Ireland*, Brandon, London, (1998), p. 3.
[41] George Boyce and Alan O'Day, 'Revisionism' and the 'revisionist' controversy,' *The Making of Modern Irish History*, London, (1996), p. 2.
[42] James Scott Wheeler, *Cromwell-in-Ireland*, Dublin, (1999), p. 3.
[43] Patrick Francis Moran, D.D., *Historical Sketch of the Persecutions Suffered by the Catholics of Ireland Under the Rule of Cromwell and the Puritans*, Dublin, (1885).

but one in which, decency, and liberal toleration, came shining through.'[44] In a more balanced assessment, Sir Charles Firth informed his 'Edwardian readers that Oliver was the greatest figure of his generation, albeit too much of a partisan to be a national hero.' [45]

In contrast, art, was used by Cromwell's detractors, to create a negative image. A copy of the painting above, appears in John Adair's *By the Sword Divided – Eyewitnesses of the English Civil War*, London, (1983), which portrays, 'the King saying goodbye to his children – in a rather fanciful 19th century version of the scene, which wrongly shows Cromwell as present.'[46]

William Lamont has recently emphasised that:

> English demonisations of Cromwell, in the nineteenth century were not unknown. In Flora Thomson's

[44] Gaunt, *op.cit.*, p. 11.
[45] Davies, *op.cit.*, p. 5.
[46] John Adair, *By the Sword Divided - Eyewitnesses of the English Civil War*, London, (1983), p. 235.

classic, *Lark Rise to Candleford*, she recalls at the end of the century in her Oxfordshire village that some of the older mothers and grandmothers still threatened naughty children with the name of Cromwell. 'If you aren't a good gal, Old Oliver Cromwell'll have 'ee,' they would say, or 'Here Comes Old Cromwell.'[47]

Finally, however, 'Cromwell emerges in the nineteenth century, either heroic or vile, according to the party or religion of the constructor.'[48] This is clearly reflected in *The Times,* articles of, 1899 and 1902. The first, recorded that:

> The 300th Anniversary of the birth of Oliver Cromwell was celebrated in the City Temple, yesterday under the auspices of the National Council of the Evangelical Free Churches. At noon, when Dr. Parker was advertised to preach, the great church was already crowded, hundreds being turned away. The audience consisted almost entirely of men, who interrupted the sermon again and again by enthusiastic cheering.[49]

The second, in March 1902, reporting a lecture Lieutenant General Sir William Butler, gave to the Irish Literacy Society, on *The Cromwellian War in Ireland*, noted how:

> Sir William proceeded to trace the history of Cromwell's campaign, commenting in severe terms on his 'duplicity, hypocrisy and cruelty.' 'For some fifty or sixty years,' he said, 'it has been the fashion of the time to speak of Cromwell as one of the greatest of men. For 200 years before our time not one historian, not one writer of any eminence, had anything

---

[47] William Lamont, 'Oliver Cromwell and English Calvinism,' in Peter Gaunt, (ed.), *Cromwell 400,* Essex, (1999), p. 68.

[48] Barnard, *op.cit.*, p. 181.

[49] *The Times,* 'Tercentenary of Oliver Cromwell,' 27th April, (1899), p. 7.

good to say about him, but we had changed all that. His eulogies could now be counted by the thousand, his admirers by the million....' 'The two chief objects of his effort were plunder and persecution.'[50]

Although, intended to be complimentary, during the 1930s and 1940s, it was fashionable to portray Cromwell, as a military dictator, and compare him with Hitler and Mussolini.[51] A good example was Maurice Ashley's, *Oliver Cromwell: the Conservative Dictator* (1937), and as Roger Howell points out 'despite Ashley's opening announcement about resisting, the 'temptation to indulge in modern comparisons or analogies,' to a large extent he did exactly that, as his subtitle suggests.'[52]

On the whole, 'American historians were unfriendly to Cromwell, since their instincts, induced them to sympathise with, his republican opponents and critics.' However, President Theodore Roosevelt wrote a biography of Cromwell, in which he insisted, that Cromwell; was 'the greatest Englishman of the seventeenth century' and had in fact, headed a movement, that produced the 'English speaking world, as we know it.'[53]

Whilst considering American historians, we must turn to W.C. Abbott (1869-1947), editor of *The Writings and Speeches of Oliver Cromwell,* (4 Vols), Cambridge, Massachusetts, 1937-47).[54] As R.S. Paul pointed out in 1955, 'Abbott, stamps his own assessment on Cromwell as a product of the present century, just as surely as the Protector's letters and speeches show him to have been a child of his own century.' This mistake led Abbott to identify Cromwell, with twentieth century dictators, an idea which became

---

[50] *The Times,* 'Sir William Butler on Cromwell,' 26th March, (1902), p. 4.

[51] Gaunt, *op.cit.*, p. 11.

[52] R.C. Richardson, 'Cromwell and the inter-war European dictators,' in R.C. Richardson (ed.), *Images of Oliver Cromwell*, Manchester, (1993), p. 113.

[53] Ashley, *op.cit.*, p. 49.

[54] W.C. Abbott, *The Writings and Speeches of Oliver Cromwell*, 4 Vols., Cambridge, Mass., (1937-47).

'increasingly and embarrassingly marked through his work.'[55]

According to Abbott, Cromwell, was 'a military dictator, whose rule was more distasteful to the men of his own time – even his own party – than even the Stuart tyranny, which he replaced.' Moreover, 'he ruled England, not to mention Ireland and Scotland, with an iron hand. His immediate methods and results, were not as different from those of the dictatorships of our time, as we should like to think.' During this troubled Century, these comparisons, were understandable, and led to a re-appraisal of Cromwell, in terms of its own traumatic times.[56]

Since many modern historians have relied heavily on Abbott, it must be emphasised, that his 'presentation of documents, has been criticized in both plan, and execution.' Furthermore, 'Abbott was not wholly an admirer of Cromwell, whose actions and whose cause, he criticised freely and forcefully.' Moreover, 'it is in his sympathetic attitude to the Royalist cause that Abbott differed chiefly from S.R. Gardiner and C.H. Firth.'[57] Furthermore, 'a hint of unscrupulousness, is discovered in Abbott's methods and some of the stories of Cromwell's enemies, are taken at face value in his work.'[58] For example Abbott asserted that, 'Murphy's careful scholarship, is at all times reliable.'[59]

It is therefore, easy to agree with John Morrill, who has argued that 'Abbott, will in my view, remain more a testimony of wasted effort, than a positive spur to research.'[60] David Smith has argued, 'Abbott's edition, is spoiled by many factual errors, by failure to

---

[55] Robert S. Paul, *The Lord Protector, Religion and Politics in the Life of Oliver Cromwell*, London, (1955), p. 415.

[56] R.C. Richardson, 'Cromwell and the inter-war European dictators,' in R.C. Richardson, (ed.), *Images of Cromwell*, Manchester, (1993), p. 118.

[57] P.H. Hardacre, 'Writing on Oliver Cromwell since 1929,' *The Journal of Modern History*, Vol. XXXIII, No. 1, (1961), p. 2; E.S. de Beer in *History*, Vol. XXIII, (1938), pp. 120-29; 'examples of transcribing slips are given in *Journal of Modern History*, XI11, (1941), pp. 241-43.'

[58] Ashley, *op.cit.*, p. 19.

[59] Abbott, Vol. II, *op.cit.*, p. 250.

[60] Morrill, *op.cit.*, p. 629.

explain, his editorial policy regarding the wide discrepancies, between original sources and some very unreliable texts.'[61] It seems that this criticism, has been largely ignored. Biographers of Cromwell, will of course, continue to find what they look for.[62] However, as Lamont and Oldfield remind us; 'criticism of Cromwell is weak in documentation.'[63]

Modern historians, tend to be non-judgemental of Cromwell, but instead, place him in the context of his own mid-seventeenth-century times. 'In demythologizing Cromwell, it is hoped that a more accurate historical picture will be discovered.'[64] However, in this Book, the focus, will be on the Irish aspects of the Cromwell image, in order, to separate myth, from reality. Cromwell's storms of Drogheda and Wexford, have caused the most controversy. Surprisingly these events were not the subject of 'condemnation or debate at the time or before the Restoration.'[65] Although, Cromwell had left Ireland two and a half years before, the re-conquest was complete and though the subsequent settlement, had been decided long before he became the Lord Protector, both conquest and settlement, have been inevitably and wrongly identified, with Cromwell.[66]

The problem is of course, most Historians, have not, based their research on original, primary source documentation. Instead, the history of Cromwell and Ireland has been largely based on the assumptions of previous writers, and their analysis of the facts, taken from secondary works. Therefore, as far as possible, I have used, original, primary resource material, to write this book, and allowed Cromwell, and Historical documents, to speak for themselves. Whilst at the same time, challenging many of the myths developed, in the historiography, about Cromwell in Ireland.

(

---

[61] Smith, *op.cit.*, p. 10.
[62] Pennington, *op.cit.*, p. 605.
[63] William Lamont and Sybil Oldfield, *Politics, Religion and Literature in the Seventeenth Century*, London, (1975), p. 151.
[64] Gaunt, *op.cit.*, pp. 11-12.
[65] Morrill, *op.cit.*, p. 267.
[66] Roger Howell, Jnr., *Cromwell*, Boston, (1977), p. 146.

CHAPTER TWO

The Cessation of Arms 1643 to Cromwell's Arrival in Ireland 1649

The myths that have developed surrounding Cromwell's Irish Campaign 1649-50, cannot be fully understood in isolation but need to be placed in a wider context. A critical period, were the years between the close of the rebellion, in 1643, until Cromwell's arrival in Ireland in 1649.

To understand the events and legacy of 1641 they must be placed in historical context. Ireland was England's most important colony in the seventeenth century. Following the Reformation, the wars in Ireland, became more than locally significant due to the religious differences. This was because the majority of both the native Irish, and English Lords, who had settled the area around Dublin known as 'The Pale,' since Henry II remained Roman Catholic. Moreover, Henry VIII's son, Edward VI, and his daughters, Mary and Elizabeth, continued some of their fathers Irish policies.[1] Mary in order to strengthen English rule started the plantation of Ireland. She began by seizing land in Leix and Offaly and gave it to English Catholic settlers, renaming the counties as Queens and Kings counties. Following this Elizabeth I tried to establish Protestantism, by introducing acts of Parliament, which made Roman Catholic services unlawful. Throughout her reign Elizabeth continued the plantation of Ireland with Protestant settlers from mainland Britain. At the same time she had the whole of Ireland surveyed and divided into shires.[2]

---

[1] Maurice Ashley, *England in the Seventeenth Century*, London, (1954), p. 224.
[2] J.C. Beckett, *A Short History of Ireland*, London, (1973), p. 55; R. Dunlop, 'The Plantation of Munster,' *English Historical Review,iii*, (1888).

In 1596 following the Desmond, Rebellion Edmund Spencer believed that extensive colonisation of Ireland by English settlers was necessary in order to strengthen English rule and the Protestant faith. As a result further plantation of Ireland began. Following the flight of prominent Ulster Earls to the continent in 1611, and after the previous revolt of Sir Cahir O'Doherty in 1608, James I confiscated land in many areas of Ulster, and granted it to English and Scottish settlers.[3] Thus a new militant Protestant minority was located within a largely Roman Catholic population. In 1633 Sir Thomas Wentworth, who later became the First Earl of Strafford, was appointed as Charles I's Lord Deputy in Ireland; who continued the policy of strengthening English rule, through further settlement with English settlers.[4]

By the 1640s, Irelands inhabitants, consisted of three, main groups; the 'Gaelic, or native Irish,' the Norman Irish, or 'Old English' and the 'New English,' who were, Protestant colonists, who had settled in Ireland after the Reformation. Many native Irish of course, by this time had also become completely anglicised, therefore, Anglo-Irish.[5] It has been estimated, that by 1640 the 'Old English,' owned over a third of Ireland's land. Moreover, 'As Catholic, men of property, they were liable to be drawn two ways, by any threatening polarisation of Irish society.' For example, with the threat of losing his land to a plantation scheme, Ormond protested that 'he was the first Englishman, to be treated as if he, was Irish.'[6] Sir William Petty, in his survey of Ireland, estimated that by 1641, the population of Ireland was almost a million and a half, and living amongst them, there were about 'two hundred and sixty thousand Protestants.'[7] The New English, unlike the Normans, who were

---

[3] Jane H. Ohlmeyer, 'The Wars of the three Kingdoms,' *History Today,* November, (1998), pp.17-18.; also see Jonathon Bardon, *A History of Ulster*, Belfast, (1992), p. 127.
[4] Ashley *op.cit.,* p. 224.
[5] C.V. Wedgewood, *Thomas Wentworth First Earl of Strafford 1593-1641, A Revaluation*, London, (1961), Paperback edition, London, (2000), pp. 127-128.
[6] Conrad Russell, 'The British background to the Irish Rebellion of 1641,' *Historical Research*, No. 61, (1988), p. 168.
[7] James Anthony Froude, *The English in Ireland in the Eighteenth Century*, 3 vols., London, (1887), vol. 1, p. 78.; William Petty, Sir, *The Political Anatomy of Ireland*, London, (1691), p. 17.

largely warriors, intended to exploit the agricultural opportunities in Ireland, build towns, ports, and develop a more profitable way of life. This was completely out of character, with the Gaelic civilization, which was still primitive, and nomadic. The Gaelic Irish, lived by a clan system, herding their cattle from place to place. Their customs were largely ignored by the new English settlers. This form of English colonial expansion would be repeated in later centuries in other parts of the world, creating the same bitterness. In addition to these factors, when the majority of the Irish, rejected the new English religion, problems were bound to follow.[8]

Despite Wentworth' successes, in Ireland, such as the suppression of piracy and promoting the growth of the linen industry, his attempts to force the Thirty-nine Articles of the Anglican church, on both the Irish Catholics and the Ulster Presbyterians, was extremely unpopular, as was his plan to plant large areas of Connaught with settlers.[9]

For Charles I, the Bishops' Wars, were a disaster, from both a political and military perspective. He refused to acknowledge his losses and set about raising an army of 10,000 men, to be led by Wentworth. These Irish troops, would invade Western Scotland, while the Scottish Royalists, contained the Covenanters. Wentworth was appalled, that the King would arm, a Catholic army 'of naked and inexperienced Irishmen;' or as many O's, and Mac's, as would startle a whole council abroad,' and include among its leaders, the sons of the treacherous Earl of Tyrone. Despite his misgivings, Wentworth continued to recruit this 'New Irish Army,' which eventually assembled during the summer of 1640.[10] The majority of the soldiers recruited for the 'New Irish Army' were later to form the 'backbone of confederate armies.'[11]

---

[8] Wedgewood, *op.cit.*, pp. 127-128.

[9] Ashley, *op.cit.*, p. 224. Wedgewood, *op. cit.*, pp. 171-173.

[10] Jane H. Ohlmeyer, 'The Marquis of Antrim: A Stuart turn kilt,' *History Today*, March (1993), p.15

[11] Rolf Loeber and Geoffrey Parker, 'The Military Revolution in Seventeenth-Century Ireland,' in Jane H. Ohlmeyer, (ed), *Ireland from Independence to Occupation 1641-1660*, Cambridge, (1993), p. 73.

The Kings first attempt in April, to call a Parliament and have it finance his wars against the Scots, failed as this 'Short' Parliament, refused to discuss money until its grievances were met and it was dissolved. Continued military defeats for the King, forced him to summon a new Parliament, which met in November 1640, known as the 'Long Parliament.' However, instead of providing the much needed resources it impeached Wentworth. Moreover, the Irish Parliament called to finance the 'New Irish Army,' responded in the same way. It also condemned Wentworth's administration. However, Wentworth's execution, on 12th May 1641, brought temporary respite for the King.[12] Although the King's own plan, 'The Antrim Plot', did not directly give rise to the insurrection, his negotiations with the Irish nobility in the summer of 1641 to effect a *coup*, encouraged the outbreak of rebellion.[13]

Meanwhile in Ireland, Wentworth's 8,000 to 10,000 strong, 'New Irish Army,' who had not been paid, because his efficient administration had been withdrawn, were, becoming dangerous.[14] On 22nd October 1641, an attempt to capture Dublin Castle, failed, as the plot was betrayed at the last moment, and Lord Maguire and other conspirators were arrested. Nevertheless, the same night, the Irish uprising, began in Ulster.[15] Large areas of Ireland, were soon overrun by groups of native Irish joining the rebels, who then were joined by the Old English Lords of the Pale.[16] This started, a

---

[12] Jane H. Ohlmeyer, 'The Antrim Plot' of 1641 – A Myth?' *The Historical Journal* Vol. 35, No. 4, (1992), pp. 905-6.

[13] Keith Lindley, *The impact of the 1641 Rebellion upon England and Wales 1641-5, Irish Historical Studies*, Vol. XVIII, No. 70, September, (1972), p.165.

[14] Wedgewood, *op.cit.*, p. 392. also see Hugh Kearney, *Strafford in Ireland 1633-41: A Study in Absolutism*, Cambridge, (1989), p. 213.

[15] Froude, *op.cit.*, p. 110.; The various plots in Ireland, are discussed in Martyn Bennett, *The Civil Wars in Britain and Ireland 1638-1651*, Oxford, (1997), pp. 91-92., and, Jane H. Ohlmeyer, *Civil War and Restoration in Three Stuart Kingdoms: the Career of Randal MacDonnell, Marquis of Antrim 1609-1683*, Cambridge, (1993), pp. 96-101.; M. Percival-Maxwell, 'Ulster in the context of political development in three kingdoms,' in Brian MacCuarta, S.J., (eds), *Ulster 1641: Aspects of the Rising*, Belfast, (1993), p. 106.; Conrad Russell, *The Fall of the British Monarchies 1637-1642*, Oxford, (1991), p. 392.

[16] Maurice Ashley, *The Greatness of Oliver Cromwell*, London, (1957), p. 227.

decade of ferocious warfare in Ireland, and 'destabilised the military and political situation, in England and Scotland,'[17] and thereby, 'triggered the first English Civil War.'[18]

In August 1642 the King raised his standard at Nottingham which marked the start of the 'First English Civil War.'[19] Therefore, any, chance of swiftly suppressing, the rebellion in Ireland, had been spoilt because, of the 'shortage of arms, men and money,' which caused the Parliamentary war-effort there, to almost grind to a halt.[20] At first, Roman Catholics were prohibited, from joining Royalist forces, but on 27th September 1642, the King, authorised Catholics to take up arms on his behalf.[21] Meanwhile, 'the Catholic war-effort in Ireland gained momentum.'[22] This was largely due to the fact that the 'Catholic insurgents were now bound by an oath of association which allowed them to organise themselves into a formal confederation, modelled on the English Parliament, with its 'capital' at Kilkenny.'[23]

As early as the spring of 1643, the King needed troops, to strengthen his armies, in England. In April, he instructed Ormond, to open negotiations with the Irish Confederation.[24] Because he hoped to pacify the Irish Catholics and use, the English regiments in Ireland, against the English Parliament.[25] Finally, Ormond signed his name to a ceasefire, known as, the Cessation of Arms on 15th September 1643. This Cessation also released the stretched English army, which had been struggling against the Irish, to fight for the King in England. Furthermore, the Confederacy also agreed, to

---

[17] Scott Wheeler, 'Four armies in Ireland,' in Jane H. Ohlmeyer, (ed.), *Ireland from Independence to Occupation 1641-1660*, Cambridge, (1995), p. 43.

[18] Ohlmeyer *op.cit.*, p. 21. *The Wars of The Three Kingdoms*

[19] Samuel Rawson Gardiner, *History of The Great Civil War, 1642-44*, Vol. I, (1888), Reprinted (1987), p. 1.

[20] Jane H. Ohlmeyer, (ed), 'A failed revolution,' in *Ireland from Independence to Occupation 1641-1660*, Cambridge, (1995), pp. 11-12.

[21] K.J. Lindley, The Part Played by the Catholics in The English Civil War, (Unpublished Ph.D Thesis), University of Manchester, (1968), p. 71.

[22] Wheeler, op.cit., p. 47. *Four Armies in Ireland*

[23] Ohlmeyer, *op.cit.*, p. 12. *Independence to Occupation*

[24] John Kenyon, *The Civil Wars in England*, London, (1996), p. 90.

[25] Gardiner, *op.cit.*, Vol. I, p. 120. *Civil War*

send £30,000 towards their maintenance. Politically the Cessation did the King more harm than good, because; of the English hatred of Catholicism during these years.[26] Nevertheless, twelve English regiments of Foot, and one of Horse, serving in Ireland, began leaving for England. After their arrival in England, these troops, found themselves, scornfully 'accused of having abandoned English settlers to the mercy of the rebels.'[27]

However, prior to the cessation, the 'assemblies' of England, Scotland and Wales, signed the Solemn League and Covenant in September, in which, they were each required, to provide mutual assistance against the King.[28] With this agreement, the Covenanters, led by the Earl of Argyle, thus formalised their role in Ireland, and committed a Scots army of 20,000, men to the war in England.[29]

Meanwhile, in Ireland, Robert Monro the Commander, of the Scots army in Ulster would not accept the 'cessation' protesting to Ormond that 'a ceasefire would only favour the Irish rebels by allowing them to concentrate on expelling the Scots.'[30] This ceasefire was an embarrassment to English Royalists who did not want to appear pro-Catholic. Nevertheless, despite the perilous state of the King's affairs, many could not accept his decision, and had no option but to change their allegiance. From the 'parliamentary perspective a united Ireland however tenuous the union – constituted a major strategic threat because the King now had access to previously unexploited assets in terms of men and money.'[31]

Nevertheless, between the summer 1643 and March 1644, as many as 'seventeen thousand six hundred trained soldiers,' sailed from Ireland, to strengthen the King's forces in England. The majority, of those who landed at Chester, were allotted to Sir John

---

[26] Austin Woolrych, *Battles of the English Civil War*, London, (1991), p. 48.

[27] Peter Young and Richard Holmes, *The English Civil War, A Military History of The Three Civil Wars 1642-1651*, London, (1974), p. 165.

[28] Martyn Bennett, *The Civil Wars in Britain and Ireland 1638-1651*, Oxford, (1997), p. 162. Gardiner, *op.cit.*, Vol I, pp. 229-236, *Civil War.*

[29] Jane H. Ohlmeyer, 'The civil wars in Ireland,' in John Kenyon and Jane H. Ohlmeyer, (eds.), *The Civil Wars, A Military History of England, Scotland and Ireland 1683-1660*, Oxford, (1998), p. 32.

[30] James Scott Wheeler, *Cromwell-in-Ireland*, Dublin, (1999), p. 19.

[31] Kenyon and Ohlmeyer, *op.cit.*, p. 87.

Byron. However, Byron's army was defeated at the Battle of Nantwich later in 1644. Although, it suited the Parliamentary propaganda machine, to describe, Byron's army as 'Irish Papist,' in reality, the majority were Protestant Englishmen, who had volunteered, for service in Ireland in 1642, to help put down the uprising.[32] However, as many as 1,500 English soldiers, from Ireland, were taken prisoner after the battle, but were enlisted into the Parliamentary army soon afterwards.[33]

To understand the confusing military campaigns, which took place in Ireland during this critical period some basic knowledge of the military situation is necessary. By 1644 'four armies' or, what have recently been described as 'groups of armies,' were actively engaged in the Irish Civil Wars. These groups of armies, Protestant and Catholic were dispersed throughout Ireland in no less than 'three to four hundred garrison towns and castles.'[34]

The Protestant armies consisted of the Scots army in Ulster, under the command of Robert Monro, based mainly in County Antrim,[35] and parliamentary regiments under the command of Michael Jones in Dublin, Sir Charles Coote in Connaught and Lord Inchiquin in Munster.[36] There was also the Royalist Army commanded by Ormond. 'The Catholic armies comprised the Confederate provincial armies of Ulster, Leinster and Munster, under the respective commands of Owen Roe O'Neill, Thomas Preston and Theobald Viscount Taaff.' Modern historians now generally agree that from the summer of 1642 the Irish Confederates, who by now controlled most of the country, 'not only possessed sufficient military force to defeat their domestic enemies, whether Parliamentary, Scottish, or (prior to 1643) Royalist, but also despatch expeditionary forces to Britain.'[37]

As early as 1644 Charles I had asked the Confederation to

---

[32] John Kenyon, *op.cit.*, p. 90.
[33] Woolrych, *op.cit.*, p. 52.
[34] Wheeler, *op.cit.*, p. 43, *Four armies in Ireland,*; Ian Gentles, *The New Model Army in England, Ireland and Scotland, 1645-1653*, Oxford, (1992), p. 382.
[35] Wheeler, *op.cit.*, p. 43. *Four Armies in Ireland*
[36] Tom Reilly, *Cromwell, An Honourable Enemy*, London, (1999), p. 27.
[37] Wheeler, *op.cit.*, p. 43. *Four Armies in Ireland*

supply him with 10,000 Irish Catholic Soldiers. Although, other members of the Royalist Party, regarded this move unwise, because, in return for Catholic troops, the Confederation demanded full toleration for Catholics, money to support the clergy and an independent Irish Parliament. Consequently, these demands were put off. However, after Papal Nuncio Rinuccini arrived in October 1645, Confederate demands were increased. However, 'Ormond dismissed these demands as unthinkable.'[38] Nevertheless without Ormond's knowledge, Charles I, ordered the Earl of Glamorgan to make a secret treaty with the Confederates. In this treaty Glamorgan, promised further religious concessions in return for Irish Catholic troops. However, Rinuccini rejected this treaty, because he believed that Glamorgan had no authority, to grant the concessions he had promised.[39]

On the 30th March 1646 following negotiations, it was finally decided that Ormond would only sign the political articles of the treaty, while the religious articles of the treaty, were to be left for the King's decision. To further complicate matters Rinuccini denounced this 'Ormond Peace' and arrested the Catholic delegates who had agreed to it. Nevertheless, although the Irish Confederates were ready with their soldiers, it was too late because Chester had capitulated by this time along with the other suitable ports of entry into England. As a result the King was forced to admit that he had 'no horse nor ports in our power to secure them' perhaps fortunately for his reputation.[40]

Despite factionalism, however, throughout 1646 the Confederates enjoyed major military success.[41] Preston, with 6,000 men under his command moved into Connaught in June, laying siege to Roscommon and captured a number of smaller strongholds around Limerick.[42] However, the greatest Confederate victory occurred at the Battle of Benburb on 5 June 1646 when O'Neill's

---

[38] Kenyon, *op.cit.*, p. 156.
[39] Gardiner, *op.cit.*, Vol., III, pp. 30-42. *Civil War*
[40] Kenyon, *op.cit.*, p. 155.
[41] Ohlmeyer, *op.cit.*, p. 90. *The Civil Wars in Ireland*
[42] Wheeler, *op.cit.*, p. 55, *Four armies in Ireland*

army clashed with Robert Monro's Covenanter army on the banks of the River Blackwater.[43] O'Neill's army of 5,000 foot and 500 horse practically annihilated Monro's army of a similar number. Although, a few of Monro's officers were taken prisoner for ransom, no quarter was offered to the common soldiers, and at the end of the day, 3,000 Scots lay dead on the battlefield.[44] O'Neill's victory was soon "heralded as a 'Gaelic apex.'"[45] However, Confederate victories were short lived, as they were spoilt by internal rivalry. This was 'partly political and partly personal,' between O'Neill, and Preston who now commanded the Confederate army in Leinster.[46]

The political and military crisis came to a head, when Rinuccini appointed a new Supreme Council at Kilkenny, who wanted freedom from Ormond's authority. Soon afterwards, the Supreme Council ordered Confederate forces to attack Dublin, because by the winter of 1646 it was obvious that the Parliamentarians, were their only real enemy. Their armies reached Lucan but were dispersed by troops from the Dublin garrison. As a result a large scale but premature attack failed, largely because 'O'Neill and Preston failed to act decisively,' and the siege was abandoned.[47] At this stage, the Irish commanders, were as divided, as the Irish themselves. On the one hand, Clanricarde, Preston, and Taaff, followed the orders, of the Supreme Council of Kilkenny. Whilst on the other hand, Owen O'Neill, remained faithful to Rinuccini.[48]

Soon after, Ormond, seeing no further prospect of assistance from the King, opened negotiations with Parliament.[49] Subsequently in June 1647, having obtained immunity for his personal estates, Ormond handed over Dublin and all remaining Royalist garrisons

---

[43] Edward Furgul, 'The civil wars in Scotland,' in John Kenyon and Jane H. Ohlmeyer, (eds.), *The Civil Wars, A Military History of England, Scotland and Ireland 1638-1660*, Oxford, (1998), p. 61.
[44] Gardiner, *op.cit.*, Vol. III, p. 152. *Civil War*
[45] Bennett, *op.cit.,* p. 253.
[46] Kenyon, *op.cit.*, p. 163; Beckett, *op.cit.*, p. 77.
[47] Ohlmeyer, *op.cit.*, p. 91, *The civil wars in Ireland*
[48] Gardiner, *op.cit.*, Vol. IV, p. 163. *Civil War*
[49] Kenyon, *op.cit.*, p. 163.

in Ireland, to the Parliamentary Commander, Michael Jones.[50] Throughout, the summer of 1648, Irish armies, were occupied with their own internal disputes and bickering. Thus, there was little chance of them being available for service in England, or defeat Parliamentary forces in Dublin. Consequently, Ormond's, duties in Ireland, were postponed.[51] Ormond then left Ireland for England, and later joined the exiled Royalist court in France.[52]

Following Ormond's departure, Confederate forces began, a number of military campaigns. Preston, captured Carlow in May, followed by Naas, and Maynooth, by July. He then, decided, to capture Trim, in order to further isolate Dublin.[53] However, on 1st August, Jones marched northwards out of Dublin; on 4th August, he met up with Sir Henry Tichborne, now serving, as the Parliamentary Governor of Drogheda, and they combined their forces. This army consisted of 5,000 foot, and 1,500 horse. On the other hand, Preston had as many as 7,000 foot and 1,000 horse under his command. Finally, on 8th August 1647, the two armies clashed at Dungan's Hill, located near Trim. Although half of Preston's men were killed on the battlefield, the rest escaped into a bog. Almost at once, Jones surrounded the bog, with his horse, and ordered his foot to pursue the enemy. At the end of the day, most of Preston's officers were taken prisoner. However, no more than 288 common soldiers, escaped with their lives. This included, 'four hundred of the hardy band which had followed Alaster Macdonald, in the Highlands under the leadership of Montrose.'[54]

In October 1647 Jones began several skilfully planned military campaigns. He was able to scatter O'Neill's forces in most of Leinster. This allowed him to strengthen the strategic parliamentary garrisons along the River Boyne, including Drogheda. By this time, Jones appeared to have tipped the military balance, in favour of

---

[50] Ohlmeyer, *op.cit.*, p. 91.*The civil wars in Ireland;* Keith Roberts, *Cromwell's War Machine, The New Model Army 1645-1660,* Barnsley, (2005), pp. 233-234.
[51] Gardiner, *op.cit.*, Vol. IV, p. 163. *Civil War*
[52] Kenyon, *op.cit.*, p. 163.
[53] Ohlmeyer, *op.cit.*, p. 91. *The civil wars in Ireland*
[54] Gardiner, *op.cit.*, Vol. IV, p. 105. *Civil War*

Parliament.[55] As O'Neill was no longer in the North at this stage Monck marched with his army of 1,400 foot and 600 horse to assist Jones. Reports indicate that their combined army amounted to 6,000 foot and 1,600 horse. Together they captured many fortresses, including the stronghold at Athboy, right under the nose of O'Neill.[56]

Meanwhile, Lord Inchiquin, who's 'savage destructiveness,' had earned him the nickname, 'Murrough of the burnings,' by the Irish, pursued, his campaign in Munster, with vigour sacking Cashel on 3rd September.[57] Although, Lord Inchiquin's greatest victory, occurred on 13th November 1647, at the battle of Knocknannus, near Mallow. Inchiquin, annihilated the Confederate army, of 4,000 men, commanded by Lord Taaff, who had also, been reinforced, by Alaster Macdonald's highlanders, despatched there by O'Neill, thus, destroying their forces in Munster. Furthermore, as happened at Dungan Hill, the common soldiers, were denied quarter, and their officers taken prisoner.[58]

Just as the Confederate, and Royalist, causes in Ireland, seemed doomed, Ormond returned from France in September 1648, with orders to agree terms with the Confederation. Ormond successfully concluded a treaty, known as the 'Second Ormond Peace.' In return, for a promise, of greater religious toleration, the Confederates agreed to recognise royal authority.[59] At this time Lord Inchiquin, the Parliamentary Commander in Munster, who had been fighting the Irish Confederates, with 'singular brutality,' changed sides and declared for the King, which enhanced the 'Ormond Peace.'[60] This enabled Ormond, to unite the Catholic Confederate forces, with his own Protestant Royalist force, and the other Munster Protestants, led by Lord Inchiquin.[61] This was intended, to be a final attempt to create an army, capable, of

---

[55] Ohlmeyer. *op.cit.*, p. 91. *The Civil Wars in Ireland*

[56] Gardiner, *op.cit.*, Vol. IV, p. 108. *Civil War*

[57] *Ibid*, pp. 106-107.; Ronald Hutton, *The British Republic, 1649-1660*, London, (1990), p. 47.

[58] Gardiner, *op.cit.*, Vol. IV, p. 109.

[59] Wheeler, *op.cit.*, p. 60. *Four Armies in Ireland*

[60] Woolrych, *op.cit.* p. 155. ; Gardiner, *op.cit.*, Vol. IV. p. 110. *Civil War*

[61] J.G. Simms, 'Cromwell at Drogheda,' in David Hayton and G. O'Brien, (eds.), *War and Politics in Ireland 1649-1730*, London, (1986), p. 1.

defeating Parliamentary forces in Ireland, before invading mainland Britain, in the name of Charles I.[62]

The war in England had the effect of dividing Irish Protestants into two factions, firstly those who supported the King and secondly those who supported Parliament. However, Parliament's victory in England led Catholics and Royalists to make a common cause. In addition, Parliament's shoddy treatment of some of its own supporters in Ireland, caused them to defect, Lord Inchiquin being a classical example. Moreover, 'mutual suspicions meant, that a coalition between these three groups, was very slow to form, but, in January 1649, it was complete, when Charles I was executed.'[63] However, on 5th February 1649, the Covenanters, proclaimed, Charles II as King.[64] Whilst on 17th March 1649, the English Parliament, abolished the monarchy, as 'unnecessary, burdensome, and dangerous, to the liberty, safety, and public interest, of the people.' Finally, on 19th May 1649, England, was declared, to be a Commonwealth.[65]

Meanwhile in Ireland the situation remained confused, because Owen Roe O'Neill was attempting to negotiate an independent peace agreement with George Monck, the Parliamentary commander in the North.[66] Whilst in Ulster, the Scottish Presbytery, had divided into two factions. On the one hand there were the 'Resolutioners,' who supported Charles II. On the other hand there were the 'Remonstrants,' who chose to support Parliament.[67] The Scottish Resolutioners were outraged at the execution of Charles I and as a result the Scottish army in Ulster also joined Ormond's

---

[62] Raymond Gillespie, 'The Irish economy at war 1641-1642,' in Jane H. Ohlmeyer, (ed.), *Ireland from Independence to Occupation 1641-1660*, Cambridge, (1995), p. 175.

[63] Ronald Hutton, *The British Republic 1649*-1660, London, (1990), pp. 46-7.

[64] Maurice Ashley, *The English Civil War*, London, (1974), Paperback edition, (1998), p. 173.

[65] David L. Smith, *Oliver Cromwell, Politics and Religion in the English Revolution, 1640-1658*, [documents and commentary], Cambridge, (1991), p. 30.

[66] Norah Carlin, 'The Levellers and the conquest of Ireland 1649,' *The Historical Journal*, 30, 2, (1987), p. 276.

[67] T.C. Barnard, 'Planters and policies in Cromwellian Ireland', *Past and Present*, (1973), p. 55.

coalition. Thus Ormond was able to put together a formidable Royalist army in Ireland,[68] whose only 'purpose was to take over the whole realm and invade England in the name of Charles II.'[69]

During Charles I's trial, Ormond had invited the Prince of Wales, to Ireland, with the intention of leading an invasion into England. The Prince of Wales preferred to mount an attack from Scotland but his cousin, Prince Rupert, had already sailed with his fleet to Munster where it remained for most of 1649 at Kinsale.[70] Occasionally, annoying 'Parliamentary shipping with a fleet of privateers.' However, Prince Rupert, was no match against, Robert Blake, Edward Popham, and Richard Deane, who had recently been appointed, to take command of the Parliamentary Navy.[71]

It is now clear, why the re-conquest of Ireland became a priority for the English Parliament. A war cabinet was organised following the King's execution. This cabinet included Cromwell, Vane, Martin, Colonel Jones and Thomas Scot who finally planned the expedition. Their opinion was, that a combined force of 12,000 foot and horse would be required to undertake this task. The re-conquest of Ireland was not open to question. Firstly, it was axiomatic that it belonged to England, as it had under Charles I. Secondly, there existed widespread opinion that retribution was needed for the killing of thousands of English colonists during the insurrection of 1641. Thirdly, Ireland had to be quickly subdued as Ireland was now a dangerous base for the invasion of England by the Royalists. 'Even the Levellers did not, for the most part, question these assumptions.'[72] From a Parliamentary perspective a major military offensive in Ireland could no longer be postponed.[73] Consequently in March 1649, the English Parliament chose Oliver Cromwell to command an expeditionary force of 12,000 New Model soldiers.

---

[68] Simms, *op.cit.*, p. 1.
[69] Hutton, *op.cit.*, p. 47.
[70] Simms, *op.cit.*, p. 1.
[71] Alan Freer, 'Until the Age of Nelson, Robert Blake was England's greatest admiral,' *Military History* April, (2006), p. 20.
[72] Gentles, *op.cit.*, p.350; see also Norah Carlin, 'The Levellers and the conquest of Ireland in 1649,' *The Historical Journal*, 30, 2, (1987), pp.269-88, esp. p.266.
[73] Carlin, *Ibid.*, p. 276.

They also supplied him with 'a large artillery train, 130 ships and a war chest of 100,000 pounds.'[74] Perhaps John Maudit's view was typical of most Englishmen at the time, when he wrote to Cromwell in July 1649 before he sailed for Ireland:

> you are sent over not to harm or oppress the innocent,
> but to subdue and chastise the rebellious and take account
> of the cruel massacres and abundance of blood of
> the Lords own dear ones which they have shed.[75]

A similar view was echoed by the Earl of Pembroke, in his speech to the New Model Army before it left for Ireland. 'You are going a hunting of rebels into Ireland. I wish you good sport in catching your game.'[76]

Fortunately, for the new Republic, Lieutenant General Michael Jones, in Dublin, Sir Charles Coote, at Londonderry, and George Monck, at Dundalk, remained loyal to their cause. Because, by June 1649, Parliament had few garrisons in Ireland. These included Dublin, Drogheda, Derry, Trim and Dundalk along with some smaller ones like Ballyshannon.[77]

Unfortunately, for Cromwell, only one month prior to his arrival in Dublin the Governor of Drogheda, had been forced to surrender to Lord Inchiquin. In June Ormond had despatched Inchiquin, along with his Munster Army, to capture the town.[78] Although Drogheda was courageously defended by Parliamentary soldiers they were forced to surrender on the 11th July 1649, simply because they had run out of ammunition.[79] However, Gardiner noted, 'of the 700 [Parliamentary] foot and 255 horse of which the garrison comprised,

---

[74] Ohlmeyer, *op.cit.*, p. 90. *The Civil Wars in Ireland*
[75] Chris Durston, 'Let Ireland be quiet: opposition in England to the Cromwellian conquest of Ireland,' *History Workshop Journal*, No. 21, Spring, (1986), p. 106.
[76] *Ibid.*
[77] Gentles, *op.cit.*, p. 357.
[78] Samuel Rawson Gardiner, *History of the Commonwealth and Protectorate, 1649-1656*, Vol. I, (1903), pp. 90-97.
[79] Wheeler, *op.cit.*, p. 61. *Cromwell-in-Ireland*, citing, TT, E566 (7), *A Modest Narrative of Intelligence*, 21-28 July 1649, 132-4; TT, E531 (11), *Moderate Messenger*, 25 June-2 July 1649, 59-60.

no fewer than 600 foot and 220 horse, took service with the victorious [Royalist] party.'[80]

After strengthening the Drogheda garrison with his own troops, Lord Inchiquin, turned his attention to Trim and Dundalk. However, most of the parliamentary soldiers, manning the garrison at Dundalk, had deserted, which forced George Monck to surrender.[81] Meanwhile, on 25th July 1649, encouraged by Inchiquin's victories, at Drogheda and Dundalk; Ormond, moved most of his troops to Rathmines, south of Dublin, leaving Lord Dillon at Finglas, with 2,000 foot and 500 horse. On 27th July, Ormond was joined by Inchiquin accompanied by the majority of his forces, to decide, the course of action to be taken; regarding the possibility, of Cromwell landing in Munster. Finally however, Inchiquin, was despatched with a regiment of horse to Munster, whilst, Ormond, prepared to besiege Dublin.[82]

Cromwell was fortunate that, even before he arrived in Ireland, Michael Jones, had defeated Ormond, at the Battle of Rathmines on 2nd August 1649, capturing his munitions and smashing his army.[83] Here Jones, 'with enterprising opportunism' and reinforced by three regiments, dispatched by Cromwell from Chester, attacked 1500 of Ormond's, soldiers encamped at Baggarath, located only one mile from Dublin.[84] This attack had the effect of a rout, which spread to Ormond's army, encamped at Rathmines. Having been just awakened from sleep, Ormond, in vain, ordered his troops to stand firm. However, 'one regiment after another either threw down their arms or ran.' Furthermore, although Ormond called on his other regiments at Finglas, they refused to muster, despite urgent orders from their officers. This was a grave day for the Royalists, because at the end of the day, Jones, claimed to have killed 4,000 men and taken 2,517 prisoners.[85] On the other hand, Ormond estimated that the number of those killed were no more than 600, and alleged, that most of them were; 'butchered in cold blood after

[80] Gardiner, op.cit., Vol., I p. 97. C&P.
[81] Wheeler, op.cit., p. 61. Cromwell-in-Ireland
[82] Gardiner, C&P, Vol. I, op.cit., p. 100.
[83] Ohlmeyer, op.cit., p. 98. The Civil Wars in Ireland
[84] Ashley, op.cit., p. 228. Greatness of Oliver Cromwell
[85] Gardiner, C&P, Vol. I, op.cit., pp. 101-2.

they had laid down their arms upon promise of quarter and had been for almost an hour prisoners, and divers of them murdered after they were brought within the works of Dublin.'[86]

It has been shown that between the years of 1643 and 1649, there were a number of major battles fought in Ireland. These included the battle of Benburb, 5th June 1646, Dungan's Hill, 8th August 1647, Knocknanuss, 13th November 1647, and Rathmines, 2nd August 1649. Although the Confederates, were victorious at the battle of Benburb, they were defeated in all the others and suffered heavy losses.[87] However, there seems little doubt that the Royalists defeat at Rathmines was the real turning point of the war.

Looking at Rathmines, from a Parliamentary perspective, as Whitelock put it, 'there was never a day in Ireland like this.' In addition 'news of the battle was to spur recruitment in England.'[88] This victory was to invigorate Cromwell's expeditions, allowing his army to land unchallenged at Ringside, on 15th August 1649, whilst the 'Royalists were still licking their wounds from an unexpected defeat.'[89] There seems little doubt that Jones' recent victory had cleared the way for Cromwell's success; because he met not a united vigorous and successful enemy, but one already shattered and divided against itself.[90]

On the day of his arrival in Ireland, Cromwell made a speech, to the citizens of Dublin:

> That God brought him thither in safety so he doubted
> not, but by his divine providence, to restore them all
> to their lost liberties and properties and that all those
> who heart's affections were real for the carrying on
> of the great work against the barbarous and
> bloodthirsty Irish, and the rest of their adherents and
> confederates, for the propagating of the Gospel of

[86] *Ibid*, p. 102. ; Gilbert, *op.cit.*, Vol. II, p. 271. Ormond to Byron, 29th September 1649.
[87] Kenyon and Ohlmeyer, *op. cit.*, p. 84.
[88] Gentles. *op. cit.*, p. 357.
[89] Ashley, *op.cit.*, p. 228. *Greatness of Oliver Cromwell,*
[90] Wilbur Cortez Abbott, *The Writings and Speeches of Oliver Cromwell*, Vol. II, Cambridge, Mass., (1939-40), p. 105.

> Christ, the establishing of truth and peace, and restoring that bleeding nation to its former happiness and tranquillity, should find favour and protection from the Parliament of England and himself, and withal should receive such endowments and gratuities as should be answerable to their merits.[91]

Cromwell's speech, clearly outlined his purpose for being in Ireland, and offered 'peace and protection' from the Parliament of England to the Irish people, should they help him in his endeavours.[92] Cromwell's real purpose was plain, - the assertion of English (and in the context, Parliamentary), control in Ireland. Such support was manifest when Cromwell remained in Dublin for two weeks 'gathering intelligence and organising his army.'[93] In the words, of Lieutenant-Colonel Baldock, 'However he may have obtained them, Cromwell never seemed to have lacked good spies, and his wonderful military judgement sifted the wheat from the chaff, in their reports with infallible accuracy.'[94] Finally, Cromwell issued proclamations against 'profane swearing and drunkness,' prohibiting his troops from 'plundering or doing any wrong or violence' towards the Irish people, 'unless they be in arms or office with the Enemy,' and assuring any who supplied his army and garrisons with provisions that they would receive payment in cash and protection.[95] Charles Firth, emphasised this was a clear demonstration of the fact that 'no other General [in Ireland], was more careful to protect peaceable peasants from plunder and violence.'[96] It was against this background, that Cromwell and his army, marched out of Dublin, on or about 30th August 1649, to face the Royalist garrison at Drogheda.[97]

---

[91] Charles L. Stainer, (ed.), *Speeches of Oliver Cromwell 1644-1658*, London, (1901), pp. 76-77. [Substance only].
[92] *Ibid.*
[93] Ashley, *op.cit.*, pp. 228-9.
[94] T.S. Baldock, *Cromwell As A Soldier*, London, (1899), p. 382.
[95] Peter Gaunt, *Oliver Cromwell*, Oxford, (1996), p. 115.
[96] Charles Firth, *Oliver Cromwell and the Rule of the Puritans in England*, Oxford, (1900), p. 254.
[97] J.G. Simms, 'Cromwell at Drogheda 1649,' *The Irish Sword*, (1974), p. 214.

The mythical illustration, 'Cromwell's Massacre at Drogheda', by Henry Doyle, as it appears in Mary Francis Cussack's *Illustrated History of Ireland*, 1868.

CHAPTER THREE

Myths and Cromwell's Storm of Drogheda 1649

Beside the Garrison about four thousand of the Catholic citizens were deliberately massacred. [Patrick Francis Moran][1]

The major myths, surrounding Cromwell's storm of Drogheda in 1649, can be summarised as follows: firstly, that the civilian inhabitants of the town were all Irish Catholics;[2] secondly, the garrison, comprising of 3,000 men, were also Irish Catholics;[3] thirdly, after Cromwell had induced the garrison to surrender, by offering quarter for their lives, he then broke his word, and ordered indiscriminate massacre of the whole garrison;[4] fourthly, Cromwell also put to the sword, the bulk of the civilian inhabitants, sparing, neither woman nor children;[5] finally, none of the garrison's soldiers escaped, except, for one lieutenant.[6]

Simon Shama in *A History of Britain, The British Wars 1603-1776*, (2001), more recently emphasised that, the vast majority of the inhabitants of Drogheda, when it was stormed by Cromwell in 1649, 'were neither Catholic, nor Gaelic Irish, nor were any of

---

[1] Patrick Francis Moran, DD, *Historical Sketch of the Persecutions Suffered by the Catholics of Ireland Under the Rule of Cromwell and the Puritans.* Dublin, (1885), p. 93.

[2] *Ibid.*

[3] Denis Murphy, Rev., S.J., *Cromwell in Ireland, A History of Cromwell's Irish Campaign*, Dublin, (1883), p. 86.

[4] Moran, *op.cit.*, p. 90.

[5] Edward Hyde, Earl of Clarendon, *The History of the Rebellion and Civil Wars in England*, Oxford, (1888), Vol. V. II, p. 102.

[6] Peter Gaunt, *Oliver Cromwell*, Oxford, (1996), p. 112.

them unarmed civilians, the women and children, of Father Murphy's largely mythical history, published in 1883'[7] and in Moran's *Historical Sketch of the Persecutions Suffered by the Catholics of Ireland Under the Rule of Cromwell and the Puritans* (1885). Moreover, as Robert Kee has highlighted:

> Cromwell's ruthless action at Drogheda cannot be seen simply as the crude anti-Irish racialism of Irish nationalist legend. The garrison at Drogheda was commanded by an English Catholic, Sir Arthur Aston, and was largely under English officers - all Royalists fighting Cromwell in this the last stage of the great 'Civil War.'[8]

There is little doubt that the controversy, surrounding Cromwell's Storm of Drogheda; has plagued historians for centuries. The purpose of this Chapter, is to challenge the myths, surrounding this event, that were created, then developed by early Royalist propaganda. A more objective picture needs to be drawn, as the Royalist myth has been used to depict Cromwell 'as a monster of cruelty, differing from the other great generals and statesmen in English history' and, secondly, because 'it has been frequently assigned as the main reason for poisoning Anglo-Irish relations to modern times.'[9] While the reporting of events at Drogheda, have had repercussions to the present day, at the time it made little impact, except on Royalist morale.[10]

It was largely Moran's assertion, in the nineteenth century that 'beside the garrison, about four thousand of the Catholic citizens, were deliberately massacred'[11] which developed the myth, that the inhabitants of Drogheda in 1649 were Irish Catholics. The

---

[7] Simon Schama, *A History of Britain, The British Wars 1603-1776,* London, (2001), p. 203.

[8] Robert Kee, *Ireland: A History,* Boston, (1980), p. 46.

[9] Maurice Ashley, *The Greatness of Oliver Cromwell,* London, (1957), p. 253.

[10] Ian Gentles, *The New Model Army in England, Ireland and Scotland, 1645-1653,* Oxford, (1992), p. 362.

[11] Moran, *op.cit.,* p. 93.

evidence has never supported this claim, and in fact, the inhabitants of Drogheda were mostly New English settlers.[12] Although up until the end of August 1649, the Town Sherriff, of Drogheda was actually a Scotsman.[13]

Sir, Phelim O'Neill tried to capture Drogheda during the unsuccessful siege which began on 21 November 1641 and lasted until March 1642, when eventually, the besiegers were forced to withdraw.[14] In fact, Drogheda was 'one of the major English enclaves, that held out from the rebellious native Irish.' Moreover, 'Those that were supportive of the insurrectionists either fled or were expelled from the town.' Furthermore, the vast majority of the citizens of Drogheda, supported the English government or whichever faction was in power at the time. For example, from 1641-7 the town was under the control of Protestant Royalists, commanded by Ormond, on the other hand, from 1647 until 11the July 1649; it was under the jurisdiction of Michael Jones the Parliamentary Governor of Dublin. [15] By August 1649 Drogheda, had remained an English Protestant enclave, for the best part of a decade.

Unfortunately for Cromwell, only one month prior to his arrival in Dublin, the Governor of Drogheda, Sir Henry Tichborne, had been forced to surrender to Lord Inchiquin.[16] Although Drogheda, was courageously defended by Parliamentary soldiers, the Governor was forced to surrender simply, because he had run out of ammunition.[17]

---

[12] Ernest Hamilton, Lord, *The Irish Rebellion of 1641*, London, (1920), p.367; Reilly *op.cit*, p. 8.

[13] J.T. Gilbert, (ed), *A Contemporary History of Affairs in Ireland from A.D. 1641-1652*, (3. Vols), Dublin, (1879-80), Vol. 1I. p. 247.

[14] Rolf Loeber and Geoffrey Parker, 'The Military Revolution in Seventeenth-Century Ireland,' in Jane H. Ohlmeyer, (ed), *Ireland From Independence to Occupation, 1641-1660.* Cambridge, (1995), p. 77.

[15] Tom Reilly *Cromwell, An Honourable Enemy*, London, (1999), p. 8.

[16] Samuel Rawson Gardiner, *History of the Commonwealth and Protectorate, 1649-1656*, London, (1903), Vol., I p. 97.

[17] James Scott Wheeler, *Cromwell-in-Ireland*, Dublin, (1999), p. 61, citing, TT, E566 (7), *A Moderate Narrative of Intelligence*, 21-28 July 1649, 132-4; TT, E531 (11), *Moderate Messenger*, 25 June-2 July 1649, 59-60.

Throughout the 1640s, Drogheda never had been, an Irish Confederate garrison. Moran's suggestion that 4000 Catholics, inhabited Drogheda and that the garrison comprised 3000 Irish catholic Confederate soldiers was pure fiction. As Tom Reilly has stressed, by 1649 the Irish population of the area, was forced to live in cabins outside the town walls, only a small number were permitted to reside within the town boundaries in a confined area, known as 'Irish Street.'[18]

Popular historical opinion, created the myth, that the soldiers in the garrison of Drogheda, mainly consisted of Irish Catholics. This is pure fiction and is not supported by the evidence. Although on this point there has been deliberate contradiction. For example, 'Clarendon says: 'As to the garrison, most of them were English'. In another place, he speaks of, the 'massacre of that body of English at Tredagh.' Ormond says, 'they were chiefly Catholic' and 'Irish writers interpret this to mean Irish Catholic.'[19] Winston Churchill refers to, 'the flower of the Irish Royalists and English Volunteers.'[20] Patrick Corish argues, 'How many of them were English and how many of them were Irish, seems beyond establishing, but the serving officers, were chiefly English, as was the Commander Sir Arthur Aston, a Catholic Royalist.'[21]

The Military Lists and Muster-Rolls for 30th August 1649, only two days before the approach of Cromwell, makes it clear that the garrison at Drogheda, was manned by 320 horse and 2,221 foot-soldiers. This included the entire force of Royalist artillery, which consisted of 'one master-gunner, two gunners and three gunner's mates, – who were: the Town Major, his man Clarke of the Store, William Wade, gunner George Calluert, gunner Phebus Bagnall, gunner's mate Thomas Paine, gunner's mate Robert Evans, Carpenter John Keane, his mate and William Purchase-Smyth,' all

[18] Reilly, *op.cit.*, p. 9.
[19] Frederick Harrison, *Oliver Cromwell*, London, (1922), p. 148.
[20] Winston Churchill, *The Island Race*, London, (1964), p. 170.
[21] Patrick Corish, 'The Cromwellian Conquest 1649-53,' in T.W. Moody, F.X. Martin and F.J. Byrne, (eds.), *History of Ireland, Vol. 3, Early Modern Ireland 1534-1692*, Oxford, (1976), pp. 339-40.

of whom appear to have been English.[22] In addition, 'Ormond's soldiers consisted of not only many recent English settlers, but also Royalist refugees from England, who had no claim to be Irish in any sense.'[23] It appears that half of Ormond's soldiers defending Drogheda, were either English, or Anglo-Irish Protestants.[24] The others seem to have been mostly English Catholics.[25] This completely refutes the myth that the garrison consisted of 3,000 men, who were mostly Catholic Irishmen.

Given the fact that Drogheda, was a Parliamentary garrison up until 11th July 1649, when captured by Lord Inchiquin, it would be highly unlikely that Catholic Priests or Friars would be living in the town prior to this.[26] Moreover, when Ormond strengthened the garrison, with his own troops, prior to Cromwell's arrival, each regiment travelled there with its own Chaplin, as the Muster Rolls show.[27] Even Ormond's own Regiment, had a 'Catholic priest who was Chaplin to the Catholics in his Regiment.'[28] Apparently this was not unusual, for example, it was reported that at Duncannon, the 'Catholic priest and the Protestant Minister, were on the best of terms and shared use of the garrison chapel.'[29] Reilly concludes; 'The two main church buildings in 1649, were of Protestant British origin.'[30]

To place the events in historical context, Ormond having been defeated at Rathmines, used his remaining horse and deceit, to obtain the surrender of Ballyshannon, convincing its Governor that he had captured Dublin.[31] Two days after Cromwell's arrival in Ireland, Ormond visited Drogheda, on the 17th August, intent on

---

[22] Gilbert, *op.cit.*, Vol. II, p. 496.

[23] Ronald Hutton, *The British Republic 1649-1660*, London, (1990), p. 47.

[24] Wheeler, *op.cit.*, p. 87. *Cromwell in Ireland*

[25] D.M.R. Esson, *The Curse of Cromwell: A History of the Ironside Conquest of Ireland, 1649-53*, Totowa, New Jersey, (1971), p. 112.

[26] Gilbert, *op. cit.*, II, p. 247.

[27] *Ibid*, p. 496.

[28] Thomas Carlyle, *Oliver Cromwell's Letters and Speeches with Elucidations*, (second revised edition), (3 Vols in One), London, (1846), p. 350.

[29] Gardiner *op. cit.*, Vol., I, p. 137.

[30] Reilly, *op. cit.*, p. 8.

[31] Gentles *op.cit.*, p. 357.

reinforcing it, as a bastion against Cromwell's advance. To this end he dismissed the Lord Inchiquin appointed Governor, Lord Moore, and replaced him with an English Catholic, Sir Arthur Aston. Ormond then withdrew to Tecroghan, north of Trim, to the residence of Sir Luke Fitzgerald. Aston, had previously served as the Governor of Reading in 1643 and Oxford throughout 1644. It was here, that he had lost his leg, after a fall from his horse, which had been replaced by a wooden one. Reports indicate that Aston was 'notorious for his stern and unbending nature.' [32]

Most of the inhabitants of Drogheda, did not support Aston, and some were actively plotting to betray him, to Parliamentary Commanders in Dublin. These facts are supported by the following contemporary documents. On 25th August 1649 Aston wrote to Ormond:

> My Lorde,
>
> Your Exellency was no sooner out of towne, but I meete with sum people whome I believe know not well my constitution ; your Exellency will by theas small enclosed coppies perceive whot inclination Me Lady Wilmut hath, to do mischiefe if it lay in her power. By her commaunde these papers weare to have been sent to Dublin, her owne boye was of them, the berer who I feare is of to smale a sise to bee hanged. The Lord Blanyes daughters writ too of the papers, and my Lady Wilmot herself the therde, I have put my wifes uncle Frank More under arrest for I cannot well disieste shutch knavish foolings. As for the ladies, I say nothing to them until I have your Exellencys positive orders how to proceede against them; as for the other too named, to wit Kerkham and Owins, I will examine the business and with your exellencys permission proseed with them accordingly. This

---

[32] Gardiner, *op cit.*, Vol., I, p. 110.

Kerkham is Me Lord Moores shurgin. Sum halfe an howre before I sawe the boye (but he was already taken), My Lady Wilmot sent unto mee to desire leave to sende a messenger to Dublin. I answered I had no commission to doe itt, but it seems she had nottis that the boy was then brought to mee, with occationed this motion of herrs, I beseech your Exellencys expres commaundes to turne her and her malignant family out of the towne, for thoughe she bee my grand mother, I shall make powder of her of her else if she playmee shutch foule playe. I humbly crave yor Exellencys speedy commaundes herein, for they are very dangerous company, as the case standes with mee, who is for ever Me Lord,

Yor Excilence faithfull and most humble servant,
Arthur Ashton.
Drogheda, this 25ᵗʰ August, in the evening. [33]

It can be established from Aston's letter, that those plotting against him, included his own grandmother Lady Wilmot, two of Lord Blaynes daughters, Kerkham and Owens. Whilst the ex Governor Lord Frank Moore, was placed under arrest. Moreover, Lady Wilmot had sent her young boy with correspondence and secret information, for Parliamentary Commanders, Leiutenant Colonel Foulkes and Colonel Jones, at their Dublin garrison. However, Lady Wilmot's boy was stopped and arrested, and the following documents were intercepted by Aston, who enclosed them in his letter to Ormond.

Enclosures in Aston's Letter.
Sir,
I am now to crave your advice and Coll. Johnes, and what I shall doe, ffor I am in a verie great strate and

---

[33] Gilbert, *op cit.*, Vol. II. Part II, p. 234.

sad condition. Their fore let me here from you speedily. I am your faithfull friend. Poore Franke and I are in one condition.

M. Wilmot.

Sir-
I must beg one favour from you, which is to send me a protection for Mr Cercom [Kerkham], who I will confidentlt engage myselfe, woold have beene at Dublin longe since, had not his goodness taken greate pittie on me.
I must beg the same favour for my poore cozen Owens, who on my worde is much a servant to that cause as anye one can be. And had not his greate charge hindered him he woold have been their, for on my credit his heart is their. And I hope you will cosider him. And it shall always owne as a special favour to him, who is most really your faithfull servant,

A.B. [Mrs Blayny]

Sir,
The hearing of your coming this way is a greate joy to me, but it has driven all the Lords away. And My Lady Moore. I have more to wryte but I leave you to the boy to learne more newes. Sir, I hear there is one Captain Kitely who intends to come to this partie, with manye more of his comrades; and my uncle is desirous you should know it. Sir, I must now give you thankes for your token I received by Mr. Backster, and desire you to be assured I am the same you left me; and will be.
I am you faithful servant.

A.B. [Mrs Blayny]

The following letters from Aston to Ormond seeking the exchange of female Parliamentary prisoners in Drogheda, for Royalist Coalition prisoners in Dublin.

Aston to Ormond

I would have taken it for a very great favour, if yor Exelency would have been pleased to have sent yor positive answer, what I should have doon with my femall traytors, and so have taken mee of the busines, by reson my neere relation unto sum of them, but thay shall not fare the better for that ; if the begun unusual coors by Jones, for the exchange of women may bee observed, I would not doubt, but to get honester and better subjects for them.

May it, pleas yor Exlens,
Arth Aston[34] Trogodaghe, 27th Aug, 1649

In the meane time, I wish I weare well cleard of theas femall spies that are here, I beseetch yor Exellency's express order, for if the oulde lady were not so neer in relation unto mee as she is, I shoulde have been very sparing of any serrimonyous proceedings with her.[35]

Yor Exlens most humble servant
Arth Aston[36] Trogodaghe 27th Aug, 1649

Ormond to Aston

Sir,- Women is given much to make little factions ; I do not much apprehend this, but it is fit you know all I

---

[34] *Ibid*. p. 235 -236.
[35] *Ibid*. p. 234-235.

doe. If you cannot beter imploy your men, it were not amis partys were sent to interrupt the Dublin market, and destroy corne and hay, I rest

Yor affectionate servant: Ormond
Endorsed : 28 Aug., 1649. A coppy of yr letter to Art Aston.[37]

In reality of course, Ormond, remained at Tecroghan with 3000, men, a long way from Drogheda and too far away to be of any military assistance to Aston. Furthermore 'in justification for his timid behaviour, he afterwards explained that his troops were in such low spirits that he did not dare bring them close to the enemy.'[38] Aston was in an increasingly untenable position. He was running out of food, munitions and money to pay his men, plus, the additional troops, promised by Ormond; had still not arrived. Whilst at the same time parliamentary supporters within the town itself were plotting against him. It was hardly the best scenario, for a Commander, about to undergo trial by siege from Cromwell's army.[39]

Most recently, Tristram Hunt in *The English Civil War at First Hand*, (2002), has asserted that at Drogheda, 'four thousand confederate troops lost their lives,'[40] when in fact, O'Neill's confederate army, failed to march to Drogheda. This is demonstrated by the fact, that desperate to increase the troops, in place to confront Cromwell, Ormond sent the Catholic Bishop of Raphoe, and Colonel Mervyn Audley, to ask Owen O'Neill, to lead his confederate Catholic Army of Ulster, to Drogheda.[41] Mervyn, deserted to the Parliamentary commander Sir Charles

---

[36] *Ibid.*, p. 235 -236.
[37] *Ibid.*, p. 238.
[38] Gentles, *op.cit.*, p. 358.
[39] Trevor Royle, *Civil war – The War of the Three Kingdoms, 1638 – 1660*, London, (2004), Paperback edition, London, (2005), p. 528.
[40] Tristram Hunt, *The English Civil War at First Hand*, London, (2002), p. 230.
[41] Gardiner, *op.cit.*, p. Vol. I, p. 111; Ormond to O'Neill, 23rd August 1649, Gilbert, *op.cit.*, Vol. II, p. 230.

Coote and the bishop later reported, that O'Neill himself, was at Coote's headquarters. On 5th September, Ormond was informed by Daniel O'Neill, that Owen O'Neill could not leave Coote's headquarters, 'because of a swelling in his knee.' Ormond realised, he could gain no support from the Confederate army, nor from Inchiquin, nor Clanricarde, who had both failed to send the required reinforcements. Colonel Trevor, responded but so slowly that Cromwell would be at Drogheda before he arrived. To make matters worse, Ormond faced the desertion of Captain Wentworth and one hundred and fifty of Inchiquin's horse, to the Parliamentary camp. Divisions within Ormond's army, and between the English and the Irish, were playing into Cromwell's hands.[42]

By 30th August all regiments allocated for the defence of Drogheda by Ormond, had arrived there. According to the Muster Rolls, see Appendix 1. The garrison consisted of 2552 men, including officers.[43] They were the 'flower of Ormond's army,' which included his own regiment, under the command of Sir Edmund Verney, who had previously arrived there to support, the three regiments of foot, which were already in Drogheda, when it was attacked by Jones. Gardiner argues, 'The other three regiments, one under Colonel Byrne, which had been left behind by Inchiquin, consisted of Englishmen and Protestants, whilst the other two under Wall and Warren were for the most part, if not altogether, composed of Irish Catholics.'[44] J.G. Simms argues, 'Ormond's regiment is likely to have had a good proportion of Protestants.'[45] On the other hand Barry Taylor argues, 'more than half of Ormond's army comprised of English Catholics.'[46] Although Reilly is probably correct, in believing that the defenders of Drogheda 'were a mixture of Irish and English Protestants, and Catholics.'[47]

---

[42] *Ibid*, p. 114; Daniel O'Neill to Ormond, 5th September 1649, Gilbert, *op.cit.*, Vol, II, p. 251.

[43] *Ibid.,* Vol, II pp. 496-499. *Contemporary History*

[44] Gardiner, *op.cit.*, pp. 110-111.

[45] J.G. Simms, 'Cromwell at Drogheda 1649,' *The Irish Sword*, XI, (1973-74), p. 4.

[46] Barry M. Taylor, 'Siege and slaughter at Drogheda,' *Military History*, October, (1999), 16, (4), p. 62.

[47] Reilly, *op.cit.*, p. 114.

On 1ˢᵗ September 1649 Aston wrote to Ormond again:

May it pleas yor Exellency

Yesternight, late, I received yor Exellencys letter…The Bishop of Dronmore writ unto Collonell Warren which hee showed mee, that theare was com unto this towne too fryers who intended no good. It may bee my fortune to light upon them which if I doe, upon my credit wee shall have a troubles worse then I have had with my grandmother, who with much adoe hath yelded yesternight to leave this place and goe to Mellefant, but sore against her will, and highly offended with mee,who am very glad to be rid of her upon anye tear mes, with her deer son Franke. Yesterday I had intelligence that the rebels [Parliamentary forces] have put sum greate cannon a ship borde to bring along with them heether. Thay bring 8 ships a longe with them, and other cannon and mortar peese thay intend to bring by lande; thay have provided skaling lathers to bringe with them…I meete with sum asignements, passes, and protections signed by yor Exellency I believe not rightly made use of. One was given unto the Scotch Sherrif here, who under the culler of free tradinge, without eather my knowledge or the Mayors, hath carried away a great part of his goods and himselfe lefte the toune.
Yor Exlence most faithfull and most humble servant, Arthur Aston.
Trogodaghe,this ferst September, 1649
Endorsed : Sr Ar : Astons. Dated 1. Rec. Sept., 1649. Concerning some fryers wich the Bishop of Dronmore writt to Collonell Warren were gone to Drogheda to doe mischiefe, etc.[48]

---

[48] Gilbert, *op.cit.*, Vol. II. p. 247.

It can be seen in Aston's letter, that Lady Wilmot, along with her son Frank were expelled from the town and sent to Mellifont. However, it is not clear what happened to Lady Blaney's daughters, Captain Kitely, his comrades, and the other conspirators.

Cromwell's first objective, was the control of Drogheda, which would enable him to secure the road from the north, along which Lord Ardes was advancing with Scottish regiments from Ulster to reinforce Aston at the garrison.[49]

On 30th August, Cromwell left Dublin and marched North with his army of 12,000 men, arriving before Drogheda on 2nd September.[50] His smaller pieces of artillery were soon in position. However, it was not until 5th September, that Cromwell's heavy guns were safely landed at the mouth of the river Boyne, which were then hauled overland. Finally by 9th September, Cromwell's artillery was ready for action.[51]

Built by the Normans in the twelfth century, the geography of Drogheda, only 23 miles from Dublin, was vital to the siege. It was a fortressed, town surrounded by a stone wall, about one and a half miles long. The walls were twenty feet high, six feet thick with built in firing steps for the defenders. The defences of Drogheda had several advantages. The river Boyne, separated the town into two parts, North Town and South Town, which were linked by a narrow drawbridge.[52] In Cromwell's time, there were five gates and eleven towers, on the South side of town and seven gates and nineteen towers, on the North side.[53] A successful siege, or assault on the town, therefore, would have required a much larger force than the one commanded by Cromwell.[54]

---

[49] Gardiner, *op.cit.*, Vol., I, p. 110 - 14.

[50] Gaunt, *op.cit.*, p. 115.

[51] Esson, *op.cit.*, p. 112; Rolf Loeber and Geoffrey Parker, 'The military revolution in seventeenth-century Ireland,' in Jane H. Ohlmeyer, (ed.), *Ireland from Independence to Occupation 1641-1660*, Cambridge, (1995), p. 77.

[52] Gardiner, *op.cit.*, Vol., I., p. 114.

[53] Simms, *op.cit.*, p. 3.

[54] Gardiner, *op.cit.*, Vol., I, p. 114.

[55] James Scott Wheeler *op.cit.*, p. 87. *Cromwell in Ireland.*

James Scott Wheeler, in his book *Cromwell in Ireland*, (1999), has asserted that Cromwell had stationed 'cavalry patrols,' outside the Northern walls of Drogheda, to prevent the defenders escape in that direction.[55] However, there is simply no evidence of this, nor does Wheeler produce any to support his claim. Because, in reality Cromwell never invested the northern half, of the town, until after the storm. He relied on his heavy guns to make breaches in the southern wall, which could then be stormed, a technique he had perfected during the English Civil War.[56] This argument is supported by the evidence of Sir Edmund Verney, who wrote to Ormond on 9th September, that 'The enemy hath no forces on the North side of the Boyne.'[57] Further supported by the evidence of Cromwell himself, who explains to Parliament:

> If we had divided our forces into two quarters to have besieged the North Town and the South Town, we would not have had correspondency between the two parts of our Army, but they might have chosen to have brought their Army, and have fought with which part 'of ours' they pleased, and at the same time [the enemy] have made a sally with 2,000 men upon us, and have left their walls manned; they having in the Town the number hereafter specified, but some say 4,000.[58]

Because the Storm of Drogheda; has passed into 'Irish demonology,' perhaps it should be made clear what happened there. Cromwell had nothing but contempt, for the casual plunder and slaughter, on both sides, which was a feature of Irish campaigning. This is demonstrated by the fact, that he had his men under firm control, hanging two of them, for daring to steal hens from the Irish only two days before the storm. 'He hoped that with his reputation, his siege train and formidable, army he could induce

---

[56] Simms, *op.cit.*, p. 5.
[57] Robert Murray, 'Cromwell at Drogheda: a reply to J.B. Williams,' *The Nineteenth Century*, Vol. LXXII, (1912), p. 1231.
[58] Carlyle, *op.cit.*, pp. 298-9. Letter XCIX.

the enemy towns to surrender peaceably and thereby save lives.'[59] Cromwell demonstrated this, when he deployed his eleven siege guns in front of Drogheda. He expected the governor to surrender peacefully, and sent terms under a white flag.[60]

On Saturday 7th September 1649, Aston ordered a sally of 2000, horse and foot, under the command of Captain Plunket, who attacked the Parliamentary forces, at St John's Hill, killing a Lieutenant-Colonel, a sergeant and nine or ten common soldiers, wounding many others. There were no casualties, on Astons side, save for Captain Plunket, being shot in his leg. On Sunday 8th September 1649, Aston writes to Ormond, describing his sally on the 7th September desperately requesting Ormond to send him more money, men, munitions, food and supplies.[61]

Antonia Fraser, wrongly asserts, 'On the 10th September Cromwell issued his first official summons to Sir Arthur Aston to surrender the town.'[62] When in fact, the evidence shows Cromwell sent his first official summons to Aston on Monday 9th September 1649. Cromwell recorded that, 'upon Monday the 9th of this instant, the batteries began to play. Whereupon I sent Sir Arthur Ashton, the then governor, a summons,':

> Having brought the army belonging to the Parliament of England before this place to reduce it to obedience, to the end effusion of blood may be prevented, I though fit to summon you to deliver the same into my hands to their use. If this be refused you will have no cause to blame me. I expect your answer, and rest.[63]

Your servant
O. Cromwell

---

[59] Paul Johnson, *Ireland Land of Trouble, A History from the Twelfth Century to the Present Day*, London, (1980), p. 44.
[60] Ashley, *op.cit.*, p. 230.
[61] Gilbert, *op. cit.*, Vol. II. p. 236.
[62] Antonia Fraser, *Cromwell, Our Chief of Men*, London, (1973), Paperback edition, London, (2004), p. 417.
[63] Carlyle, *op.cit.*, p. 297.

In marked contrast to Cromwell, Tom Reilly wrongly asserts, 'Monday was the tenth' and says, 'Cromwell continues the error, as to the day of the month throughout the letter.'[64] However, he does not give an explanation, or produce evidence, in support this sweeping statement. However, using the actual date simply destroys his assertions. There is no doubt, Cromwell knew exactly what day and date it was, as his official reports to parliament show.

Further Cromwell says: 'To which receiving no satisfactory answer, I proceeded that day [9th Sept], to beat down the steeple of the Church, on the South side of the Town, and to beat down a Tower, not far from the same place, which you will discern by the chart enclosed.'[65] Although there is no record of the chart surviving to date, he was referring to St. Mary's Church, which can be seen in the bottom right hand corner of the maps of Drogheda.[66] Cromwell positioned his two batteries opposite the wall at the south-eastern corner, with St. Mary's Church just behind it.

By late afternoon on Tuesday, the 10th September, he had demolished the steeple of the church and had made a small breach near the corner of the wall, with a much larger breach in its southern face. Cromwell refers to breaches 'on the east and south wall' and 'of being stormed.'[67] Although Cromwell recorded that he had sent his summons on Monday 9th September, Aston apparently did not receive it until the following morning Tuesday 10th September. This is confirmed by the letter Aston wrote to Ormond that morning:

---

[64] Reilly, *op.cit.*, p. 273.

[65] Carlyle, *op.cit.*, p. 297.

[66] There are two maps: the first is a map of Drogheda as it was in 1657 by Robert Newcomen and appears in John Dalton's, *The History of Drogheda-with its Environs*, Dublin, (1844). The second map of Drogheda based on this map has been inserted by the author.

[67] Simms, *op.cit.*, p. 6; see also Loeber and Parker, *op.cit.*, p. 81.

My Lorde,

This morning, about 8 of the clock, I received the enclosed summons…Since the summons I heard no answer but by the mouth of the cannon which hath ever since without intermission played upon our walls and works. They have made a very great breach near the church [of St. Mary]…speedy help is much desired…Living I am and dying I will end, my hand,

Yours truly,

Excellency's most humble servant'.
Arthur Ashton , Trogodaghe, 10ᵗʰ September.[68]

Samuel Rawson Gardiner, Antonia Fraser, and Ian Gentles, have all wrongly asserted that Cromwell's storm of Drogheda began at 5.o'clock on the 11ᵗʰ September 1649, and this mistake has been copied into many other histories;[69] despite primary documentary evidence to the contrary. Although, in all fairness, to Ian Gentles, who says Cromwell's storm began on the 11ᵗʰ September, in his narrative, but actually inserts the correct date of the storm, the 10ᵗʰ September, in the notation at the bottom of his map of Drogheda in the same book.[70]

Most recently Tom Reilly, in *Cromwell – An honourable Enemy*, (1998),[71] and James Scott Wheeler, in *Cromwell in Ireland*, (1999),[72] have also asserted that Cromwell's, storm of Drogheda began at 5.o'clock, on 11ᵗʰ September. In contrast, examination of the primary documents make it clear that the battle for Drogheda was all over by this time both in the South and North Towns, by the evening of the 11ᵗʰ. On the one hand, Reilly asserts, that

[68] Gilbert, (ed.), *op.cit.*, Vol. II, p. 259.
[69] Gardiner, *op.cit.,* Vol., I, p. 116., Fraser, *op.cit.*, p. 419, Gentles, *op.cit.*, p. 360.
[70] Gentles, *op.cit.,* p. 360.
[71] Reilly, *op.cit.*, p. 66.
[72] Wheeler, *op.cit.*, p. 86.

Cromwell gets his day and dates wrong, whilst, on the other hand, Wheeler, in his narrative concerning events at Drogheda, makes no reference, nor does he cite Cromwell's report to Parliament at all.[73] In marked contrast to Reilly and Wheeler, Cromwell makes it very clear that the 'batteries began to play' on Monday 9th September, and continued up to the storm, which began at 5.o'clock, on Tuesday 10th September 1649. Cromwell says in his report to Parliament:

> *Upon Tuesday the tenth instant, about five of the clock in the evening we began the storm,* and after some hot dispute, we entered about seven or eight hundred men, the enemy disputing it very stiffly with us ; Colonel Castle being shot in the head, whereupon he presently dyed, and divers soldiers and officers doing their duty killed and wounded. There was a tenalia to flanker the south wall of the town, between Duleek Gate, and the corner tower before mentioned, which our men entered where they found some *forty or fifty of the enemy, which they put to the sword,* and this they held.[74]

Cromwells report continues:

> 'Although, our men that stormed the breaches were forced to recoil as before expressed, yet being encouraged to recover their loss, they made a second attempt.' This forced the enemy, to 'quit his entrenchments; and after very hot dispute, the enemy having both horse and foot, and we only on foot, within the wall, the enemy gave ground, and our men became masters; of their entrenchments, and of the church, which indeed although they made our entrance the more difficult, yet this proved of excellent use to us, so the enemy could not annoy us with their horse, but

---

[73] *Ibid.*, pp. 83-88.
[74] Carlyle, *op.cit.*, p. 297. Letter XC1X.

thereby we had advantage to make good the ground, that so we might let in our own horse, which accordingly was done though with much difficulty.'[75]

Ormond writing to Lord Byron, 29th September 1649 confirmed that Cromwell:

Continued his Battering all Munday and Tuesday, till about four of the clock in the afternoone. Having made a breach which he judged assaultable, he assaulted it and being twice beaten off, the third time he carryed it.[76]

Noting how the battle continued, Cromwell observed that, 'The enemy retreated, divers of them into the Mill-Mount; a place very strong and of difficult access; being exceedingly high, having a good graft, and strongly pallisaded.' Furthermore, 'The governor Sir Arthur Ashton, and divers considerable officers being there, our men getting up to them were ordered by me to put all to the sword.'[77]

It was at this point, according to Ormond, relying on the evidence of Lord Inchiquin, that some offer of quarter was given and accepted by some of his officers and soldiers, who agreed to lay down their arms.[78] Ormond's allegation, is supported by an anonymous letter from Drogheda, appearing in *Perfect Diurnall* E,553,17., describes the taking of the Mill-Mount, from the Parliamentary side at the time:

The mount was very strong of itself, and manned with 250 of their principal men, Sir Arthur Ashton being in it, who was the Governor of the Town, when they saw their men retreat, were so cast down and disheartened that they thought it in vain to make any further resistance, which, if they had, would have killed some hundreds of our men before we could

---

[75] *Ibid.*, p. 297.
[76] Gilbert *op.cit,.* Vol. II, p. 271. Ormond, to Lord Byron, 29th September, 1649.
[77] Carlyle, *op.cit.*, p. 298.
[78] Gilbert, *op.cit.*, Vol II, p. 271.

have taken it. Lieutenant-Colonel Axtell, of Colonel Hewson's regiment, with some twelve of his men, went up to the top of the Mount and demanded of the Governor the surrender of it; who was very stubborn, speaking very big words, but at length was persuaded to go into the windmill. On top of the Mount, and as many more of the chiefest of them it would contain, where they were disarmed, and afterwards all slain.[79]

Paul Kerrigan in *Castles and Fortifications 1485-1945*, (1995), has more recently highlighted the fact, that 'the circular structure on the Mill mount at Drogheda, named Richmond Fort by Lewis in his *Topographical Dictionary of Ireland*, (1837),' was 'according to Lewis erected in 1808.'[80] There is of course, no circular structure on the Mill Mount, in Robert Newcomen's map of 1657, which appears in this Chapter.

An account of the taking of the Mill Mount, from the Royalist side, appears in Lord Inchiquin's letter to Ormond. Inchiquin says: 'that the governor was killed in the Mill Mount, after quarter, given by the officers that first come there.'[81]

Therefore, if both the parliamentary, and the Royalist accounts, are to be believed there is clearly evidence to support, the allegation that Royalist officers and soldiers, in the Mill Mount were killed after quarter had been offered. On the other hand, there is ' no evidence or proof, that when Cromwell ordered the garrison in the Mill Mount to be put to the sword, he knew that terms of surrender had been offered.'[82] There is also no doubt that Cromwell, would not have agreed with such an action; given his overriding order against quarter. Clearly, no promise of quarter was offered by Cromwell. After ordering that Aston and his men, on the Mill-Mount, be put to the sword, in the next breath Cromwell says:

---

[79] Gardiner, *op.cit.*, Vol., I, p. 119, citing, *Perfect Duirnall*, E,553, 17.
[80] Paul M. Kerrigan, *Castles and Fortifications in Ireland 1485-1995*, Cork, (1995), p. 178.
[81] Gilbert, *op.cit.,* Vol. II, Preface, XXVII., Lord Inchiquin to Ormond, 15th September, 1649.
[82] Godfrey Davies, *Journal of Modern History,* Vol. XIII, (1941), p. 241.

And indeed, being in the heat of the action [fighting], I forbade them to spare any that were in arms in the town: and, I think, that night [10th September 1649] they put to the sword about 2,000 men[83]

Gardiner, Gentles, and more recently Wheeler, despite documentary evidence to the contrary, have suggested that the battlefield, extended to the North Town, on the same night that Cromwell stormed Drogheda. Further, Gardiner suggests, that whilst the battle continued in the South Town and huge numbers of Aston's men who Gardiner refers to as' flying wretches,' somehow escaped across:

'the narrow passage of the bridge, and the slaughter continued as pursuers and pursued breasted the steep hill on the northern side of the Boyne. A thousand were slain in or around St.Peter's Church at the top of the hill'[84]

However, Gardiner, provides no documentary evidence to support this contention. This is because there is no documentary evidence of any battle taking place in the North Town. In marked contrast both Cromwell and Lord Inchiquin say that only a few escaped across the bridge to the North Town on 10th September 1649. Writing to Ormond on 15th September 1649, Inchiquin says:

That there was never seen *so cruel a fight* our horse doing beyond expectation, and *some few of them..* retreated over the bridge and gott out of town on the north side, where these men cum off, saw them charging through cromwell's foot – neare Sunday Gate.[85]

---

[83] Carlyle, *op.cit.*, Vol., p. 298.
[84] Gardiner, *op.cit.*, p. 119.
[85] Gilbert, *op. cit.*, Vol. II, p. xxvii.

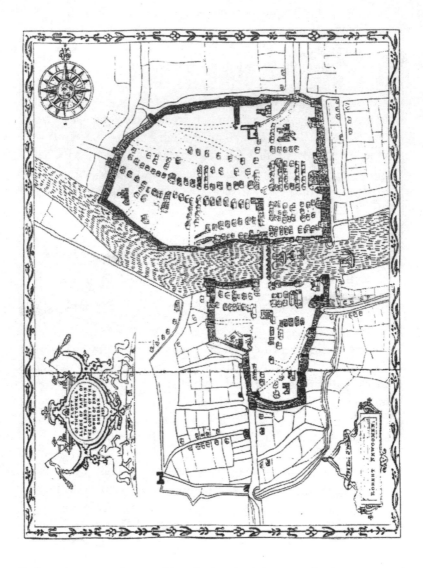

Robert Newcomen's map of Drogheda only eight years after it was stormed by Cromwell and the New Model Army in 1649.

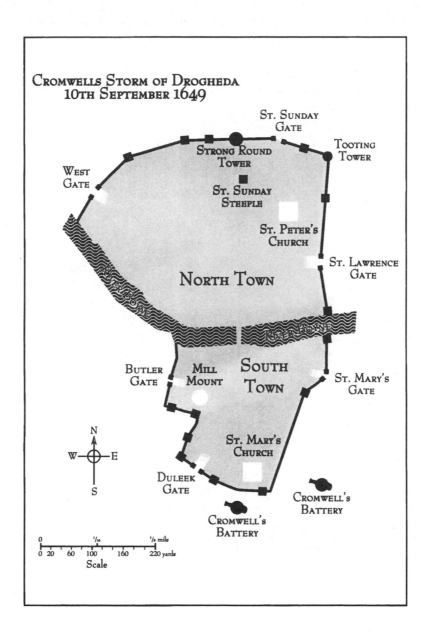

CROMWELLS STORM OF DROGHEDA
10TH SEPTEMBER 1649

ST. SUNDAY GATE

TOOTING TOWER

STRONG ROUND TOWER

WEST GATE

ST. SUNDAY STEEPLE

ST. PETER'S CHURCH

ST. LAWRENCE GATE

RIVER BOYNE

NORTH TOWN

RIVER BOYNE

BUTLER GATE

MILL MOUNT

SOUTH TOWN

ST. MARY'S GATE

N
W — E
S

ST. MARY'S CHURCH

DULEEK GATE

CROMWELL'S BATTERY

CROMWELL'S BATTERY

0   1/16   1/8 mile
0   20   60   100   160   220 yards
Scale

There is no doubt that huge numbers of Royalist soldiers, did not escape across the bridge to the North Town. Only a few soldiers were pursued across the bridge and killed.[86] It is also clear, that Cromwell was talking about the battle continuing in the South Town. Up until this time the whole of the North Town had still been in Royalist hands.

Cromwell's report, concerning the night of Tuesday 10th September 1649, continues : 'divers of the officers, and soldiers, being fled over the Bridge into the other part of town, [North Town], where 100 of them, possessed St. Peters church steeple, some the *West Gate*, and others a *Strong Round Tower,* next to the Gate called St. Sundays. These being summoned to mercy, refused, whereupon, I ordered the steeple of St. Peters church to be fired.'[87] According to Cromwell's letter to Parliament this was the end of any fighting, or action on 10th September 1649, save for placing guards around the towers containing enemy soldiers. It must be noted, the *West Gate* and the *Strong Round Tower*, which, Cromwell, refers to can be clearly identified in the maps of Drogheda, appearing in this Chapter.

By wrongly suggesting, that Cromwell's storm began at 5.o'clock, on 11th September, instead of Tuesday 10th September, the following primary evidence is concealed, and three key points, must be emphasised, regarding the events that occurred on Wednesday 11th September 1649, the day after the storm:

Firstly, Cromwell writes :

> It wasn't until the next day, {Wednesday 11 September} the other two Towers {*West Gate* and *Strong Round Tower* next to the Gate called St. Sundays} were summoned ; in one of which was about six or seven score [120-140 men] ; but they refused to yield themselves : and we knowing that hunger must compel them, set only good guards to secure them

[86] Williams, J.B., 'Fresh light on Cromwell at Drogheda,' *The Nineteenth Century*, (1912), p. 483
[87] Carlyle, *op. cit.*, p. 298.

from running away until their stomachs came down. From one of the said Towers, notwithstanding their condition, they killed and wounded some of our men. When they submitted, their officers were knocked on the head ; and every tenth man of the soldiers killed ; and the rest shipped for the Barbadoes, the soldiers in the other Tower were spared, as to their lives only; and shipped likewise for the Barbadoes, all the rest of the soldiers in the other town [North Town] were all spared, as to their lives only, and shipped likewise to the Barbadoes.[88]

The second point says :

'the soldiers in the other Tower were spared, as to their lives only; and shipped likewise for the Barbadoes'.[89]

The final point, that seems to have been accidentally, or deliberately overlooked, by some historians to fit the myth or legend, when Cromwell made clear in his letter to Parliament:

all the rest of the soldiers in the other town [North Town] were all spared, as to their lives only, and shipped likewise to the Barbadoes.[90]

Cromwell makes it clear, that on the day after the storm Wednesday 11th September 1649 only 10 or 12 officers were knocked on the head along with every tenth soldier, a maximum of 20 men. The rest of the soldiers in both towers and all the soldiers in the North Town were all spared and shipped to Barbadoes.

Reilly, suggests that the defenders, who opened fire from one of the towers, killing and wounding, some of Cromwell's men who were guarding the tower, was 'probably Tooting Tower.'[91] However,

---

[88] *Ibid.*, p. 299.
[89] *Ibid.*,
[90] *Ibid.*,
[91] Reilly, *op.cit.*, p. 78.

it is more likely, that the defenders fired from the *Strong Round Tower,* near Sundays Gate, as indicated by Cromwell, which can be clearly seen in Robert Newcomen's map of 1657 as it appears in this Chapter.

According to the accounts made by Gardiner, Fraser, Gentles, Reilly and Wheeler, Cromwell would have been still creating, and entering, the breaches in the south wall, with his heavy guns, and did not start the storm until 5.o,clock, on 11th September. The primary documents, of course refute this contention. The capture of Drogheda was virtually all over by this time. This is further demonstrated by the fact that on Thursday 12th September, Cromwell wrote the following letter to the Chief Commanding Officer, at the garrison in Dundalk, which signified that Drogheda had been captured by Parliamentary forces:

For the Chief Officer Commanding in Dundalk: These

'Tredagh' 12th September 1649
Sir,

I offered mercy to the Garrison of Tredagh, in sending the Governor a Summons before I attempted the taking of it. Which being refused brought evil upon them.

If you being warned thereby, shall surrender your Garrison to the use of the Parliament of England, which by this I summon you to do, you may thereby prevent effusion of blood. If, upon refusing this offer, that which you like not befalls you, you will know whom to blame.

I rest,
Your Servant,
Oliver Cromwell.[92]

---

[92] Carlyle, *op.cit.*, p. 295. Letter XCVII.

James Scott Wheeler in his account suggests, that none of Aston's men escaped from the North Town of Drogheda. He asserts that, 'an English Cavalry screen outside the Northern Wall prevented [the defenders] retreat in that direction.'[93] He provides no documentary evidence to support this contention, and appears to rely purely upon his own views and opinions. Remembering of course, Cromwell had no forces North of the Boyne prior to the night of Tuesday 10th September. The evidence of Lord Inchiquin when writing to Ormond on 15th September 1649 makes it clear that:

> Many men, and some officers, have made their escapes out of Drogheda, some of every regiment have come unto me...Garret Dungan is one, and is now at Tecraghan...Lieutenant Collonell Cavanagh is escaped to Mark Trevor, who is at Carrickmacross.[94]

The fact that some of Aston's men escaped from Drogheda is also supported by the evidence of Cromwell in his letter to John Bradshaw, written on the 16th September 1649 says:

> I do not think thirty of the whole number escaped with their lives and those that did are in safe custody for Barbadoes...I do believe, neither do I hear that any officer escaped with his life, save only one lieutenant, who, I hear going to the Enemy said that he was the only man that escaped of all the garrison.[95]

The fact that 'many men, and some officers' escaped from Drogheda is also confirmed by Ormond who, writing to the king says, 'some escaped by a miracle.'[96]

Obviously Cromwell was not aware that 'many men, and some officers' made their escape from Drogheda. This is understandable

---

[93] Wheeler, *op cit.*, p. 87. *Cromwell in Ireland*
[94] Gilbert, *op.cit.*, Vol. II, p. xxiii.
[95] Carlyle, *op.cit.*, p. 295. Letter XCVIII.
[96] *Ibid.*, p. 271.

because, as was proven earlier, Cromwell never invested the northern half of the town, prior to the siege.[97] James Burke agrees, that 'despite Cromwell's assertion that all officers perished, apart from one lieutenant, a small number did manage to evade capture.' Further he says 'it is quite probable that a couple of hundred of the garrison would have survived. Cromwell's army, had been concentrated on the southern side of the town, and many of the soldiers stationed on the northern half would have had the opportunity to escape over the northern walls.'[98] W.C. Abbott, on the other hand, argues 'it would appear that a few hundred escaped over the walls, though Cromwell declared, that not thirty escaped with their lives.'[99]

Burke, and Abbott, probably were correct in believing, that many soldiers escaped over the northern walls, but the majority are more likely to have escaped through Sunday's Gate, as indicated by Lord Inchiquin, in his report to Ormond.[100] They would have had plenty of time to escape through the numerous exit gates in the North Town, which up until this time was still in Royalist hands.

Recent maps, appearing in the works of Gardiner, Fraser, Gentles, Reilly, and Wheeler, do not show or demonstrate the fact that Sunday's Gate, was a clear exit point throughout Cromwell's siege of Drogheda, as they appear to have overlooked this. However, Sunday's Gate is shown clearly as an exit point in Ravell's map used by Dennis Murphy, in his *Cromwell in Ireland,* (1883), [101] also refer to Robert Newcomen's map of 1657, in this Chapter.[102]

The significance of Sunday's Gate, is important because by not showing the Gate, it makes it appear, that the defenders were trapped in the town with no means of escape, when fleeing, from

---

[97] Carlyle, *op.cit.*, p. 298-9.
[98] James Burke, 'The New Model Army and the problems of siege warfare 1648-51,' *Irish Historical Studies*, Vol. XXVII, No. 105, May, (1990), pp. 12-13.
[99] Abbott, *op.cit.*, Vol. II, p. 120.
[100] Gilbert, *op.cit.*, p. xxvii.
[101] Murphy *op.cit.*, p. 85.
[102] Map, taken from John Dalton, 'Dublin and Drogehda Railway,' in *The History of Drogheda with its Environs*, (1844).

Cromwell's army coming from the South Town. Remembering of course whilst the battle continued on the 10th September 1649, in the South Town and on Mill Mount, which is also located in the South Town, the whole of the North Town, was still in Royalist hands.

Not only, does James Scott Wheeler wrongly suggest, that Cromwell's storm of Drogheda, began at 5.o'clock on Wednesday 11th September 1649, he implies that the soldiers, in the towers, and the North Town, were dealt with, on the night of the storm. Further he says, 'over the next two days any remaining prisoners were murdered, closing the curtain on the blackest episode in Cromwell's career.'[103] There is simply no documentary evidence of this and Wheeler is merely expressing his own opinion. In fact the primary documents I have produced refute this contention. Wheeler of course, does not even refer to Cromwell's own account.

The Military Lists and Muster-Rolls for 30th August 1649, only two days, before the approach of Cromwell, makes it clear that the garrison of Drogheda, was manned by 320 horse and 2,221 foot-soldiers.[104] From these muster rolls, and Cromwell's official account of those killed at Drogheda, the numbers of soldiers defending the garrison can be ascertained.

Cromwell summarises Royalist losses as follows:

> The following Officers and Soldiers were slain at the storming of Tredagh, Sir Arthur Ashton, Governor: Sir Edmund Varney, Lieutenant Colonel Finglass, Major Fitzgerald, with eight Captains, eight Lieutenants, and eight Cornets all of Horse; Colonel's Warren, Wall, and Bryne of Foot, with their Lieutenants, Majors and C; the Lord Taaffs Brother an Augustin Friar; forty-four Captains, and all their Lieutenants, Ensigns, and C; 220 Reformadoes and Troopers; 2,500 Foot soldiers besides Staff Officers, Surgeons and C&; [105]

---

[103] Wheeler, *op.cit.*, p. 87. *Cromwell in Ireland*
[104] Gilbert, *op.cit.*, Vol 11. Appendix, pp. 496-9.
[105] Carlyle, *op.cit.*, p. 302.

It must be noted the words 'and many inhabitants,' do *not* appear at the end of Cromwell's letter printed in Carlyle. They do appear however, in a copy printed in Abbott, II, p. 131. Carlyle writes, 'Parliamentary History (xix 207-9), has copied this letter from the old pamphlet, (as usual giving no reference), and after the conclusion ; 'Surgeons and C&,' has taken the liberty of adding these words, 'and many inhabitants' of which there is no whisper in the old pamphlets ; a very considerable liberty indeed.'[106] Nevertheless, even if Cromwell had used the phrase 'and many inhabitants,' it would have referred to armed inhabitants, because, if, new model soldiers, had killed any unarmed inhabitants at Drogheda, they would have been clearly disobeying Cromwell's orders.

Ian Gentles, has asserted that, ' according to official estimates there were 3,100 soldiers in the town, of whom 2,800 were killed, as well as many inhabitants, including every friar, who could be found. The final toll may thus have been in the neighbourhood of 3,500 soldiers, civilians and clergy.'[107] Gentles of course, does not cite documentary evidence in support his allegation. This is because there is no evidence whatever, to suggest Cromwell's men killed unarmed inhabitants at Drogheda.

Even overestimating Cromwell's figures of deaths and executions at Drogheda, historical records show that in total no more than 2,860 defenders were killed. This figure includes at least five Catholic Friars, who were executed by Cromwell's men. They included 'Father Peter Taaff, John Taaff, Robert Netterville, Dominick Dillion, and Richard Overton,'[108] who had served as officers.[109] This is confirmed by Cromwell who explains to Parliament:

> I believe all their friars were knocked on the head promiscuously but two; the one of which was Father Peter Taaff, brother of the Lord Taaff whom the soldiers took the next day, and made an end of. The other was taken in the Round Tower, under the repute

[106] *Ibid.*
[107] Gentles, *op.cit.*, p. 361.
[108] Reilly, *op.cit.*, p. 79.
[109] Esson, *op.cit.*, p. 112.

of a Lieutenant and when he understood that the officers of that Tower had no Quarter he confessed he was a friar; but that did not save him.[110]

Furthermore, Reilly suggests that 3000 Royalist defenders were killed, but there is no documentary evidence of this, and conflicts with Cromwell's account. In addition Reilly claims that; 'these numbers do not suggest that there was any hand to hand combat within the walls of town, just plain butchery.' However both Cromwell's and Inchiquin's account refute this allegation.[111] In fact, Cromwell also summarises the New Model Army's losses, as follows:

> 'A great deal of loss fell upon Colonel Hewson's, Colonel Castle's, and Colonel Ewer, having two officers in his field regiment shot; Colonel Castle, and Captain of his regiment slain; Colonel Hewson's Captain Lieutenant slain. I do not think we lost 100 men upon the place, though many *be wounded*.'[112]

To briefly summarise the events at Drogheda so far. On Monday 9th September 1649, Cromwell opened fire on the southern walls of the town with his heavy guns. The following day, Tuesday 10th September, Cromwell's guns continued to play on the town walls, until he had blown a hole in the South wall; large enough for his men to enter. Then, at 5 o'clock on Tuesday 10th September, his men began the storm of the south town. The main battle occurred in the South Town, and on the Mill Mount, also located in the South Town. It was here, according to Cromwell, that 'about 2,000 men were put to the sword.' It is also highly likely that more than 2,000 defenders were put to the sword in the South Town. Because only a few of Aston's men escaped across the drawbridge, to the North Town, where only 100 of them possessed the steeple of St. Peters church, 'some the *West Gate*, and others a *Strong Round Tower*, next to the Gate, called St. Sunday's.' When, the 100 soldiers in

---

[110] Carlyle, *op.cit.*, p. 299.
[111] Reilly, *op cit.*, p. 74.
[112] Carlyle, *op.cit.*, p. 299.

the steeple, refused to surrender, Cromwell, ordered the steeple to be fired and the soldiers were killed. According to Cromwell, that was the end of the action on the 10th September, save, for placing guards around the towers containing enemy soldiers. Meanwhile, a few of Astons men who had escaped over the drawbridge, also on the 10th September, charged through Sundays Gate. It is also clear that many other soldiers also escaped from the North Town, although the exact number is not known. However, Lord Inchiquin does say ' Many men, and some officers,have made their escapes out of Drogheda, some of every regiment have come unto me.' This was also later confirmed by Ormond.

On the following day, Wednesday 11th September, which Cromwell refers to as ' the next day' the Soldiers in the towers were dealt with. It must be noted, that only about 10 or 12 officers, were knocked on the head, along with every tenth soldier, from the tower that contained [120-140] men, a maximum of 20 were killed, and the rest were all spared. Further, the soldiers in the other Tower, were also all spared, along with all the rest of the soldiers in the North Town. All those that were spared were taken prisoner and shipped to the Barbadoes. Therefore, according to Cromwell only about 20 officers and men, were killed on this day, Wednesday 11th September 1649, the day after the storm.

On Thursday 12th September 1649, whilst still at Drogheda, Cromwell writes his letter to the Officer Commanding Dundalk. Furthermore, on the 14th September, Cromwell issued a pass of safety, for the peaceful behaviour of the troops as follows:

> To Henry Parker
> Ordering the protection of Christopher of St Lawrence and certain of the inhabitants of Tredagh and the peaceful behaviour of troops.
>
> At the camp before Tredagh this 14th September 1649
> O. Cromwell[113]

---

[113] W.C. Abbott, *The Writings and Speeches of Oliver Cromwell*, Cambridge, Mass., (1937-47), Vol. II, p. 22.

Not only does Reilly wrongly assert, that Cromwell's storm began, on the 11th September, 1649, he has completely over-looked the primary evidence of events, which took place in the North Town on the second day. Reilly says, 'The day after the storm, aside from negotiating with the soldiers in the towers, Cromwell had a busy day. He found time, however, to write a letter to the commander of Dundalk.' [114] This statement by Reilly is incorrect, firstly, because, Cromwell's storm began on the 10th secondly, Cromwell negotiated with the soldiers in the towers on the day after the storm which was the 11th and finally writes to, The Officer Commanding Dundalk, on Thursday 12th September. Furthermore, Reilly asserts :

> The slaughter continued all through the night of the 11th September 1649. Having learned that Mass had been celebrated for soldiers in St. Peter's Church, Cromwell thought that it was 'remarkable that these people at first set up the mass in some places in the town that had been monasteries, but afterwards grew so insolent, that the last lord's Day before the storm, the protestant's were thrust out of the great church called St. Peter's and the had public Mass there'. He adds a chilling confirmation that the area in and around the church was consumed with Puritanical rage as 'in this very place near one thousand of them were put to the sword fleeing thither for safety'.[115]

To begin with, there is not a scrap of documentary evidence to support Reilly's claim, that, 'the slaughter continued all through the night of the 11th September 1649,' but there is substantial documentary evidence, to refute the views expressed by Reilly. He is merely expressing his own opinion, without evidence. Furthermore, the passage in Cromwell's report which Reilly refers to, reads as follows, Cromwell says:

---

[114] Reilly, *op.cit.*, p. 82.
[115] *Ibid.*, p. 77.

It is remarkable that these people at the first set up Mass in some places of the town that had been monasteries; but afterwards grew so insolent that the last Lord's Day before the storm, the Protestants were thrust out of the great church called St. Peter's, and they had public Mass there; and in this very place near one thousand of them were put to the sword, fleeing thither for safety.[116]

It should be remembered that Godfrey Davies stressed in the *Journal of Modern History*, (1941), that Cromwell wrote very long sentences, which frequently ran into each other. Punctuation marks like colons, semi-colons, and commas, other than full stops were not used by Cromwell. His original letters were written in black ink, and punctuation marks, were inserted when they were being transcribed into print by Carlyle.[117]

There is no documentary evidence to suggest, that any slaughter, took place in Drogheda North Town. Other than, Cromwell's own account of the battle that took place predominantly in the South Town, on 10th September 1649. The only documentary evidence of action in the North Town, on the night of the 10th September 1649, was regarding the burning of St Peter's Church steeple. However, there is considerable documentary evidence, to show that there was no Cromwellian slaughter in the North Town, where St Peter's church was located, and detailed accounts, of the taking of the two towers, and defenders escapes, through Sunday's Gate. These documented facts, provide evidence of only a small number of deaths, and a great number of prisoners sent to Barbadoes.

By asserting, that Cromwell's storm began on 11th September 1649, instead of the actual documented date 10th September 1649, Cromwell's vital evidence, regarding the day after the storm is concealed. Because it shows, that there was a no large scale slaughter in the North Town. Therefore, if we accept Cromwell's evidence of what actually occurred on the day of the storm, Tuesday

---

[116] Carlyle. *op.cit.,* p. 299.
[117] Godfrey Davies, *Journal of Modern History,* Vol. X111, (1941), p. 241.

10th and, what occurred on Wednesday 11th September 1649, which was the day after the storm, then the following alternate interpretation should be considered:

> It is remarkable, that these people[Aston's soldiers] at the first set up the Mass in some places of the town that had been monasteries; but afterwards grew so insolent, that the last Lord's day before the storm[Sunday 8th September 1649, before Cromwell stormed the town] the Protestants were thrust out of the great church called St. Peter's and they [Aston's soldiers] had public Mass there; and in this very place near one thousand of them[Protestant Parliamentary sympathisers] were put to the sword, fleeing thither for safety.[118]

Otherwise Cromwell, would be contradicting himself, in his earlier report regarding, what actually, occurred on the 10th and 11th and it is highly unlikely that he would make such an error on such an important point.

The evidence of Aston's letters show, that he had serious problems with parliamentary supporters, and prisoners in the town, and was trying to arrange prisoner exchange for these people. It is possible that those killed in Drogheda, were Parliamentary Protestant sympathisers, seeking to support Cromwell, who were a thorn in the side of Aston, and who he could do without, whilst facing trial by siege by Cromwell.

In addition, the following facts relating to Cromwell's report to be considered, firstly: It is remarkable that the monasteries and churches, that were no longer in use following the insurrection 1641, were used by the Aston's men. Secondly, 'These people' obviously refer to Aston's men. Thirdly, the Protestants, who lived mainly in houses in the North Town were worshipping at St. Peter's Church, which was a Protestant Church, up until Sunday 8th September. Fourthly, according to Cromwell, the Protestants were

---

[118] *Ibid.*, p. 299.

thrust out of the Church, on the Sunday 8th September, which was the day before Cromwell opened fire with his batteries and had not even entered the town. Fifthly, there is no doubt that 1000 of Aston's soldiers, did not survive the Battle in the South Town, to flee over the bridge in large numbers, and only a few soldiers took refuge in the Towers, and St Peter's Church Steeple, whilst some also escaped through Sunday's gate and various other exits.

There was, no documented evidence of any killings in the North Town, other than Cromwell's own account, and no documented, eye witness accounts, by either side in existence, for the killing of town citizens to date. Cromwell, could not have been responsible for the near 1000 people being put to the sword, in the North Town, in or around St. Peter's Church, as he did not, enter into the North Town, until 10/11th September 1649. Any killings, in Drogheda, prior to that date, would have to have been under the jurisdiction and authority, of Aston as Governor of Drogheda. Remembering of course, that the vast majority of the soldiers defending the North Town were all spared, and shipped to the 'Barbadoes' as slaves.

In his letter to Parliament concerning the capture of Drogheda, Cromwell explains his actions to Parliament as follows:

> I am persuaded that this is a righteous judgement of God upon these barbarous wretches who have imbrued their hands in so much innocent blood, and that it will tend to prevent the infusion of blood for the future, which are the satisfactory grounds for such actions, which otherwise cannot but work remorse and regret.[119]

Antonia Fraser, referring to the above passage of Cromwell's account asserts that: 'Cromwell had summed it up from his own point of view, first of all, the Irish, those massacrists of 1641 (who Cromwell had somehow convinced himself were now congregated within the walls of Drogheda), had richly deserved their fate.'[120]

---

[119] *Ibid.*, p. 299.
[120] Fraser *op. cit.* p. 423.

On the other hand, Ian Gentles says, 'It was a startling doctrine which held a town that had at no time been in the hands of Confederate Catholics responsibility for the massacre which they had unleashed in 1641.'[121] A similar view is expressed by Martyn Bennett, in *The Civil Wars 1637-1653*, (1998), who asserts, 'Cromwell concocted a series of lame excuses for the butchery, centring on retribution for the 1641/2 massacres, which had already acquired mythical status. He ignored the fact that Drogheda had at the time been in Protestant hands.'[122] There is no historical documentary evidence to support these assertions.

There is no doubt that Fraser's, Gentles, and Bennett's assertions, are based largely upon biased, mythical and fictional historical narratives. Furthermore, in the words of Lieutenant-Colonel Baldock, 'However, he may have obtained them, Cromwell never seemed to have lacked good spies, and his wonderful military judgement, sifted the wheat, from the chaff, in their reports with infallible accuracy.'[123] There is no doubt that Cromwell knew his enemies well, and who his friends were, within and outside the walls of Drogheda. It is more likely that Cromwell's meaning, could be interpreted as follows:

> I am persuaded that this is a righteous judgement of God upon these barbarous wretches [Aston's Soldiers] who have imbrued their hands in so much innocent blood, [Protestant Parliamentarian Supporters, thrust out of the church] and that it will tend to prevent the infusion of blood for the future, which are the satisfactory grounds for such actions, which otherwise cannot but work remorse and regret.[124]

The allegation, that New Model soldiers killed unarmed citizens at Drogheda, must be treated as a myth, because in reality it has

---

[121] Gentles, *op.cit.*, p. 362.
[122] Martyn Bennett, *The Civil Wars* 1637-1653, Stroud, (1998), p. 91.
[123] T. S. Baldock, *Cromwell As A Soldier*, London, (1899), p. 382.
[124] Carlyle, *op. cit.*, p. 302.

never been supported by evidence. This myth, was created and developed, by Royalist historian, Lord Clarendon, who says that Cromwell's men 'put all the citizens who were Irish, man, woman and child to the sword.'[125] Clarendon, was unable to produce evidence to support his allegation, and relied on Ormond's report, which merely described his defeat at Drogheda, as: 'making as many several pictures of inhumanity as are described in the *Book of Martyrs* or *The Relation of Amboya*.'[126] Again it is discovered that these allegations are not supported by an eyewitness account. Certainly Lord Inchiquin, makes no mention of unarmed citizens being killed.[127]

Clarendon's myth, was further developed by Dr. George Bate's account. After asserting that 4,000 were killed at Drogheda he says:

> ...neither the gown nor the dwelling house offered any protection, nor was there any great respect had to either sex. The soldiers continued for three days in cruelly slaying the townspeople that carried arms, whom they dragged out of their lurking holes nay, and those who after the third day came creeping out of their hiding places were most inhumanely put to death.[128]

In reality, Bate's story was not an eyewitness account, because he never visited Drogheda, or Ireland, for that matter. Neither is the story supported by other eyewitness accounts. Although, Bate had previously served as a physician to Cromwell in England, after the Restoration of the monarchy in 1660, he became the personal physician to Charles II. Consequently Bate's account was largely a work of Royalist propaganda.[129]

---

[125] Clarendon, *op.cit.*, Vol. V, p. 102.
[126] Gilbert, *op.cit.*, Vol. II, p. 271.
[127] *Ibid.*, p. xxvii.
[128] Reilly, *op.cit.*, pp. 100-1.
[129] *Ibid.*

Clarendon's and Bate's unfounded allegations, were simply repeated word for word, by the Rev. Denis Murphy, in *Cromwell In Ireland*, during the nineteenth century.[130] Followed by Patrick Francis Moran, in his *Historical Sketch of the Persecutions Suffered by the Catholics of Ireland Under the Rule of Cromwell and the Puritans*. Moran, asserts that 'beside the garrison about four thousand of the Catholic citizens were thus deliberately massacred.'[131] As Trevor Royle has recently emphasised later, descriptions of Cromwell's storm of Drogheda were 'carefully collected and disseminated by the Irish Clergy' as Moran's account shows:

The city being captured by heretics, the blood of Catholics was mercilessly shed in the streets, and in the dwelling-houses, and in the open fields; to none was mercy shown, not to women, nor to the aged, nor to the young. The property of the citizens became the prey of the parliamentary troops; everything in our residence was plundered; the library, the sacred chalices, of which there were many of great value, as well as all the furniture, sacred and profane, were destroyed. On the following day, when the soldiers were searching through the ruins of the city, they discovered one of our fathers named John Bathe[Taaffe], with his brother, a secular priest: suspecting that they were religious, they examined them, and finding that they were priests, and one of them, moreover, a Jesuit, they led them off in triumph, and accompanied by a tumultuous crowd, conducted them to the market-place, and there, as if they were at length extinguishing the Catholic religion and our society, they tied them both to stakes fixed in the ground, and pierced their bodies with shot till they both expired.[132]

---

[130] Murphy, *op.cit.*, p. 109.
[131] Moran, *op.cit.*, p. 93.
[132] Royle, *op.cit.* p. 529; Moran, *op.cit.* p. 51

Acquiring the status of 'fact,' by constant repetition, this myth was further developed in the twentieth century by Hillaire Belloc, in *Cromwell* (1936), who says, 'Not only were the whole garrison put to the sword, but all the civilian population as well, save for some insignificant remnant, there was a general murder of men, women and children on every side.'[133] Belloc, also fails to produce evidence, and cites Clarendon, to support his unfounded allegations. Peter and Fiona Somerset-Fry, in *A History of Ireland,* (1988), further develop this myth, by asserting Cromwell's men 'put the defenders to the sword then streamed through the street mercilessly killing about a thousand of the townspeople.'[134] There is simply no evidence to support this contention nor do they cite any. Nevertheless the myth is further developed by R.F. Foster, in *Modern Ireland 1600-1972*, (1988), who asserts, 'Cromwell's tactics were decisive. The tone was set by his massacre of the civilian population at Drogheda.'[135]

The success of these now powerful myths, is demonstrated by Ronald Hutton, who points out that whilst on holiday in Ireland in the summer of 1988, he watched a promotional video produced by the Irish Tourist Board.

> When it introduced the town of Drogheda, it spoke of the time in 1649, when Cromwell stormed the place and killed every man, woman and child within it, as a black day which will live on in the hearts of Irish people for ever. Enquiries in England revealed that this was also the general impression of the events of Drogheda and Wexford, which the republican army took a few weeks later.[136]

This myth, has continued to be repeated in many histories, most recently James Lydon, in his *The Making of Ireland-From Ancient*

---

[133] Hillaire Belloc, *Cromwell*, London, (1936), p. 281.

[134] Peter and Fiona Somerset-Fry, *A History of Ireland*, London, (1988), p. 154.

[135] R.F. Foster, *Modern Ireland, 1600-1972*, London, (1988), p. 102.

[136] Ronald Hutton, *The British Republic 1649-1660*, London, (1990), p. 47.

Times to Present, (1998), where he asserts, 'the slaughter of innocent civilians quickly revealed the ruthless side of Cromwell.'[137] Naturally Lydon, does not cite any evidence to support his allegation, probably due to the fact he could not find any.

In dismissing the allegations, made by Clarendon, which were later developed into myth by later writers, it must be emphasised; that Cromwell's orders at Drogheda, were quite specific, he forbade his men to spare anyone in the town bearing arms.[138] This would have included, Ormond's soldiers, and any armed citizens, involved in the defence of the town.[139] Although it is possible that some unarmed citizens were accidentally killed; 'there is simply no evidence of this from an eyewitness and only rumours and reports at second hand.'[140] One such report, was the fictional account of a massacre of women and children made by Thomas-a-Wood to his brother Anthony.[141]

It must also be emphasised, that the evidence of Cromwell himself supports the fact that no unarmed citizens were killed by Cromwell. At Youghal, months later, Cromwell replied to the Bishops appeal of Clanmacnoise, for unity, in which he placed the blame for the insurrection on the Irish clergy.[142] In this Declaration...for the Undeceiving of the Deluded and Seduced People,[143] Cromwell asked them: 'give us an instance of man, since my coming into Ireland, not in arms, massacred, destroyed, or

---

[137] James Lydon, *The Making of Ireland-From Ancient Times to Present*, London, (1998), p. 192.

[138] Carlyle, *op.cit.*, p. 298.

[139] Hutton, *op.cit.*, p. 47.

[140] James Anthony Froude, *Ireland in the Eighteenth Century*, London, (1901), p. 125.

[141] Hutton, *op.cit.*, p. 47, 'the sources are listed accurately in Samuel Rawson Gardiner, *History of the Commonwealth and Protectorate*, (1903), Vol., I, pp. 112-24, 127-33'; Bennett, *op.cit.*, p. 330; Reilly, *op.cit.*, pp. 101-3.

[142] Gentles, *op.cit.*, p. 371.

[143] Carlyle, *op.cit.*, pp. 332-43. *A Declaration of the Lord Leiutenant of Ireland. For the Undeceiving of Deluded and Seduced People: which may be satisfactory to all that doe not wilfully shut their eyes against the light. In answer to certain later Declarations and Acts, framed by the Irish Papish Prelates and Clergy, in a Conventicle at Clanmacnoise.*

banished; concerning the massacre or the destruction of whom, justice hath not been done, or endeavoured to be done.'[144] Two very important points support Cromwell's statement. Firstly, there is no doubt that a man such as Cromwell could not have made such an unambiguous statement of denial, if he had been aware that a slaughter of non-combatants had been committed by his men.[145] Secondly, the Bishops,' made no mention of those 'many inhabitants,' 'butchered at Drogheda, or Wexford, lately,' and on the contrary, they were more concerned with warning the people of Cromwell's 'shews of clemency.'[146]

The allegation, that Cromwell massacred all the soldiers of the garrison, after they had surrendered is another myth, which is not supported by the evidence. This myth was first created by Ormond, who declares in a letter to Byron of 29th September 1649, that:

> Cromwell's officers and soldiers promised quarter to such as would lay down their arms, and performed it, as long as any place held out, which encouraged others to yield. But when they had once all in their power, then the word no quarter went round, and the soldiers were many of them forced against their wills to kill the prisoners. The cruelty exercised there for five days after the town was taken, would, [he declared], 'make as many several pictures of inhumanity, as are to be found in *The Book of Martyrs* or in *The Relation of Amboya*'.[147]

This allegation, was simply repeated word for word, in the nineteenth century by the Rev. Denis Murphy in his *Cromwell-in-Ireland*, (1883), and many other histories.[148]

This myth, was further developed by Thomas Coonan *in The Irish Catholic Confederacy and the Puritan Revolution,* (1954),

---

[144] *Ibid.*
[145] Harrison, *op.cit.*, p. 148.
[146] Carlyle, *op.cit.*, p. 331.
[147] Gilbert, *op.cit.*, Vol. II, p. 271.

who asserts that: 'The evidence for the charge, that Cromwell massacred the soldiers of the garrison after they surrendered on quarter is impressive.'[149] However, Coonan does not provide, new evidence to support his allegations, but simply repeats Ormond's account. In reality, of course there is, no evidence to suggest that the entire garrison, surrendered and were slaughtered. Furthermore Lord Inchiquin's account, contradicts Ormond's statement, when he reported to Ormond, 'there was never seen so cruel a fight our horse doing beyond expectation.' In addition, Inchiquin makes no mention of 'the slaughter of the citizenry.' in relation to Cromwell's capture of Drogheda.[150]

With respect to Cromwell's severity at Drogheda, James Scott Wheeler has recently asserted, that, 'there is no justification we can make today for a soldier, even in the violent seventeenth century, to have refused to accept the surrender of enemy soldiers.'[151] Wheeler, has overlooked the fact that Cromwell, was not bound by the twentieth century, rules of war, but acted at all times in strict accordance with the rules of war at the time.[152] Furthermore, in the seventeenth century the rules of war were quite clear. Defending armies risked more, from what Ormond called, 'Colonel Hunger and Major Sickness,' apart from the assault itself. A besieged town, risked massacre, if it rejected terms to surrender before investment. Garrisons which held out, were put to the sword to avoid costly sieges elsewhere.[153] As Wellington, was later to put it, 'The practice of refusing quarter to a garrison which stands on assault is not a useless effusion of blood.'[154]

It should be remembered that on 26th December 1643, Lord Byron summoned a Parliamentarian detachment at Barthomley

---

[148] Murphy, *op.cit.*, p. 109.
[149] Thomas Coonan, *The Irish Catholic Confederacy and the Puritan Revolution*, Dublin, (1954), p. 296.
[150] Gilbert, *op.cit.*, Vol. II, p. xxii.
[151] Wheeler, *op.cit.*, p. 87. *Cromwell-in-Ireland*
[152] David L. Smith, *Oliver Cromwell, Politics and Religion in the English Revolution, 1640-1658*, Cambridge, (1991), p. 7.
[153] Johnson, *op.cit.*, p. 44.
[154] Ashley, *op.cit.*, p. 231.

Church, in Cheshire. The troops refused to surrender, consequently, Byron stormed the church. Afterwards he wrote: 'I put them all to the sword, which I find to be the best way to proceed with these people, for mercy to them is cruelty.'[155] Byron's brutal action, was of course in accordance with the seventeenth century rules of war, which is probably, why Byron, survived without a blemish on his reputation. When George Monck's storm of Dundee, of 1651, was followed by a massacre, he also survived with his reputation untainted.[156]

Cromwell sent a party of his horse to Dundalk, which the enemy quitted, and he says 'we are possessed of another castle they deserted between Trim and Tredagh, upon the Boyne.' Further he says 'I sent a party of horse and dragoons, to a house within five miles of Trim, there being in Trim, some Scots companies, which Lord Ardes brought to assist the Lord of Ormond. But on the news of Tredagh, they ran away, leaving their great guns behind them, which we also possessed.'[157]

The main justification offered, for Cromwell's severity at Drogheda, has been that it would demoralise other garrisons, and speed a general submission. As we have seen initially, this may have been the case, in regions close to Drogheda, but in the more remote areas, reports had little impact as we shall see in the remaining chapters.[158]

To conclude, at Drogheda, Cromwell offered terms to the garrison, warning the governor of the consequences should he refuse. His summons was refused and the storm began. After this initial rejection Cromwell refused subsequent quarter to the garrison, in accordance with the contemporary rules of war. Furthermore, in dismissing as myths the claims made in biased historical accounts; firstly, the majority of the inhabitants of Drogheda, in September 1649, were not in fact all Irish Catholics. The inhabitants were

---

[155] Peter Young and Richard Holmes, *The English Civil War – A Military History of Three Civil Wars 1642-1651*, London, (1975), p. 174., quoting, *Mercurius Civicus*, No. 35, p. 374.
[156] Ashley, *op.cit.*, p. 232.
[157] *Ibid.*, p. 299. Letter XCVIII.
[158] Barnard, *op.cit.*, p. 181.

New English and Scottish settlers who were Protestants. There were of course a small number of Irish Catholics living in the Irish section of the town.

There is also no doubt, that the garrison of 3,000 men, who were not Irish Catholics. The majority of the soldiers defending the garrison, like its inhabitants, were mostly English. Approximately half were Catholics and the other half Protestants. The officers were English, some of whom were Catholics like the governor Sir Arthur Ashton. On the other hand, Colonel Byrne commanded a whole regiment of Protestant Englishmen. In addition, 'Ormond's soldiers included, not only of many recent English settlers, but also royalist refugees, from England who had no claim to be Irish in any sense.'[159]

As Ernest Hamilton emphasised: 'Cromwell's alleged massacre of Drogheda, is invariably cited as an example of Cromwell's brutality to the Irish; but as a matter of fact, the vast majority of the victims were English. Practically all the officers and by far the greater part of the garrison were English. As to this point there is absolutely no room for doubt.'[160] Patrick Corish agrees, 'How many of them were English and how many of them were Irish, seems beyond establishing, but the serving officers, were chiefly English, as was the Commander Sir Arthur Aston, a Catholic Royalist.'[161] The myth that the soldiers, and the greater part of the garrison, were Irish Catholics, was created then developed in the nineteenth century, for propaganda and partisan purposes and is not supported by the evidence I have produced.

There is nothing to support the other popular belief that after Cromwell had induced the garrison to surrender by offering quarter for their lives, he then broke his word and ordered indiscriminate massacre of the whole garrison. In contrast, research shows whilst there is some evidence that some Royalist officers and soldiers were put to the sword, on the Mill Mount, after quarter had been given by the first officer who went there, there is no proof that this

---

[159] Hutton, *op.cit.*, p. 46.
[160] Hamilton, *op.cit.*, p. 367.
[161] Corish, *op.cit.*,p. 339-40.

occurred with Cromwell's knowledge. There is also evidence that the remainder of the garrison did not surrender and were killed fighting. Lord Inchiquin, when referring to the Royalist defenders of the garrison, says 'that there was never seen so cruel a fight our horse doing beyond expectation.' Moreover, Cromwell's orders at Drogheda were quite specific, he forbade his men to spare any bearing arms in the town. In addition to Cromwell's own letters, the two authentic documents presented in this Chapter, one of them from a Royalist officer seem to disprove conclusively the story of a general massacre.[162] There is also sufficient conflicting evidence to strongly challenge the myth that the whole garrison was slaughtered after they had surrendered.

Finally, the popular belief that Cromwell put to the sword the bulk of the civilian inhabitants sparing neither women nor children is not supported by evidence. Although it is possible that some unarmed inhabitants were accidentally killed; there is actually no evidence of this from an eyewitness but only rumours and reports at second hand. One such report was the fictional account of a massacre of women and children made by Thomas-a-Wood to his brother Anthony.[163]

There was, no documented evidence of any killings in the North Town, other than Cromwell's own account, and no documented, eye witness accounts, by either side in existence, for the killing of town citizens to date. Cromwell, could not have been responsible for the near 1000 people being put to the sword, in the North Town, in or around St. Peter's Church, as he did not, enter into the North Town, until 10/11th September 1649. Any killings, in Drogheda, prior to that date, would have to have been under the jurisdiction and authority, of Aston as Governor of Drogheda. Remembering of course, the vast majority of the soldiers defending the North Town, were all spared, and shipped to the 'Barbadoes' as slaves.

In fact on 14th September 1649 Cromwell issued a pass of safety offering protection to the inhabitants and the peaceful behaviour of troops. It must be remembered if New Model soldiers had killed

---

[162] Froude, *op.cit.*, p. 148.
[163] Hutton, *op.cit.*, p. 47.

any unarmed inhabitants at Drogheda they would have disobeyed Cromwell's orders. He forbade his men to spare any bearing arms. The popular belief that none of the garrison's soldiers escaped except for one lieutenant, is also a myth. Lord Inchiquin reported to Ormond 'many men, and some officers, have made their escapes out of Drogheda, som of every regiment have come unto me...Garret Dungan is one, and is at Tecraghan...Lieutenant Collonell Cavenagh is escaped to Mark Trevor, who is at Carrickmacross.'[164]

Finally, it has been demonstrated in this Chapter, that there are, more believable explanations, and assessments, than those manifest in the myths, which have been developed in fictional accounts, and frequently repeated in every generation.

---

[164] Gilbert, *op.cit.*, Vol. II, p. xxiii.

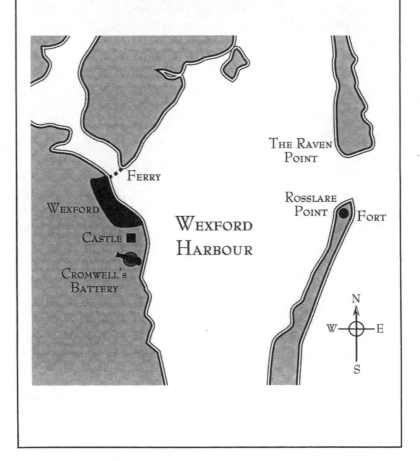

CROMWELL'S SIEGE OF WEXFORD
1-11 OCTOBER, 1649

THE RAVEN POINT

FERRY

WEXFORD

CASTLE ■

WEXFORD HARBOUR

ROSSLARE POINT   ● FORT

CROMWELL'S BATTERY

N
W ─⊕─ E
S

CHAPTER FOUR

Myths And Cromwell's Storm Of Wexford

300 women were put to death in the public square. They flocked around the great cross, which stood there, in the hope that Christian soldiers would be so far softened by the sight of that emblem of mercy, as to spare the lives of unresisting women. But the victors, enraged at such superstitions, and perhaps regarding their presence there as proof that they were Catholics, and therefore fit objects of their zeal, rushed up and put them all to death [Rev. Denis Murphy, S.J.][1]

The major myths, surrounding the events at Wexford, can be summarised as follows: all the inhabitants were Irish.[2] The majority, of the unarmed, inhabitants were indiscriminately killed;[3] two or three hundred women, were put to death in the market cross.[4] Cromwell, exterminated the citizens of Wexford, by the sword.[5] It will be argued, that other interpretations, based on evidence available, reveal that such claims remain myths, without much historical validity.

---

[1] Rev. S.J. Denis Murphy, *Cromwell in Ireland – A History of Cromwell's Irish Campaign*, Dublin, (1883), p. 341.
[2] Patrick Francis Moran, D.D., *Historical Sketch of the Persecutions Suffered by the Catholics of Ireland Under the Rule of Cromwell and the Puritans*, Dublin, (1885), p. 104.
[3] Patrick Corish, 'The Cromwellian Conquest, 1649-1653,' in T.W. Moody, F.X. Marten and F.J. Byrne, *A New History of Ireland, Vol. III: Early Modern Ireland*, Oxford, (1976), p. 341.
[4] Murphy, *op.cit.*, p. 341.
[5] Moran, *op.cit.*, p. 104.

Cromwell, left the garrison behind him at Drogheda, and marched South; back to Dublin. Simultaneously, 5,000 men, under the command of Colonels Venables, and Theophilus Jones; were sent to reduce, enemy held territory, in the North. Cromwell, marched out of Dublin, on or about 23rd September, determined, to take Wexford. Cromwell, as usual maintained discipline, on the march and encountered no resistance.[6] Cromwell writes:

For the Honourable William Lenthall
Speaker of the Parliament of England.
Wexford, 14 October 1649

Sir
The army marched from Dublin, on or about the 23rd September into the County of Wicklow, where the enemy had a Garrison about fourteen miles from Dublin, called Killencarick, they quitting, a company of the Army was put therein. From thence a passage over the River Doro about a mile above the Castle of Arklow, which was the first seat and honour of the Marquis of Ormond's family. Which he had strongly fortified but it was upon, the approach of the Army quitted; wherein we left another company of foot.

From thence the Army marched towards Wexford; where in the way was a strong and large Castle, at a town called Limbrick, the ancient seat of the Esmonds; where the Enemy had a strong Garrison; which they burnt and quitted, the day before our coming thither. From thence we marched towards Ferns, an Episcopal seat, where was a Castle; to which I sent Colonel Reynolds with a party to summon it. Which accordingly he did, and it was surrendered to him; where we having put a company.

---

[6] Samuel Rawson Gardiner, *History of the Commonwealth and Protectorate 1649-1656*, Vol. I, London, (1903), pp. 126-7.

Cromwell then

> advanced the Army to a passage over the River
> Slaney, which runs down to Wexford; and that night,
> we marched into the fields of a Village called
> Enniscorthy, belonging to Mr. Robert Wallop; where
> was a strong Castle very well manned and provided
> for by the enemy; and close under it, a very fair House
> belonging to the same worthy person – a Monastery
> of Franciscan Friars, the considerablest in all Ireland;
> they ran away the night before we came. We
> summoned the Castle; and they refused to yield at
> the first; but upon better consideration, they were
> willing to deliver the place to us; which accordingly
> they did; leaving their great guns, arms, ammunition
> and provisions behind them.[7]

Cromwell, was not with his army, at the conclusion of the march,
when they took Killencarrick and Arklow. Limbrick, Ferns and
Enniscorthy, also surrendered, to Cromwell's men, without
violence.[8]

Wexford, was a fortressed town similar to Drogheda. The town,
was surrounded by, high stonewall, and lined with ramparts of earth
fifteen foot thick.[9] In addition, a castle, guarded the southern end
of the town, built outside the wall. The town itself, stretched along
the whole length of the harbour.[10]

Popular historical opinion, created the belief, that all of the
residents of Wexford, in 1649 were Irish,[11] but this view is not
supported by the evidence. Modern research, has revealed that in
the middle of the 1640s, a cosmopolitan community including English,

---

[7] Thomas Carlyle, *Oliver Cromwell's, Letters and Speeches with Elucidations*,
(2nd revised edition), (3 Vols. in one), London, (1846), p. 302.
[8] *Ibid.*, pp. 302-3.
[9] *Ibid.*, p. 303.
[10] Gardiner, *op.cit.*, Vol., I, p. 127.
[11] Moran, *op.cit.*, p. 104.

Flemish, and French, as well as Irish residents, was thriving in Wexford. Contemporary accounts; indicate that, 'there were about forty privateering vessels in the harbour, when it was stormed by Cromwell in, 1649.'[12] In fact, after the outbreak of the first English Civil War, in August 1642, Wexford soon developed, into a major base, for piracy.[13] Whilst at Ross, on 14th November 1649, Cromwell, reported to Parliament :

> Your ships have taken some good prizes. The last was thus; There came in a Dunkirk man-of-war with 32 guns; who brought in a Turkish man-of–war whom she had taken, and another ship of 10 guns laden with poor-john and oil. These two your ships took. But the man-of-war whose prizes these two were, put herself under the Fort of Duncannon, so that your ships could not come near her. It pleased God that we had two demi-cannon with the foot, on shore; which being planted, raked through, killing and wounding her men ; so that after ten shot she weighed anchor, and ran into your Fleet, with a flag of submission, surrendering herself. She was well manned, the prisoners taken being two hundred and thirty.-I doubt the taking of prisoners of this sort will cause the wicked trade of piracy to be endless.[14]

> Your most humble and faithful servant,

> Ross, 14th November, 1649, Oliver Cromwell.

Throughout the winter, of 1642-1643, the Confederation of Kilkenny, ordered Dunkirk privateers, who were, operating in the

[12] John Kenyon and Jane H. Ohlmeyer, (ed), *The Civil Wars - A Military History of England, Scotland and Ireland 1638-1660*, Oxford, (1998), pp. 96-97.
[13] Bernard Capp, *Cromwell's Navy: The Fleet and the English Revolution, 1645-1660*, Oxford, (1989), p. 17.
[14] Thomas Carlyle, *Oliver Cromwell's Letters and Speeches with Elucidations*, (second edition), (1846), II, p. 94. Letter CXVI.

Irish Sea, to capture, 'enemy shipping.'[15] Moreover, 'The activities of privateers, had cost the lives of countless English seamen, who had been ruthlessly hanged, or thrown overboard, when their ships were captured, both in the Channel, and the Irish Sea.'[16]

Martyn Bennett in *The Civil Wars 1637-1653*, (1998), has wrongly suggested: 'In fact, Wexford people, had been only marginally if at all, involved in the murders, of 1641,'[17]during the uprising. This of course, is contradicted by the evidence, because in marked contrast to Drogheda, the majority of the inhabitants, of Wexford, had taken side with the rebels, during the Irish insurrection in 1641. Over 2,000 men from the County of Wexford, had joined the Irish rebel forces, including eight hundred, from the town. The Confederation of Kilkenny, even appointed their own Govenor at Wexford.[18] Moreover, on 29th July 1642, a Protestant Nicholas Rochford deposed:

> The gentlemen of the county [names given] had declared themselves to be in rebellion, and made captains among themselves to command the several inhabitants within the parishes of the said town...the men under the command of the captains numbered 800.[19]

Furthermore, eighty Protestants were crammed into a frigate, and because it was overloaded, it sank in the harbour. Not surprisingly, only one man survived. John Archer deposed:

> More than threescore passages being on ship board at Wexford intending to goe to England were wilfully cast away by the Irish owners or seamen for their wealthes sake, and as the said passengers did swymm

---

[15] Capp, *op.cit.*, p.17.
[16] C.V. Wedgewood, *Oliver Cromwell*, London, (1939), pp. 70-1.
[17] Martin Bennett, *The Civil Wars 1637-1653*, Stroud, (1998), p. 92.
[18] Tom Reilly, *Cromwell, An Honourable Enemy*, London, (1999), p.133.
[19] *Ibid.*

to shore they were thrust back into the sea againe and drowned by the saylers and rebells on shore, none escaping but the seafaring men, and one Papist woman who made the boast thereof at her returne to Wexford.[20]

After his defeat at Drogheda, Ormond initially, intended to abandon Wexford. However, it was rife with factions, and these divisions, played into Cromwell's hands. On the one hand, the party, that supported the Nuncio Rinuccini, wished to surrender to Cromwell. On the other hand, the Confederates, who wanted to hold out, and insisted, that Ormond send only Catholic soldiers, to reinforce the garrison; at Wexford.[21] It was the Confederates, who were successful, and Ormond despatched 1,500 soldiers of Castlehaven's Ulster foot, to bolster defence.[22]

Cromwell finally appeared before Wexford, with an army of approximately, 7,000 foot, and 2,000 horse.[23] Cromwell says: 'Upon Monday, the first of October, we came before Wexford, into which the enemy had put a garrison consisting of their army, this town until then been so confident of their own strength, as that they would not at any time suffer a garrison to be imposed on them.'[24] In other words the garrison had refused to take on reinforcements. Cromwell, summoned the governor as follows:

> To the Commander-in-Chief of the Town of Wexford
> Before Wexford 3rd October 1649
> Sir,
> ...having brought the Army belonging to the Parliament of England before this place, to reduce it to obedience; to the effusion of blood may be prevented, and the Town and Country about it

---

[20] *Ibid*.
[21] Gentles, *op.cit.*, pp. 364-5.
[22] Gardiner, *op.cit.*, Vol., I, p. 129.
[23] *Ibid*, p. 127.
[24] Carlyle, *op.cit.*, p. 303.

preserved from ruin, I thought fit to summon you to deliver the same to me, to the use of the State of England. By this offer, I hope it will clearly appear where the guilt will lie, if the innocent persons should come to suffer with the guilty.

I expect your speedy answer; and rest,

Your servant, Oliver Cromwell.[25]

However, Cromwell's summons, was met with delaying tactics, from the governor David Sinnot, who corresponded with him for a week.[26] Cromwell, finally replies :

For the Commander-in Chief Chief, in the Town of Wexford
Before Wexford, 11th October, 1649

Sir,

I have had the pleasure to pursue your Propositions; to which I might have returned an Answer with some disdain. But, to be short – I shall give the Soldiers and Non-commissioned Officers quarter for life, and leave to go to their several habitations, with their wearing clothes they engaging themselves to take up arms no more against the Parliament of England. And to the Commissioned Officers quarter for their lives, but to render themselves Prisoners. And as for The

---

[25] Carlyle, *Ibid*, p. 303. Letter CI. ; Other contemporary accounts of the taking of Wexford can be found in Col. Deane's narrative in HMC, *Leyborne-Popham*, p. 47, and two anonymous letters in *A Very Full and Particular Relation of the Great Progress... toward the Reducing of Ireland*, (31 Oct, 1649), E576/6, pp. 50-52.

[26] James Burke, 'The New Model Army and the problems with siege warfare, 1648-51,' *Irish Historical Studies*, Vol. XXVII, p. 14.

Inhabitants I shall engage myself That no violence
shall be offered to their goods, and that I shall protect
the Town from Plunder. I expect your positive Answer
instantly; and if you will upon these terms surrender
and quite, 'and' shall, in one hour, send forth to me
Four Officers of the quality of Field Officers, and
Two Aldermen, for the performance thereof, - I shall
thereupon forbear all acts of hostility.

Your Servant
Oliver Cromwell.[27]

James Scott Wheeler, has suggested that, 'What followed is
somewhat unclear, although, Cromwell undoubtedly rejected further
negotiations.'[28] However, examination of the primary documentary
evidence, makes it very clear, as to what actually happened.
Cromwell says:

The Governor of the town having obtained from me a
safe conduct for four persons mentioned in one of
the papers, to come and treat with me about the
surrender of the town, I expected they should have
done so; but instead thereof, the Earl of Castlehaven
brought to their relief on the northside of the river
about five hundred foot, which occasioned their refusal
to send out any to treat, and caused me to revoke my
safe conduct.[29]

Meanwhile, Cromwell's heavy cannon, were landed in Wexford
harbour, and his men, began setting up their batteries, which, were
being trained on the castle.[30] Cromwell says :

---

[27] *Ibid*.
[28] James Scott Wheeler, *Cromwell-in-Ireland*, Dublin, (1999), p. 97.
[29] Carlyle, II, *op.cit.* p. 95.
[30] *Ibid*.

A day or two before our battery was planted, Ormond, the Earl of Castlehaven, the Lord of Ardes and Clanneboys, were on the other side of the water, with about one thousand eight hundred horse, one thousand five hundred foot, and offered to put in four or five hundred foot more into the town, which the town refusing, he marched away in all haste: I sent the Lieutenant-general [Jones,] after him, with about one thousand four hundred horse, but the enemy made from him.[31]

Cromwell's account continues:

Upon Thursday the 11 instant (our batteries being finished the night before) we began to play betimes in the morning, and having spent neer a hundred shot, the Governors stomach came down, and he sent to me to give leave for four persons, entrusted by him, to come unto me and offer terms of surrender, which I consending to, two field officers, with an alderman of the town, and the captain of the castle, brought out the conditions enclosed.[32]

However, before the answer was forthcoming, the garrison, was betrayed by Captain Stafford, the Castles Governor; who agreed, to allow the New Model Army to enter. At this juncture, the defenders, on the opposite wall, seeing the castle guns, trained on them panicked. Some, jumped over the earthworks, and pleaded for quarter, whilst many more, fled to the shore, trying to escape across the harbour. Cromwell's men, were first challenged by armed resistance, in the market place area. The streets, leading to the market place, had been obstructed by cables, strung from wall to wall, to prevent cavalry, from charging through. When, New Model soldiers reached the market place, they were confronted,

---

[31] *Ibid.*
[32] *Ibid.*

by a newly constructed barricade. Behind this, stood regiments of armed soldiers and armed, townsmen. Most, of the townsmen were privateers, and a long history of piracy, had made them antagonistic towards the English Parliamentarians.[33] Most recently Tristram Hunt in *The English Civil War-At First Hand*, (2003), has asserted that it was at this point, 'Cromwell happily set loose his dogs of war on an Irish race he regarded as backward and fallen,'[34] but clearly there is no evidence of this. As Cromwell explains to Parliament:

> 'Which 'Answer' indeed had no effect. For whilst I was preparing of it; studying to preserve the town from plunder, that it might be of the more use to you and your Army – and the Captain who was one of the Commissioners, being fairly treated, yielded up the Castle to us. Upon the top of which our men no sooner appeared, but the enemy quitted the walls of the Town; which our men perceiving, ran violently upon the Town with their ladders, and stormed it. And when they [the soldiers] came into the market place, the enemy making a stiff resistance our forces brake them; and then put all to the sword that came in their way. Two boatfuls of the enemy attempting to escape, being overprest with numbers, sunk, whereby were drowned near three hundred of them; I believe in all there were lost of the enemy not less than two thousand and I believe not twenty of yours killed, from the first to the last of the siege.[35]

It is clear, that this action, did not take place under Cromwell's orders, and the Parliamentary Naval Commander, at Wexford,[36]

---

[33] Gardiner, *op.cit.*, Vol., I p. 130.

[34] Tristram Hunt, *The English Civil War-At First Hand,* London, (2002), Paperback edition, (2003), p. 257.

[35] Thomas Carlyle, *Oliver Cromwell's, Letters and Speeches with Elucidations*, (2nd Revised edition), (3 Vols, in one), p. 309.

[36] Gaunt, *op.cit.*, p. 119.

Richard Dean, wrote to Edward Popham, on 22nd October 1649, that 'this action occurred without orders from Cromwell.'[37] Cromwell, estimated that enemy deaths, at Wexford, were in the region of 2,000, including 300 drowned, on the Royalist coalition side, and less than, twenty on the Parliamentary side. In actual fact, the deaths, were almost accidental. The garrison, was about to surrender, and there was, definitely no order, from Cromwell, to storm Wexford, or to put defenders, townsfolk and priests to the sword.[38] Cromwell's report continues :

> That, we intending to better to the place than so great a ruin hoping the Town might be more use to you and your Army, yet God would not have it so; but by an unexpected providence of in his righteous justice, brought just judgement on them; causing them to become a prey to the soldier who in their piracies had made preys of so many families, and now with their bloods to answer to the cruelties which they had exercised upon the lives of divers poor protestants. Two instances,' of which I have been lately acquainted with. About seven or eight score Protestants were put by them into an old vessel; which being, some say, bulged by them, the vessel sunk, and they were presently drowned in the Harbour. The other 'instance' was thus; They put divers poor Protestants into a Chapel, (which since they have used for a Mass-house, and in which one or more of their priests were now killed), where they were famished to death. The soldiers got very good booty in this place. I could have wished for their own good, and the good of the garrison, they had been more moderate.[39]

---

[37] Burke, *op.cit.*, p. 15.
[38] *Ibid.*
[39] Carlyle, *op.cit.*, p. 309.

James Scott Wheeler, in *Cromwell-in-Ireland*, (1999), asserts that, 'Unquestionably, without moral or military justification, hundreds of non-combatants were killed by the rampaging troops,'[40] but provides no evidence in support of his allegations. This now popular belief, that, the majority of 'unarmed inhabitants, were indiscriminately killed,'[41] is not supported by eye witness accounts, but is, largely based, on mythical interpretations, which, did not surface until the nineteenth century. However, there seems little doubt that armed townsmen would have been killed; it is also possible that some unarmed inhabitants were killed, but, there are no eye witness accounts of this, other than Cromwell's own account to Parliament which states:

> The town is now so in your power, that the former inhabitants, I believe scarce one in twenty can challenge any propriety in their houses, *most of them are run away,* and many of them killed in this service.[42]

However, there is no doubt, that Catholic priests and friars, at the garrison at Wexford, were executed by Cromwell's soldiers without mercy. This is clearly illustrated by the following cotemporary account:

> Some [priests] came holding forth crucifixes before them, and conjuring our soldiers (for his sake that saved us all) to save their lives; yet our soldiers would not own their dead images for our living saviour; but struck them dead with their idols; many of their priests…were slain together by our soldiers about their altar.[43]

---

[40] Wheeler, *op.cit.*, p. 98.
[41] Corish, *op.cit.*, p. 341.
[42] Carlyle, *op.cit.*, p. 309.
[43] Gentles, *op.cit*, p. 367, citing *A Very Full and Particular Relation*, *op.cit.*, p. 56.

The popular belief, that, 'Cromwell exterminated the citizens of Wexford by the sword,' is not supported by the evidence. This belief, was developed in the middle of the nineteenth century. As, Toby Barnard emphasises:

> Among the literate survivors of the wreck, the priests were best able to frame a public response. Safe in their continental houses, often after perilous adventures, they consoled their brethren by compiling martyrologies... most of these histories spiked with vitriol, found their way into print only later – some of the most important, not until the nineteenth century.[44]

A classical example, appears in Patrick Francis Moran's, *An Historical Sketch of the Persecutions Suffered by the Catholics of Ireland Under the Rule of Cromwell and the Puritans,* who cites, the unsupported martyrology; of Father St. Leger, *The History of the Jesuits in Ireland,* (1655), who says: 'On the city (Wexford) being taken, Cromwell exterminated the citizens by the sword.'[45] However, he provides no evidence whatever, to support this allegation.

The bloodshed at Wexford, is often compared to, that at Drogheda. However, there are marked differences. At Drogheda, the order to deny quarter, was given by Cromwell, as policy, after terms of surrender had been refused. In contrast, at Wexford, the deaths, were not, a direct result of Cromwell's orders.[46] Gardiner emphasised, that the soldiers, and armed townsmen, at Wexford, 'made stiff resistance,' after the defences of the town had been captured, trying to inflict, a purposeless, loss of life on the victorious enemy, and, in doing so, paid the penalty, with their own lives.'[47] Soon, after the fall of Wexford, folk stories were fabricated and repeated. Such tales as:

---

[44] Toby Barnard, 'Irish images of Cromwell,' in R.C. Richardson, (ed.), *Images of Cromwell, Essays for and by Roger Howell, Jnr.,* p. 183.

[45] Moran, *op.cit.,* p. 104.

[46] Gaunt, *op.cit.,* p. 119.

[47] Gardiner, *op.cit.,* Vol., I, p. 133.

> ...the blood of the priest staining the executioner,
> which the man could never wash off afterwards; the
> dying monk whose cowl, bullets could not penetrate;
> the English soldiers, who having donned religious
> habits, in mockery, went sick and died haunted by
> their blasphemies; and towards the end of the day, a
> beautiful woman was seen ascending into the sky,
> just over the spot where a number of religious had
> died.[48]

These events, became part of an apparently, systematic propaganda war, against Cromwell, and, an accepted fact, among the more credulous of the Irish population. The mythical belief, that two or three hundred women, were put to death, in the market cross by New Model soldiers,[49] is pure fiction. This myth, appears to have been created by Royalist propagandist, James Heath, in his biography *Flagellum,* published after the Restoration in 1663. Heath, portrayed 'two hundred women, many of them of high rank, asking for mercy,...with the command of their charming eyes and those melting tears, – but, it was denied to them.'[50] In the nineteenth century, the Rev. Denis Murphy, enlarged and developed, Heath's myth, as follows:

> 300 women were put to death in the public square.
> They had flocked round the great cross which stood
> there, in the hope that Christian soldiers would be so
> far softened by the sight of that emblem of mercy, as
> to spare the lives of unresisting women. But the victors,
> enraged at such superstitions, and perhaps regarding
> their presence there as proof that they were Catholics,
> and therefore fit objects of their zeal, rushed up and
> put them all to death.[51]

---

[48] Antonia Fraser, *Cromwell, Our Chief of Men*, London, (1973), Paperback edition, (2004), p. 432.
[49] Murphy, *op.cit.*, p. 167.
[50] Fraser, *op.cit.*, p. 431.
[51] Murphy, *op.cit.*, p. 167.

However, Murphy does cite, Abbe Macghegans, *History of Ireland,* (1758), in support of his allegations. Macghegans account, did not appear, until the middle of the eighteenth century, and there were, no eyewitness reports, in this source, regarding the alleged event, so it cannot be taken seriously.[52] Patrick Corish, citing Heath, further develops this myth thus, - 'within a few years of the Restoration the story of 200 women massacred there had found its way into print. This, may mean that the full truth could now be openly told, or, it may mark, the beginning of a legend. Truth, or legend, it came to be accepted as truth.'[53] A classical example, of developing the myth further, without citing evidence appears in Robert Kee's *Ireland A History* (1980), in which it is asserted, 'Wexford, suffered even worse than Drogheda, being stormed, while still negotiating surrender. Cromwell's men ran amok in the town, killing at least 2,000, of whom 200, were said to be women, and children, slaughtered in the market-place.'[54] However there is simply no evidence of 200 women and children being slaughtered in the market place, nor, does Kee cite any.

In dismissing the myth, that all of the inhabitants of Wexford, in 1649, were Irish, it has been demonstrated, that the cosmopolitan community of the town, was made up of English, Irish, French, and Flemish privateers.[55] In respect, to the other myths, that the majority of the unarmed inhabitants were indiscriminately killed, or that, Cromwell exterminated the citizens of Wexford, by the sword, or that two or three hundred women, were put to death in the market cross, by New Model soldiers, the following points, must be emphasised: Firstly, the cross seems to have been situated in the market place, which would have been the last place the unarmed inhabitants, would have chosen as a place of refuge, as, it was a centre of preparations, for armed resistance. Secondly, although, Cromwell, does say, of the inhabitants, 'many, were killed, in this service,' whether they were armed, or unarmed he does not

---

[52] Gardiner, *op.cit.*, Vol., I, p. 132.
[53] Corish, *op.cit.*, p. 321.
[54] Robert Kee, *Ireland: A History*, Boston, (1980), re-issued, (1993), p. 48.
[55] Kenyon and Ohlmeyer, *op.cit.*, pp. 96-7.

say, but, he does say *'most of them are run away,'* and, that about 300 were drowned, trying to escape across the harbour, because, two of their boats were overloaded. Whilst it is possible of course, that some unarmed inhabitants were killed, there is no real evidence of this, other, than rumours and reports second hand. However, Cromwell does say that, he wished the soldiers had been more moderate. Thirdly, if any large numbers of women, or unarmed citizens, were deliberately killed, it would, have been recorded, somewhere, in Ormond's extensive correspondence, and of course it was not.[56] Fourthly, the storming of Wexford, took place without Cromwell's orders.[57] Finally, the strongest, reason to dismiss, the myths relating to, Cromwell's behaviour, at Wexford, is that, they have never been supported, by eye-witness accounts. They were, later interpolations from afar.[58]

---

[56] Gardiner, *op.cit.*, Vol., I, pp. 132-3.

[57] Gaunt, *op.cit.*, p. 119.

[58] Barnard, *op.cit.*, p. 183.

CHAPTER FIVE

Myths Associated with other Aspects of Cromwell's Military Campaign

Cromwell landed on our shores [Ireland] firmly resolved to acquire popularity amongst his fellow Puritans by extermination of the Irish papists. [Patrick Francis Moran].[1]

Two popular beliefs have been associated with Cromwell's military campaign in Ireland. The first is that it was a war fought by English Protestants against Irish Catholics.[2] The second is that Cromwell ordered wholesale and indiscriminate massacre of ordinary unarmed, Catholic citizens in the towns that he besieged.[3] Other interpretations of these issues, based on the evidence available suggest such beliefs are invalid.

The popular belief that Cromwell's military campaign in Ireland, was fought on the basis of English Protestant, against Irish Catholic, is not supported by evidence. Historical, research has firmly established that at the time of Cromwell's arrival in Ireland, Ormond had rallied all the parties in Ireland against the new republic. These Irish parties included English Catholics of the Pale, Old Irish Catholics, Episcopalian English Royalists, and the Scottish Presbyterians in Ulster, who, while they all had their own agenda,

---

[1] Patrick Francis Moran, DD, *Historical Sketch of the Persecutions Suffered by the Catholics of Ireland under the Rule of Cromwell and the Puritans*, Dublin, (1885), p. 90.

[2] John Gillingham, *Cromwell, Portrait of a Soldier*, London, (1979), p. 113.

[3] J.C. Davis, *Oliver Cromwell*, London, (2001), p. 108.

were united in their attempt to get Charles II on the throne.[4]

Cromwell, 'restricted his military campaign to only some of those areas where English rule had been previously well established, and where deserters from Royalist armies made his work easier.'[5] Following his victory at Wexford, Cromwell had good reason to believe that the whole of the south of Ireland would be speedily subdued. 'This was because most of the English royalists there, like Captain Stafford at Wexford were ready to betray their own cause.'[6]

Cromwell's hopes came to fruition, during the next few weeks, several towns in the province of Munster defected to Parliament. On 16th October the English soldiers along with their officers of the garrison at Cork supported by the English inhabitants declared for Parliament, expelled their governor, and drove out the Irish, wounding many of them in the process. On first news of the rising of Cork, Cromwell despatched Broghill to supervise the insurrection.[7] Cromwell writes: ' My Lord Broghil, Sir William Fenton, and Colonel Phayr, went to the town; and were received,- I shall give you My Lord Broghil's own words, - 'with all the real demonstrations of gladness an overjoyed people were capable of.'"[8]

Once Cork, had declared for Parliament, lots of other towns in the Province of Munster followed their example. These towns included: Bandon, Kinsale, and Youghal. Consequently Prince Rupert, along with his Royalist fleet was forced to make a quick retreat, due to the fall of Kinsale. This meant by the middle of

---

[4] Thomas Carlyle, *Oliver Cromwell's Letters and Speeches with Elucidations*, second revised edition, (3 Vols. in one), (1846), p. 292.

[5] Toby Barnard, 'Irish images of Cromwell,' in R.C. Richardson, (ed.), *Images of Oliver Cromwell: Essays for and by Roger Howell, Jnr.*, Manchester, (1993), p. 181.

[6] Ian Gentles, *The New Model Army in England, Ireland and Scotland 1645-1653*, Oxford, (1992), p. 368.

[7] Samuel Rawson Gardiner, *History of the Commonwealth and Protectorate, 1649-1656*, Vol, 1, (1903), pp. 136-137.

[8] Thomas Carlyle, *Oliver Cromwells, Letters and Speeches with Elucidations*, Second edition, (1846), II, p. 94. Letter CXVI.

November, Lord Inchiquin had lost most of his army causing Ormond's Irish Catholic allies, to lose confidence in him.[9]

Cromwell's next target was Waterford, a port thirty-five miles to the south. However, his way was blocked by the fortressed town of New Ross, which commanded a ferry over the river Barrow that guarded the approaches to Waterford.[10] On 17th October, Cromwell, summoned the Royalist Governor of New Ross, Sir Lucas Taaff as follows:

> For the Commander-in-Chief in Ross: These,
> Sir   17 October 1649
> Since my coming into Ireland, I have this witness for myself, That I have endeavoured to avoid effusion of blood; having been before no place, to which such terms have not been first sent as might have turned to the good and preservation of those to whom they were offered; this being my principle that the people and places where I come may not suffer, except through their own wilfulness.
>
> To the end I may not observe the like course with this place and people therein I do hereby summon you to deliver the Town of Ross into my hands, to the use of the Parliament of England. Expecting your speedy answer, I rest,
>
> Your servant,
>
> Oliver Cromwell.[11]

In reply to Cromwell's summons, Taaff requested permission, for his forces to be allowed to leave without harassment, and that religious freedom, be granted to the town's people, that chose to

---

[9] Gentles, *op. cit.*, p. 368.
[10] *Ibid.*, p. 369.
[11] Carlyle, *op.cit.*, p. 311. Letter CII.

stay behind.[12] Taaff's, request for liberty of conscience, as one of the conditions of surrender, was not acceptable to Cromwell. In keeping with the English Parliamentary view of Catholicism at the time,[13] Cromwell replied:

> For the Governor of Ross: these
> Sir   19 October 1649

> For that which you mention concerning liberty of conscience, I meddle not with a man's conscience. But if you by liberty of conscience you mean a liberty to exercise the mass, I judge it best to use plain dealing, and let you know, [that] where the parliament of England have power, that will not be allowed of. As for such of the townsmen who desire to depart and carry away themselves and goods (as you express) I engage myself they shall have three months time so to do; and in the meantime shall be protected from violence in their persons and goods, as others under the obedience of the Parliament. If you accept this offer, I engage my honour for a punctual performance hereof.[14]

> Your servant

> Oliver Cromwell.

Immediately following his reply, Cromwell demonstrated to Taaff, that there was no point in opening further negotiations, by opening fire on the walls of the fortress, with his heavy guns.[15] As a result of this, Taaff indicated, that he was ready to consider surrender.

---

[12] Gardiner, *op. cit.*, Vol., I, p. 155.
[13] Gentles, *op.cit.*, p. 373.
[14] Carlyle, *op.cit.*, p. 313. Letter CVI.
[15] Gentles, *op.cit.*, p. 373.

Cromwell replied:

> To the Governor of Ross: These
> Sir,
>
> Before Ross,   19 October 1649
>
> If you like to march away, with those under your
> command with their arms, bag and baggage, and with
> drums and colours, and shall deliver up the Town to
> me, - I shall give caution to perform these conditions;
> expecting the like from you. As to the inhabitants,
> they shall be permitted to live peaceably, free from
> the injury and violence of the soldiers. If you like
> hereof, you can tell how to let me know your mind,
> notwithstanding my *refusal* of a cessation. By these
> you will see the reality of my intentions to save blood,
> and to preserve the place from ruin, I rest,
>
> Your servant,
> Oliver Cromwell.[16]

Kevin Kelly in *The Longest War,* (1983), asserted that 'Cromwell
and the New Model Army, massacred the residents of some smaller
towns,'[17] but provides no evidence, in support of this contention.
J.C. Davis highlights the fact that, 'until recently the popular belief,
that indiscriminate massacres took place in Ireland under Cromwell,
was one widely held and not only by Irish nationalist historians.'[18]
This belief is identified by John Ardagh, in *Ireland and the Irish:
Portrait of a Changing Society*, (1994), who says, 'an Irish
rebellion was ruthlessly crushed by Cromwell, "to us he is like
Hitler," one Irishman told me, "and hundreds of thousands died."'[19]

---

[16] Carlyle, *op.cit.*, p. 312. Letter CIII.
[17] Kevin Kelly, *The Longest War*, London, (1983), p. 5.
[18] Davis, *op.cit.*, p. 108.
[19] John Ardagh, *Ireland and the Irish: Portrait of a Changing Society*, London,
(1994), p. 21.

To counter the popular belief that Cromwell, ordered wholesale and indiscriminate massacre, of ordinary, unarmed Catholic citizens, in the towns that he besieged, attention is drawn to the articles of capitulation at New Ross.

> Articles concluded and agreed upon, by and between the Right Honourable, the Lord Lieut. Of Ireland of the one part and the governor of Ross of the other part, this 19 October 1649.

> 1. It is concluded and agreed, That the governor of Ross with all under his command, may march into Kilkenny or Loughlen Bridge, with their arms, bag and baggage, drums beating, colours flying, bullet in mouth, bandeliers full of powder, and match lighted at both ends, provided they march thither in three days, and that no acts of hostility be committed during the said time.

> 2. It is concluded and greed, That such townsmen as desire to depart, and to carry away themselves and their goods, shall have three months time so to do, and in the meantime shall be preserved from violence in their persons and goods, as others under the obedience of the Parliament; and that a convoy be sent with them to secure them in their journeys.

> 3. It is concluded and agreed, that the inhabitants shall be permitted to live peaceably, and enjoy their goods and estates free from injury and the violence of the soldiers.

> 4. In consideration whereof, the governor of Ross, artillery, arms, ammunition and other utensils of war that are therein by three of the clock this present day, except such as were brought in by the said governor, or such as came in since he had the commend thereof,

and by two of the clock, to permit the Lord Lieutenant to put three hundred men into the blockhouse, gatehouse near the beach, and the white tower near the same.

5. For the performance of the Articles on the said governor's part, he is to deliver four such hostages as I shall approve.

Signed by
O. Cromwell.

Commissioners; James Crawford, Math Lynell, Thomas Gaynan, Math Dormer, Governor, Lucas Taaff.[20]

It is easy to agree with Reilly, who says, 'what is manifestly clear, is that Cromwell, is nowhere on record, as having ordered an indiscriminate slaughter of non-combatants during any battle,' in Ireland.[21] To counter the myth, that Cromwell's campaign, was fought on the basis, of English Protestant, against Irish Catholic, it must be noted that following Taaff's surrender, five hundred of Taaff's soldiers, all English by birth, joined the New Model Army.[22] Cromwell says, 'at least five hundred English, many of them Munster forces, came to us.'[23] The five hundred English soldiers, that had deserted the Royalist cause, at New Ross were a bonus to Cromwell, because, by this time his army had suffered substantial losses, due to various infectious diseases. In addition, his army had been sapped by the need to garrison the fortresses, already captured. By this time, it was unlikely that he could muster 5,000 men.[24]

---

[20] W.C. Abbott, *Writings and Speeches of Oliver Cromwell*, Vol. II, pp. 147-8.
[21] Tom Reilly, *Cromwell, An Honourable Enemy*, London, (1999), p. 7.
[22] Gardiner, *op.cit.*, Vol., I, p. 135.
[23] Carlyle, *op.cit.*, p. 315. Letter CVI.
[24] Gardiner, *op.cit.*, Vol., I, p. 135.

To counter the myth that Cromwell massacred large numbers of the Catholic inhabitants, in the towns that he besieged it must be noted, that the inhabitants of New Ross, were protected from plunder and violence, as Cromwell had earlier promised. Furthermore the Royalist soldiers of the garrison were allowed to march away with their arms, baggage, with drums beating and colours flying.[25]

In the next stage, of his campaign and following the fall of New Ross, Cromwell and his men, were forced to construct a bridge over the river Barrow, to prepare for the siege of Waterford. However Cromwell's reports, indicate that for much of this time he and 'his soldiers were unable to stir from their beds.'[26] He reported to Parliament, 'a considerable part of your army, is fitter for a hospital than the field.'[27] Cromwell writes,

> We lie with the army at Ross; where we have been making a bridge over the Barrow, and 'have' hardly yet accomplished 'it' as we could wish. The enemy lies upon the Nore, on the land between the Barrow and it; having gathered together all the force they can get. Owen Roe's men, as they report them, are six thousand foot, and about four thousand horse, beside their own army 'in this quarter'; and they give out they will have a day for it :- which we hope the Lord in His mercy will enable us to give to them, in His own good time.[28]

Waterford, the second city of Ireland, was occupied primarily by Catholics. It was a thriving centre of commerce, and was almost the equal of Dublin, in terms of both wealth and population. Located on the banks of the River Suir, its harbour, was sheltered from attack by two forts, the smaller Fort of Passage, to the west, and

---

[25] *Ibid.*
[26] Gentles, *op.cit.*, p. 369.
[27] Carlyle, *op.cit.*, p. 323, Letter CX.
[28] Carlyle *op.cit.*, II, p. 95. Letter CXVI.

Duncannon, to the east.[29] Before marching on Waterford, Cromwell dispatched Henry Ireton, with a regiment of horse and three troops of dragoons, to reduce Fort Passage. Cromwell later explained to Parliament, 'the Enemy called for quarter - and had it, and we the place.'[30]

Cromwell ordered, 2,000 troops, commanded by Michael Jones to seize control of Duncannon. Research indicates that Ormond was determined to defend Duncannon, and had recently appointed Colonel Edward Wogan as its governor, to replace Captain David Roche. Wogan, had in fact deserted from the Parliamentary army in 1648, and joined the Royalists. Ormond had also despatched 120 men from his personal bodyguard to bolster defence. Wogan was determined that Taaff's, example of Ross would not be repeated at Duncannon.[31]

Wogan, a Welsh Protestant, was one of the few royalist commanders, to successfully unite a joint force of Catholics and Protestants.[32] At Duncannon the 'Catholic priest and the Protestant minister were on the best of terms and shared the use of the garrison chapel.' Although Michael Jones was joined by Cromwell, Wogan's courageous defence proved successful. On 5th November, Jones raised the siege and marched away with his army. There seems little doubt that the 'effect of Cromwell's victories, at Drogheda and Wexford, had already worn off.'[33]

Cromwell and his forces reached Waterford on 24th November, finding the surrounding countryside unscathed by devastations of war. On 21st Lord Castlehaven had arrived at the town with relief troops to reinforce the garrison. However, despite the fact that he was a Catholic, he was refused entry, simply because he was English.[34] Because of the recent defection of the Munster Towns, the garrison, no longer trusted the English Royalists.[35] On the day

---

[29] Gentles, *op.cit.*, p. 369.
[30] Carlyle, *op.cit.*, p. 323.
[31] Gardiner, *op.cit.*, Vol., I, pp. 135-6.
[32] James Scott Wheeler, *Cromwell in Ireland*, Dublin, (1999), p. 108.
[33] Gardiner, *op.cit.*, Vol., I, p. 137.
[34] *Ibid.,* p. 141.
[35] Gentles, *op.cit.*, p. 370.

of his arrival, Cromwell summoned the town, reminding them of the fate of Wexford as follows:

To the Mayor and Aldermen of the City of Waterford

GENTLEMEN,

I have received information that you hitherto refused a garrison of the enemy to be imposed upon you; as also that some factions in the town are very active still, notwithstanding your refusals, to persuade you to the contrary.

Being come into these parts, not to destroy people and places, but to save them, that men may live comfortably and happily by their trade, (if the faults be not in themselves); and purposing also, by God's assistance, to reduce this City of Waterford to its due obedience, as He shall dispose the matter, by force, or by agreement with you upon terms wherein your own good and happiness, and of your wives, children and families may consist, notwithstanding some busy-headed persons may pretend to the contrary, knowing that if after all this you shall receive a garrison, it will probably put you into an incapacity to make any such accord for yourselves which was the cause of the ruin of the town and people of Wexford; and now I thought fit to lay these things before you, leaving you to use your own judgement therein.

And if any shall have so much power upon you as to persuade you that these are the counsels of an enemy, I doubt it will hardly prove, in the end, that they give you better. You did once live flourishingly under the power and in commerce with England. It shall be your own fault if you do not so again. I send these

intimations seasonably unto you. Weigh them well; it
so behoveth you. I rest,

Your loving friend,
O.C.[36]
[Nov.21, 1649].

However, the Mayor stalled for time, having already requested
Ormond to dispatch a strong force of Ulster Catholics, from O'Neills
army. Ormond in response complied and dispatched 1,300 soldiers,
commanded by Lieutenant-General Farrell, who arrived on the
24th. Meanwhile Henry Ireton had captured Fort Passage.[37]

By this time, Cromwell's army had been reduced to about 3,000
men. Large numbers of his men, had been dispersed in order to
secure defeated garrisons, stretching from Dublin to Wexford and
New Ross, whilst many others were sick. Moreover, Duncannon
fort was in enemy hands, Cromwell was unable to transport his
heavy artillery and supply train across the Barrow. In addition
torrential rain, 'turned his camp into a quagmire.'[38] Consequently,
on 2nd December, 'being,' as he wrote, 'as terrible a day as I ever
marched in all my life,'[39] Cromwell finally abandoned the siege of
Waterford.[40] Cromwell concludes, 'just as we marched off in the
morning – unexpected to us, the Enemy, had brought another of
near two thousand horse and foot, to increase their Garrison; which
we plainly saw at the other side of the water. We, marched that
night some ten or twelve miles through craggy country, to
KilmacThomas; a castle, some eight miles from Dungarvan.'[41]
Michael Jones was forced to stay behind at Dungarvan. There he
died of fever on 10th December; but was later buried at St Mary's
Chapel at Youghal.[42]

---

[36] Abbott, II, *op.cit.*, pp. 168-9.
[37] Gentles, *op.cit.*, p. 370.
[38] Wheeler, *op.cit.*, p. 113. *Cromwell in Ireland*
[39] Carlyle, *op.cit.*, p. 321. Letters, CXI.
[40] Gardiner, *op.cit.*, Vol., I, p. 142.
[41] Carlyle, *op.cit.*, p. 321. Letter CXI.
[42] Pauline Gregg, Oliver Cromwell, London, (1988), p. 184.

When Cromwell met up with Lord Broghill, who was leading a contingent of 1,200 horse and foot, which he had recruited in Munster, he gave Cromwell the welcome news, that the Royalist garrison at Dungarvon had also declared for Parliament that morning. The outlying garrisons of Baltimore and Castlehaven, followed suit. On 13th December, Carrickfergus, also surrendered to Coote. Thus at the close of 1649, only Waterford, on the coastline from Londonderry, to Cape Clear, was not in Cromwell's hands.[43]

At the beginning of December, Cromwell made the decision to go into winter quarters.[44] He marched from Dungarvan, to Youghal, and within a few days he was forced to discipline some of his men for looting. Moreover, on 8th December he issued the following:

Proclamation

Whereas I am informed that the horse under my command (since their being quartered within the Black-water) have and do in their several quarters take away and waste wheat and barley for their horses, and do behave themselves outrageously towards the inhabitants, not contenting themselves with such provisions as they are able to afford them, but to kill their sheep and other cattle within and as often as they please.

I do hereby straightly charge and command all soldiers to forbear such like practices upon pain of death...And I do farther will and require all officers and soldiery within the limits aforesaid, that they do not break down any stacks of barley or wheat in their respective quarters, to give the same to their horses, but that they content themselves with peas, oats, hay, and such other forage, as the country affords, paying or giving tickets at such reasonable rates for the same, as they

---

[43] Gardiner, *op.cit.*, Vol., I, p. 143.
[44] Wheeler, *op.cit.*, p. 118.

were usually sold for, before their coming into the said quarters.

Given under my hand this 8 day of December 1649,

O. Cromwell.[45]

Tom Reilly, has recently pointed out that throughout Murphy's *Cromwell-in-Ireland,* the author refuses to acknowledge these, 'emphatic resolutions' by Cromwell, because, 'They do, of course, portray a genuinely merciful individual, compared to the fiend that is depicted in that publication.'[46]

Ormond, also took the opportunity to go into Winter quarters, but his position, both from a political and military perspective was far more uncertain, than Cromwell's. Although the town of Kilkenny, had allowed him to base winter quarters there, reports, show that, 'his troops soon provoked a universal exclamation of the people due to their exactations.' Furthermore, the inhabitants of Waterford and Limerick, refused to admit his troops. Ian Gentles, draws our attention to the fact that; 'all too often it seemed that the population was readier to co-operate with Cromwell, than with Ormond. Even Royalist soldiers found the parliamentary service more attractive.'[47]

There is further evidence, to show that Cromwell's military campaign, in Ireland, was not fought, on the basis of English Protestant, against Irish Catholic. On 19th December, Cromwell, wrote to Parliament making his appraisal of the situation:

> At the present, O'Neiles party are in full conjunction with the Earl of Ormond, by which they contribute the assistance of near seven thousand effective horse and foot, these being eldest sons of the Church of Rome, most cried up and confided in by the clergy.

---

[45] Reilly, *op.cit.*, p. 216. Abbott, *op.cit.*, Vol. II, p. 175.
[46] *Ibid.*, p. 217.
[47] Gentles, *op.cit.*, p. 371.

> The rest of the army consists of the old English-Irish, some Protestants, some Papists, and other Papists Irish, who are carried by the interest of Ormond, Clanrickarde, Castlehaven, Muskery, Taaff and other old English and Irish, both lords and gentlemen, who are able to bring, and have already in the field, very considerable numbers of bodies of men not to be neglected upon any human confidence, or under-valued.[48]

As Cromwell's report to Parliament, shows he was still in a difficult situation. However, fortunately for Cromwell, new recruits began to arrive, as by now most of his men were sick, and many had died, including Michael Jones.[49]

From a Royalist perspective, there seems little doubt, Cromwell's victories, had shattered Irish confidence in Ormond. At times, the Irish stated that 'they could trust no one who did not go to the mass.' In an attempt to strengthen the Royalist alliance, the Catholic bishops met at Clanmacnoise. They issued, a call for Irish unity, in which Cromwell, was identified as their mortal enemy.[50]

The Bishops' call for unity, 'drew a ferocious response from Cromwell' and on 14 January 1650, whilst at Youghal, he drew up his 'Declaration...for Undeceiving of Deluded and Seduced People', in which he 'indicted the Irish Catholic clergy for greed, pride, cruelty and ambition.'[51] In addition, Cromwell included in this declaration his reason for being in Ireland. The movement of Protestant settlers, to the parliamentary cause, stimulated Cromwell's hope, that the Irish people could be persuaded to accept the new English Parliament. In reponse to this view he was highly critical of the Catholic Clergy.[52] Cromwell writes:

---

[48] Abbott, Vol. II, *op.cit.*, p. 179.

[49] Gentles, *op.cit.*, p. 371. Gregg, *op.cit.*, p. 184.

[50] *Ibid.*

[51] *Ibid.*

[52] Roger Howell, *Cromwell*, Boston, (1977), p. 143.

> You say your union is against a common enemy; and
> to this if you will be talking of union, I will give you
> some wormwood to bite on, by which it will appear
> God is not with you...You broke this union! You,
> unprovoked, put the English to the most unheard of
> and most barbarous massacre that ever the sun beheld.
> And at a time when Ireland was in perfect peace,
> and when, through the example of the English industry,
> through commerce and traffic, that which was in the
> natives' hand was better to them than if all Ireland
> had been in their possession and an Englishman in
> it...Is God, will God be with you? I am confident he
> will not.[53]

Cromwell, stressed that the English invasion, was based on a desire to avenge the insurrection of 1641; and to spread the benefits of England's godly way of life, rather than seize Irish lands. Cromwell writes : 'We are come to ask an account of the innocents blood that hath been shed...We come to break the power of a company of lawless rebels...we come (by assistance of God) to hold forth and maintain the lustre and glory of English liberty in a nation where we have an undoubted right to do it.' It is understandable therefore, that Irishmen may perceive Cromwell's declaration as hypocritical.[54]

By the end of January 1650, Cromwell was ready to resume his military operations. Whilst the first half of his campaign had been focused on the coastal towns, the second half would concentrate on the reduction of the inland fortresses in Munster.[55] By this time his reinforcements from England had arrived along with new uniforms, supplies, and money to pay his men.[56] Cromwell abandoned his Winter quarters at Youghal; and marched with part of his army to Fethard. After arriving before the walls of Fethard

---

[53] Carlyle, *op.cit.*, pp. 332-43.
[54] Howell, *op.cit.*, p. 143-4.
[55] Gentles, *op.cit.*, p. 372.
[56] Gardiner, *op.cit.*, Vol., I, pp. 149-50.

on 2nd February, he took 'cover in an old abbey and sent the usual summons to its governor.'[57] The governor replied:

> For Oliver Cromwell, General of the Parliamentary forces now in Ireland;
>
> May it please Your Lordship, I have received your letter about nine of the clock this night, which hour I conceive unreasonable for me to treat you. Yet if your Lordship pleases to send sufficient hostages in for such as I will employ to treat with you, I will be ready to entrust some in that business. Having no more at present. I remain,
>
> Your honour's friend and servant,
>
> Pierce Butler.
>
> From the garrison of Fethard, Feb. 2nd 1650, half an hour of nine o clock of the night.[58]

To further counter the myth, that Cromwell ordered wholesale, and indiscriminate massacre, of ordinary unarmed citizens in the towns that he besieged, it must be noted that the articles of capitulation at Fethard again emphasised; Cromwell's humanity:

> Articles of Agreement made and concluded on the 3rd day of February, 1650 between the Most Hon. Oliver Cromwell, Lord Lieutenant General of Ireland, and Lieutenant Colonel Pierce Butler, Governor of the town of Fethard, concerning the surrender of the said town as follows:

---

[57] Carlyle, *op.cit.*, p. 345.
[58] Reilly, *op.cit.*, p. 224.

1. That all the officers and soldiers shall march freely with their horses and arms and all other goods, bag and baggage, colours flying, matches lighted, ball in bouche, into any place within his Majesty's quarters or garrisons except such as are now besieged, safely convoyed thither free from violence from any of the Parliament's party.

2. That all the country families and inhabitants, as also any of the officers, may freely live and enjoy their goods either in the town or abroad; if they or any of them be disposed to betake themselves to their former habitations in the country, they may have respite of time for that, and admittance to enjoy their holdings, paying contribution, as others in the country do, and carry with them safely such goods as they have within the garrison.

3. That all clergymen and chaplains both of the soldiers, town and country, now in this garrison, may freely march, bag and baggage, without any annoyance or prejudice in body or goods.

4. That all and every the inhabitants of the said town, and their wives, children and servants, with all their goods and chattels, both within the town and abroad in the country, shall be protected from time to time, and at all times, and shall quietly and peaceably enjoy their estates, real and personal, in as free and as good condition as any English or Irish shall hold his or their estates in this Kingdom, they and every of them paying such contribution as the rest of the inhabitants of the county of Tipperary pay proportionably to their estates and no more.

In consideration whereof the said Governor doth hereby engage himself that he will deliver up the said town with all things therein, except such things as are before agreed upon, to be taken away with them by eight of the clock this morning.

Pierce Butler
Oliver Cromwell.[59]

Cromwell added, 'That night, there being about seventeen companies of the Ulster foot, in Cashel, above five miles from thence, [Fethard] they quit in some disorder; and the Sovereign and the Alderman, sent me a petition, desiring that I would protect them, which I have also made quarter'.[60]

Cromwell marched to Callen, in County Killkenny, hearing that Colonel Reynolds, had arrived there on 3 January. When he finally rendezvoused with Reynolds, he was informed by Reynolds that he had clashed with a hundred Royalist horse, and had scattered them. According to Cromwell, Reynolds had also taken prisoner, 'Lord Ossory's Captain-Lieutenant; along with another Lieutenant, and one of those, who betrayed our garrison at Enniscorthy; whom we hanged.' Moreover, 'the enemy had possessed three castles in the Town; one of them belonging to one Butler, [and] very considerable'. The other two castles, had been offered, the usual reasonable terms of surrender by Reynolds, which had been refused and as a result of this; were put to the sword. Finally, however Major-General Richard Butler surrendered his castle. Cromwell concludes, 'Butlers castle was delivered up on conditions for all to march away, leaving their arms behind them.'[61] Cromwell took Butler into custody, and later exchanged him; for new model soldiers held by Ormond.[62]

---

[59] J.T. Gilbert, (ed.), *A Contemporary History of Affairs in Ireland from AD 1641 to 1652 containing the narrative an 'Amphorismal discovery of a treasonable faction,'* 3 Vols., Dublin, (1879-80), Vol. 11, p. 215.
[60] Carlyle, *op.cit.*, p. 345. Letter CXIII.
[61] *Ibid.*, p. 345.
[62] Wheeler, *op.cit.*, p. 129. *Cromwell in Ireland*

Cromwell marched with his army and some artillery, to Cahir, arriving there on, or about, 24 February.[63] Cahir castle was located on an island, in the middle of the river Suir, which was only accessible by a drawbridge. The governor of Cahir, was 'Ormond's half brother Captain George Mathews.' The garrison had been strengthened by the arrival of a regiment of Ulster foot, who had been dispatched there by O'Neill, and who were camped outside the castle.[64] Cromwell, sent Mathews a summons offering him generous terms as follows:

> For the Governor of Cahir Castle.
> 24 February, 1650.
>
> Sir
>
> Having brought the Army and my cannon near this place- according to my usual manner in summoning places, I thought fit to offer you Terms, honourable for soldiers: That you may march away, with your baggage, arms and colours; free from injury or violence. But if I be necessitated to bend my cannon upon you, you must expect the extremity usual in such cases.
>
> To avoid blood, this is offered to you by
>
> Your Servant
> Oliver Cromwell.[65]

Mathews ignored the summons, forcing Cromwell to order a storm. However, Cromwell's men were forced to retreat as they were unable to cross the drawbridge. Consequently, Cromwell opened fire with his field guns on the castle walls. Although the Ulster foot

---

[63] Carlyle, *op.cit.*, p. 347, Letter CXIV.
[64] Wheeler, *op.cit.*, pp. 130-1. *Cromwell in Ireland*
[65] Carlyle, *op.cit.*, p. 347. Letter CXIII.

tried to retreat into the castle they were refused entry by Mathews, forcing them to negotiate terms with Cromwell. It was not long before Matthews became a party to these negotiations.[66]

Before terms were agreed on, however, according to Cromwell, some of his soldiers spent time 'beating up their quarters' and in addition, 'two Colonels, a Lieutenant-Colonel, Major and Divers Captains, all of horse: Colonel Johnson, Lieutenant-Colonel Laughern, and Major Simes, were shot to death, [as traitors], as having served under the Parliament, but now taken up arms with the Enemy.'[67]

If we examine the articles of capitulation at Cahir Castle, again, we find further evidence that Cromwell's campaign in Ireland, did not match the myths that had grown around it.

Articles for Cahir Castle

Articles made and agreed on the 24th day of Feb. 1649[-50], between his Excellency the Lord Lieutenant of Ireland on the one part, and Captain George Mathews, Governor of Cahyr Castle on the other part, concerning the surrender of the same castle;

Imprimis, that the governor and all officers, soldiers and clergymen and servants may march out with their horses and arms and bag and baggage. The English soldiers willing to serve his Excellency may be entertained. Those that will not, either English or Irish, to have liberty to live quietly in the country, laying down their arms, or passes to go elsewhere.

That the Governor may enjoy his estate which he hath as his wife's jointure, or wardship of the heiress of Cahir.

That he may have his goods and chattels and liberty for a week to carry them away; and have the

---

[66] Wheeler, *op.cit.*, p. 131. *Cromwell in Ireland*
[67] Carlyle, *op.cit.*, p. 345. Letter CXIII.

possession of the castle of Reghill for his habitation, and his corn yet remaining there, his Excellency keeping two files of musketeers there.

That the goods he hath in the castle belonging to others may be delivered to the several proprietors.

That in consideration hereof the Governor is to deliver up the said castle to his Excellency upon signing these articles.

George Mathews
O. Cromwell.[68]

After three days rest, Cromwell and his men, met with Colonel Hewson, at Gowran, which Cromwell describes as 'a popular town, where the enemy have a very strong castle.' Gowran, was under the command of an Englishman, a Colonel Hammond, who Cromwell describes as, 'a Kentishman, who was principal actor in the Kentish Insurrection, and did manage the Lord Capel's business at his trial.' Further he says 'I sent him a civil invitation to deliver up the castle unto me; to which he returned a very resolute answer and full of height.'[69]

Cromwell, having already placed his artillery in position, fired at the castle walls. However, before a considerable breach was opened, Cromwell says, 'the enemy beat for a parley for a treaty; which I having offered so fairly to him, refused; but sent him in positive conditions, that the soldiers should have their lives, and the Commission officers to be disposed of as should be thought fit; which in the end was submitted to.' Moreover, the next day, the common soldiers of the castle accepted Cromwell's offer and surrendered, Colonel Hammond, along with the other English commissioned officers.

---

[68] Gilbert, *op.cit.*, Vol. II, p. 363.
[69] Carlyle, *op.cit.*, p. 350. Letter CXVIII.

According to Cromwell: 'The next day, the Colonel, the Major, and the rest of the commissioned officers were shot to death; all but one, who delivered up the castle.' Further, 'we took a Popish Priest, who was Chaplain to the Catholics in this regiment, who was caused to be hanged. I trouble you with this, because this was the Lord of Ormond's own regiment.'[70]

Cromwell then marched to Kilkenny, north of Callan. Cromwell explains, 'upon Friday the 22nd March: and clashing with our body within a mile of the Town, we advanced with some horse very near unto it; and that evening I sent Sir Walter Butler [the governor] and the corporation a letter.'[71]

As follows:

To the Governor, and Major and Aldermen of Kilkenny:

Gentlemen
'Before Kilkenny' 22 March 1650

My coming hither is to endeavour, if God so please to bless me, the reduction of the City of Kilkenny to their obedience to the State of England; - from which by an unheard of massacre of the innocent English, you have endeavoured to rend yourselves. And as God Hath begun to judge you with His sore plagues, so will He follow you until He hath destroyed you, if you repent not. Your cause hath been judged already in England upon them who did abet your evils. By this free dealing, you see I entice you not to a compliance. You may have Terms' such as may save you in your lives, liberties and estates, according to what may be fitting for me to grant and you to receive. If you choose for the worst, blame yourselves. In confidence of the gracious blessings and presence of God with

---

[70] *Ibid.*
[71] *Ibid.*

his own Cause, which by many testimonies this is, - I shall hope for a good issue upon my endeavours.

Expecting a return from you, I rest,

Your servant,
Oliver Cromwell.[72]

Reports, indicate that the plague was raging within the walls of the town; which, had apparently spread from Galway. The inhabitants, led by the Mayor, wished to negotiate terms with Cromwell. On the other hand, the governor Sir Walter Butler, refused to surrender.[73] As a result, at 9am on 25th March, Cromwell, opened fire with his field guns, until, he had breached the town wall. However, behind the breach, the defenders had already constructed earthworks, which they had also fenced off. Kilkenny, was divided into two parts, High Town, and Irish Town. Cromwell, sent Colonel Ewer, across the river with 1,000 men, to capture the Irish town. At the same time, Cromwell ordered his men into the breach; but his men were soon beaten off.[74] This attack, according to Cromwell, 'was not performed with usual courage nor success; for they were beaten off, with the loss of one Captain; and about twenty or thirty men, killed and wounded.'[75] In his report to Parliament Cromwell says; 'and there being another walled town on the other side of the river, eight companies of foot, were sent over the river to possess, that which accordingly was effected with a similar number of losses,' of New Model soldiers. Cromwell writes, 'we made preparations for a second battery 'but' the enemy…sent for a treaty'…and after some hours, agreed to deliver up the Castle upon the Articles enclosed.'[76]

---

[72] Abbot, II, *op.cit.*, p. 224.
[73] Gardiner, *op.cit.*, Vol., I, p. 150.
[74] Wheeler, *op.cit.*, p. 134-35. *Cromwell in Ireland*
[75] Carlyle, *op.cit.*, pp. 350-1.
[76] *Ibid.*, p. 351.

Articles of agreement between the Commissioners appointed by his Excellency, Lord Cromwell, Lord Lieutenant General of Ireland, for and on behalf of his Excellency, of the one part, and those appointed Commissioners by the respective Governors of the City and Castle of Kilkenny, of the other party. March 27th, 1650.

1. That the respective Governors of the city and castle of Kilkenny shall deliver to his Excellency the Lord Cromwell, the Lord Lieutenant General of Ireland, for the use of the state of England, the said city and castle, with all arms, ammunition, and provisions of public stores therein, without embezzlement, except what is hereafter excepted, at or before nine of the clock tomorrow morning.

2. That all the inhabitants of the said city of Kilkenny and all others therein shall be defended in their persons, goods and estates, from the violence of the soldiery, and that such as shall desire to remove thence elsewhere, none excepted, shall have liberty so to do, with their goods, within three months after the date of these articles.

3. That the said Governors, with all the officers and soldiers under their respective commands in the said city and castle, and all others who shall be so pleased, shall march away at or before nine of the clock tomorrow morning, with their bag and baggage; the officers with their attendants, their arms, and with their horses not exceeding the number of one hundred and fifty horses; and their foot soldiers to march out of the town, two miles distant, with their arms, and with drums beating, colours flying, matches lighted, and ball in bouche; and then and there to deliver up the said arms to such as shall be appointed for receiving

them, excepting one hundred muskets and a hundred pikes allowed them for their defence against the Tories.

4. That the said officers and soldiers shall have from his Excellency a safe-conduct six miles from the city of Kilkenny; and from thenceforward a pass for their security out of his Excellency's quarters; the said pass to be in force for six days from the date of these presents, they marching at least ten miles each day, and doing no prejudice to quarters.

5. That the city of Kilkenny shall pay £2,000 as a gratuity to his Excellency's army; whereof £1,000 to be paid on the 30th of this month, and the other on the first day of May next following, to such as shall be by his Excellency thereunto appointed.

6. That Major John Comerford and Mr. Edward Rothe shall remain hostages under the power of his Excellency, for the performance of the said Articles, on the part of said city and garrison of Kilkenny.

7. Lastly, for the performance of all and singular the premises, the parties have hereunto interchangeably put their hands, the day and year first above written.

James Cowley
John Comerford
O. Cromwell
Edward Rothe
David Turnball.[77]

When we examine, the articles of capitulation at Kilkenny, again, we find further evidence, that Cromwell's campaign in Ireland, did not, match the myths that had grown around it.

---

[77] Gilbert, op.cit., Vol. II, p. 382.

To further, counter the popular belief that Cromwell's campaign in Ireland, was fought on the basis of English Protestant, against Irish Catholic, it must be noted that whilst negotiations were taking place at Kilkenny, Cromwell writes:

> a Lieutenant-Colonel, three majors, eight Captains, being English, Welsh and Scotch with others possessed of Cantwell Castle – very strong castle situated in a bog, - were ordered by Sir Walter Butler to come and strengthen the Garrison of Kilkenny, they sent two officers to me, to offer me the place [castle] and their service – that they might have passes to go beyond the sea to serve foreign states, with some money to bear their changes: the last whereof 'likewise' I consented to; they promising to do nothing to prejudices the Parliament of England.

O. Cromwell[78]

It must be noted, that after the articles of capitulation, had been signed, Butler, and his men, were allowed to march out of Kilkenny with arms, ammunition, with drums beating and colours flying. Furthermore, the civilian population; was protected from plunder, as Cromwell had promised.[79] On this final stage of his campaign, Cromwell, marched south to Clonmel, which was to be, his last major battle Ireland.[80]

There is further evidence, which demonstrates, that Cromwell's military campaign in Ireland, was not fought, on the basis of English Protestant, against Irish Catholic. It must be remembered; following their success in 1652, the English Parliament, introduced legislation in order to implement its plans for colonisation. In order to do this, they introduced the 'Act for the Settling of Ireland.'[81] This

---

[78] Carlyle, *op.cit.*, p. 351, Letter CXVII.
[79] *Ibid.*
[80] Gardiner, *op.cit.*, Vol., I, pp. 155-57.
[81] C.H. Firth and R.S. Rait, (eds.), *Acts and Ordinances of the Interregnum*, 3.Vols., London, (1911), Vol. II, pp. 598-603.

legislation together with the 'Adventures Act of 1642,' set out the penalties, for those involved in the rebellion, and, created the legal base for land confiscation, and settlement. Kevin McKenny, has emphasised, this legislation:

> categorized the people of Ireland, both *Protestant* and *Catholic* according to their involvement in the rebellion and, perhaps more importantly, according to their loyalty to the king, or disloyalty to the Parliament (a 'crime' which most of the British – especially Scottish – settlers of West Ulster were charged with).[82]

Samuel Rawson Gardiner stressed of course, 'as far as introducing the Act of Settlement of 1652, is concerned, there is no evidence whatever, to connect it with Cromwell.'[83] More recently Kevin McKenny, has published, the results of his computerised based research, into changing land ownership in Ireland, as a result of the so called; Cromwellian land settlements. His detailed work on West Ulster, reveals that dispossession, and survival, was not as previously believed, solely determined by ethnicity, and religion, but was also affected by 'the survival strategies and complex politicking', by individual landowners in Dublin and London.[84]

In conclusion, the popular belief that Cromwell's military campaign in Ireland, was fought, on the basis of English Protestant, against Irish Catholic, was critically examined in this Chapter.

---

[82] Kevin McKenny, 'A seventeenth-century land settlement in Ireland: towards a statistical interpretation,' in Jane H. Ohlmeyer, (ed), *Ireland from Independence to Occupation 1641-1660*, Cambridge, (1995), p. 193.; For further details also see Kevin McKenny, 'A seventeenth-century 'real estate company' The 1649 Officers and the restoration land settlement, 1641-1681' (unpublished MA thesis, NUI, Maynooth, 1989); McKenny, 'Charles II's Irish Cavaliers: The 1649 Officers and the restoration land settlement,' *Irish Historical Studies*, 28, (1993), pp. 409-25.

[83] Samuel Rawson Gardiner, 'The transplantation to Connaught,' *English Historical Review*,' Vol. 14, (1899), p. 707.

[84] Mc Kenny, *op.cit.*, p. 200.

Evidence was presented, to *show that this belief* is not supported and is therefore a myth.

In examining the popular belief, that Cromwell, was responsible for ordering wholesale and indiscriminate massacre, of ordinary unarmed Catholic civilians in the towns that he besieged, it was also shown that this belief is not supported by the evidence and is also a myth. It is clear, that in all cases Cromwell's enemies were given the opportunity to surrender, in order to save bloodshed, on both sides. In marked contrast to this myth, the articles of capitulation at the various towns, which included New Ross, Fethard, Cashel, Cahir, Gowran and Kilkenny, display Cromwell's humanity. Surrendering garrisons, were given generous terms and treated with mercy and even with honour.[85]

---

[85] Barnard, *op.cit.*, p. 183; Robert Kee, *Ireland: a History*, Boston, (1980), p. 46.

CHAPTER SIX

Myths and Cromwell's Storm of Clonmel

The Storm of Clonmel, added to the myths that emerged regarding Cromwell's actions in Ireland. Allegedly, Cromwell conspired with a Major Fennell, to betray the garrison for the sum of 500 pounds.[1] It will be argued, that this myth cannot be supported, by evidence as interpreted by later historians.

Clonmel, was another fortressed town in the province of Munster, and situated on the bank of the River Suir. In February 1650, Ormond, had placed Clonmel under the command of Hugh O'Neill, Owen O'Neill's nephew, who, like his uncle, had served in the Spanish army; and was well trained in the art of siege warfare. Reports show, that initially O'Neill's forces, consisted of only fifty-two horse, and 1,200 Ulster foot.[2] However, by April, the strength of the garrison had increased to over 2,000 men.[3] Although, Ormond had dispatched Lord Castle Connell with another 400 men to reinforce the garrison, these troops, failed to arrive before Cromwell.[4]

To place the event in historical context, after granting generous

---

[1] W.C. Abbott, *The Writing and Speeches of Oliver Cromwell*, Vol II., Cambridge, Mass., (1934-47), pp. 245-6; Denis Murphy, S.J. *Cromwell-in-Ireland*, Dublin, (1883), pp. 330-1.; James Scott Wheeler, *Cromwell-in-Ireland*, Dublin, (1999), p. 152.

[2] Samuel Rawson Gardiner, *History of the Commonwealth and Protectorate 1649-1656*, Vol. 1, London, (1903), p. 155.

[3] Ian Gentles, *The New Model Army, in England Ireland and Scotland, 1645-1653*, Oxford, (1992), p. 373.

[4] Gardiner, *op.cit.*, Vol. I, p. 156.

terms to the garrison at Kilkenny, Cromwell was delayed incorporating English troops from Lord Inchiquin's army, who had defected to the New Model Army. After completing the task he was ready to besiege Clonmel. On 27th April 1650, Cromwell appeared before Clonmel with his army.[5] He was accompanied by '8,000 infantry, 600 horse, and twelve field guns.'[6] Reports, indicate that Cromwell encamped outside the town, for a fortnight, whilst waiting for his heavy guns, and reinforcements to arrive. Finally, he opened fire on the town wall, and opened a large breach. At 8.oclock on the morning of 9th May, Cromwell ordered his men to storm.[7]

The siege at Clonmel, clearly demonstrates that Cromwell's victories at Drogheda, and Wexford, did not break Irish morale. In fact, the generous terms Cromwell had granted to other surrendering garrisons, helped to stiffen resistance.[8] Whilst, Cromwell had been encamped outside the town, the defenders were preparing for a storm. According to the contemporary accounts:

> After this Hugh Duff did set all men and maids to work, townsmen and soldiers, only those on duty attending the breach and the wall – to draw dunghills, mortar, stones, and timber, and made a long lane a man's height, and about eighty yards length on both sides up from the breach, with a foot bank at the back of it; and caused [to be] place[d] engines on both sides of the same, and two guns at the end of its invisible opposite to the breach, and so ordered all things against a storm.

---

[5] *Ibid.*, p. 155.

[6] James Burke, 'The New Model Army and problems with siege warfare 1648-51,' *Irish Historical Studies*, Vol. XXVll, No. 105, May, (1990), p. 16.

[7] Gentles, *op.cit.*, p. 374. Carlyle, *op.cit.*, p. 355.

[8] Toby Barnard, 'Irish images of Cromwell,' in R.C. Richardson (ed.), *Images of Oliver Cromwell: Essays for and by Roger Howell, Jnr.*, Manchester, (1993), p. 182.

The account continues:

> Which [storm] was about eight o'clock in the morning
> in the month of [May] and [the English] entered
> without any opposition; and but few [were] to be seen
> in the town till they so entered, that the lane was arm'd
> full with horsemen, armed with helmets, back breast
> swords, musquetoons and pistols. On which those in
> the front seeing themselves in a pound, and could not
> make their way further, cryed out, Halt! Halt! On
> which those entering behind at the breach thought by
> those words, that all those of the garrison were running
> away, and cryed out, 'Advance!' 'Advance,' as fast
> as those before cryed, 'Halt!' 'Halt!' and so advanced
> till they thrust forwards those before them, till that
> pound or lane was full, and could hold no more. Then
> suddenly rushes a resolute party of pikes and
> musqetteers to the breach, and scoured off and
> knocked back those entering. At which instance Hugh
> Duff's men within fell on those in the pound with
> shotts, pikes, scythes, stones, and casting of great long
> pieces of timber with the engines amongst them; and
> then two guns firing at them from the end of the pound,
> slaughtering them by the middle or knees with chained
> bulletts, that in less than an hour's time about a
> thousand men were killed in that pound, being a top
> one another.[9]

However, I agree with Reilly that the above 'commentary of the
unnamed officer in the regiment of Sir John Clotsworthy, must be
cautiously treated, even though it is particularly compelling. The
narrative, was written thirty-five years after the actual events, its
author being converted to the Royalist cause by this time.'[10]

---

[9] E.D. Hogan, (ed.), *The History of the War in Ireland 1641-1653 by a British
Officer in the Regiment of Sir John Clotsworthy*, Dublin, (1873), p. 108.
[10] Reilly, *op.cit.*, p. 243.

There is no doubt that at Clonmel, Cromwell, experienced the biggest defeat of his military career, 'for, four hours, he, poured men through the deadly breach, but they were continually mowed down,'[11] 'leaving wave after wave of parliamentary dead.'[12] 'Estimates of the Parliamentary dead, vary from 1,000 to 2,500.'[13] The figure of 1000, appears to be an underestimate, because the Royalist agent, Sir Lewis Dyve, wrote in his official report, 'Cromwell lost 2,500 men.'[14] Another Royalist account, conservatively estimates at least 1,500 dead.[15] On the other hand, Gardiner insists, 'not less than 2,500 dead.'[16] Most recently, Wheeler, has estimated that up to '2,000 New Model soldiers were killed or wounded.'[17]

During the night, Hugh O'Neill, and his men, crept out of Clonmel, retreating towards Waterford, after running out of ammunition and supplies, which, had prevented him holding out any longer. On the other hand, Cromwell did not have these problems, as by this time reinforcements, siege-guns, uniforms, ammunition, and provisions, were all at his disposal. It was later, revealed that O'Neill had forced the Mayor, to make terms with Cromwell, in order to aid his escape. Subsequently Cromwell agreed to terms, willingly agreeing, in return for the surrender of the town, and garrison, to grant the lives, and estates, of the inhabitants[18] as follows:

Articles between the Lord Lieutenant and the inhabitants of Clonmel touching the rendition thereof, May the 18th, 1650.

---

[11] Gentles, *op.cit.*, p. 374.

[12] Peter Gaunt, *Oliver Cromwell*, Oxford, (1996), p. 120.

[13] Ronald Hutton and Wylie Reeves, 'Sieges and fortifications,' in John Kenyon and Jane Ohlmeyer (eds.), *The Civil Wars, A Military History of England, Scotland and Ireland 1638-1660*, Oxford, (1998), p. 221.

[14] Burke, *op.cit.*, p. 19.

[15] Gentles, *op.cit.*, p. 374.

[16] Gardiner, *op.cit.*, Vol. I, p. 156.

[17] Wheeler, *op.cit.*, p. 156.

[18] Gardiner, *op.cit.*, Vol. I, pp. 156-7.

It is granted and agreed by and betwixt the Lord Lieutenant-General Cromwell on the one part, and Mr.Michael White and Mr. Nicholas Betts, commissioneries, intrusted in the behalf of the town and the garrison of Clonmel on the other part, as follows:

1st: That the said town and garrison of Clonmel, with the arms, ammunition and other furniture of war that are now therein shall be surrendered and delivered up into the hands of his Excellency the Lord-Lieutenant by eight of the clock this morning.

2nd: That in consideration thereof the inhabitants of the said town shall be protected as to their lives and estates, from all plunder and violence of the soldiery, and shall have the same right, liberty and protection as other subjects under the authority of the Parliament of England have, or ought to have and enjoy within the dominion of Ireland.

O. Cromwell.[19]

Although, the deceit, was discovered after the articles had been accepted by both sides, Cromwell kept his word and his troops entered Clonmel peaceably.[20]

An account of the storm of Clonmel, appears in *Severall Proceedings in Parliament*, dated 23 May to 6 June, which has been reprinted in Carlyle as presented below. It has been argued by some historians, that it was written by Cromwell but this remains questionable.[21]

---

[19] J.T. Gilbert, (ed.), *Contemporary History of Affairs in Ireland from AD 1641 to 1652, Containing the ...narrative an 'Amphorismal Discovery of Treasonable Faction,'* 3 Vols., Dublin, (1879-80), Vol. II, pp. 411-12.
[20] Gardiner, *op.cit.*, Vol., I, p. 157.
[21] Reilly, *op.cit.*, p. 245.

A Letter from Clonmel in Ireland

10th May 1650

Worthy Sir,

Yesterday, Thursday 9th May, we stormed Clonmel; in which work both officers and soldiers did as much and more than could be expected. We had, with our guns, made a breach in their works; - where, after an hot fight we gave back a while; but presently charged up to the same ground again. But the Enemy had made themselves exceeding strong, by double-works and traverse, which were worse to enter than the breach; and many on both sides were slain. The fierce death-wrestle, in the breaches here, lasted four hours; so many hours of hot storm and continuous tug of war, and many men were slain. At night the Enemy drew out, on the other side and marched away undiscovered to us; and the Inhabitants of Clonmel sent out for a Parley. Upon which, Articles were agreed on, before we knew the Enemy was gone. After signing of the Conditions, we discovered the Enemy to be gone; and very early this morning, pursued them; and fell upon their rear of stragglers, and killed above 200 – besides those we slew in the storm. We entered Clonmel this morning, and have kept our Conditions with them. The place is considerable and very advantageous to the reducing of these parts wholly to the Parliament of England.

(Unsigned).[22]

---

[22] Thomas Carlyle, *Oliver Cromwell's Letters and Speeches: With Elucidations*, second revised edition, (3 Vols in One), London, (1846), pp. 355-6.

Surprisingly, although Cromwell always wrote detailed reports, of all his military activity in Ireland, no report remains of the major engagement at Clonmel. It is very unlikely that Cromwell, omitted to make a detailed report of this battle. It is possible, of course, that 'a report was submitted by Cromwell only to be suppressed subsequently by Parliament, in the interests of maintaining public morale.'[23]

Recently, one of the major myths surrounding the Storm of Clonmel, can be identified in James Scott Wheeler's, *Cromwell-In-Ireland*, (1999). According to Wheeler:

> Treachery was another ploy, which Cromwell reportedly tried to use to take Clonmel. It seems that a Major Fennell, the commander of the two troops of Royalist cavalry in Clonmel, offered to open one of the gates at midnight to admit 500 English soldiers, in exchange for 500 pounds. O'Neill, who inspected his guards several times a day, suspected treachery when he noticed that Fennell's cavalry-men were posted alone at the North Gate, a post normally defended by a mixed force of Irish foot and Fennell's troopers. O'Neill took immediate action, replacing the guard with Ulster infantry. He then allowed the English to enter the gate into an ambush. A short fight ensued as the Irish surprised the attackers. The English hastily retreated, and the defenders claimed to have killed 500 Englishmen.[24]

Wheeler, cites Murphy, who relies on the anonymous author of *Aphorismical Discovery*, to support his allegations. However, it must be noted, that Wheeler in the introduction of his book, warns his readers that, 'Murphy's book is marred by his heavy reliance

---

[23] Burke, *op.cit.*, p. 17.
[24] Wheeler, *op.cit.*, p. 152.

on the highly biased source known as the *Aphorismical Discovery*, a contemporary Gaelic Irish source, that avoided no opportunity, to denigrate anyone, in Ireland, who did not adhere to, the position of, the papal Nuncio Rinuccini.'[25] In marked contrast, to this myth, Gardiner pointed out, 'I am doubtful about the story of Fennell's treachery. The alleged, attempt to storm the gate, is only mentioned by this last authority (*Aphorismical Discovery*) and seems to be, a misplaced account of what really happened in the final storm.'[26] On the other hand Burke believes, 'this seems to be a distorted account of the first assault on the town, in which Cromwell; also suffered severe losses because; of a trap set by O'Neill.'[27]

In reality, the death of 2,500 of Cromwell's soldiers, at Clonmel, was in circumstances no less severe, than the alleged massacre of enemies at Drogheda and Wexford. In marked contrast, however, while the 'events at Drogheda and Wexford, have been magnified and well publicised, the Storm of Clonmel, has been quietly passed over by Cromwell's enemies.'[28] Many histories, devote less than a sentence, to Cromwell's storm at Clonmel. This now common tendency, is most recently identified in Martyn Bennett's, *The Civil Wars in Britain and Ireland 1638-1651*, (1997), and in Tristram Hunt's, *The English Civil War At First Hand*, (2003), but there are many other examples.[29] 'Some accounts claim that two Dominican priests, and, 'not a few women' were put to the sword, but, these owe more to later myth making, than to contemporary reality.'[30]

Cromwell's storm of Clonmel, was to be his last military engagement in Ireland. The urgent need, to prepare, to meet the growing threat; from Scotland, forced the English Parliament, to

---

[25] *Ibid.*, p. 1.
[26] Gardiner, *op.cit.*, Vol, p. 157.
[27] Burke, *op.cit.*, p. 17.
[28] Barnard, *op.cit.* p. 182.
[29] Martyn Bennett, *The Civil Wars in Britain and Ireland 1638-1651*, (1997), p. 332.; Tristram Hunt, *The English Civil War-At First Hand*, London, (2002), Paperback edition, (2003), p. 258.
[30] Trevor Royal, *Civil War-The Wars of the Three Kingdoms 1638-1660*, London, (2005), p. 548.

issue orders for his recall. This, forced him to abandon all plans, of leading the Irish campaign himself, and he appointed Henry Ireton, as Lord Deputy of Ireland.[31] On 26th May 1650, Cromwell, sailed from Youghal, to Bristol.[32] His Irish campaign, which had only lasted nine months, had come to an end.[33] 'Cromwell, always prepared; to accept the teaching of events, had discovered that the way of clemency, was the shortest road to conquest.'[34] Furthermore, 'Until his death, on 3rd September 1658, Cromwell never returned to Ireland again.'[35]

In dismissing the myth, related to Cromwell at Clonmel, that he conspired with Major Fennell, to admit New Model soldiers into the garrison for five hundred pounds, it was found, that it was not supported by eye-witness accounts. It was also; demonstrated in this Chapter, that there are more, believable explanations, and assessments, than those manifest in the myth.

---

[31] Gardiner, *op.cit.*, Vol., I, p. 157.

[32] Barnard, *op.cit.,* p. 182.

[33] Antonia Fraser, *Cromwell, Our Chief of Men*, London, (1973), Paperback edition, (2004), p. 444.

[34] Gardiner, *op.cit.*, Vol., I, p. 157.

[35] Fraser, *op.cit.*, p. 355.

Henry Ireton, Cromwell's son-in-law, died of plague at
Limerick, 1651, and was buried at Westminster Abbey.
(National Portrait Gallery)

CHAPTER SEVEN

Myths Associated with Cromwell
and the Final Re-conquest of Ireland

Cromwell did not conquer the Irish and he never met any of their armies in the field [Wilbur Cortez Abbott].[1]

A major, popular historical belief, concerning Cromwell and Ireland, is that, Cromwell during his Irish campaign, accomplished the final re-conquest of the country. This belief has been highlighted, by the late Roger Howell who argued that:

> Though Cromwell had left before the conquest was completed and though subsequent settlement had been dictated in many of its outlines before he came to power, both conquest and settlement have inevitably been identified in the Irish mind with Cromwell.[2]

In this Chapter it will be argued, that 'far too much of the re-conquest of Ireland, has been attributed to Cromwell, and this, was actually accomplished, by other parliamentary commanders, including; Henry Ireton, Edmund Ludlow, Lord Broghill, Sir Charles Coote and Charles Fleetwood.'[3]

---

[1] W.C. Abbott, *The Writings and Speeches of Oliver Cromwell*, Vol II, Mass. (1937-47), p. 257.

[2] Roger Howell, Jnr., *Cromwell*, Boston, (1977), p. 146.

[3] Toby Barnard, 'Irish images of Cromwell,' in R.C. Richardson, (ed.), *Images of Cromwell: Essays for and by Roger Howell, Jnr.*, Manchester, (1993), p. 181.

Following Cromwell's departure, Henry Ireton, was appointed Lord Deputy. Although, other senior officers, in the New Model Army, such as Sir Charles Coote, Lord Broghill, General Reynolds, and even John Hewson, had shown superior military ability; but only, Cromwell's son-in law Henry, shared his religious, and political views completely.[4] The first three months, of Ireton's tour in Ireland, as Lord Deputy, were fully occupied in, the organising of five major sieges; all of which were successful. On 25th June, Tecroghan, surrendered to Reynolds; on 25th July, Carlow, surrendered to Sir Hardress Waller; on 6th August, Waterford, to Ireton himself; on 14th August, Charlemont, to Coote; and finally on 17th August, Duncannon Fort, surrendered to Cooke. Moreover, there were no, penalties imposed, or any ill treatment, upon these surrendering garrisons or their inhabitants.[5]

By the time Cromwell, left Ireland, Ormond's authority, as Lord Lieutenant had been strained under the growing wariness of Irish Catholics, towards their allies, who were, either Protestant, or not Irish. Following the death, of Owen Roe O'Neill, the assembly of Ulster, placed the 'politically astute,' though, 'militarily inexperienced' Heber McMahon, Bishop of Clogher, in command of their army. Because they believed, that he could bring together the various factions within the province.[6]

In fact, the largest battle in Ireland, took place a month, after Cromwell, had returned to England. In June 1650, McMahon marched an army of 6000 men, out of Londonderry, hoping, to destroy the Parliamentary armies led by Sir Charles Coote, and Colonel Venables, who were at some distance from one another at this stage. McMahon stormed Dungevin Fort, and even seized Ballycastle in Antrim. However, although Sir Charles Coote, commanded an army of half McMahon's numbers, he took the

---

[4] Ian Gentles, *The New Model Army,in England, Ireland and Scotland, 1645-1653*, Oxford, (1992), p. 377.

[5] Samuel Rawson Gardiner, *History of the Commonwealth and Protectorate 1649-1656,* London, (1903), Vol., II, pp. 107-108.

[6] Gentles, *op.cit.*, p. 375. Keith Roberts, *Cromwell's War Machine, The New Model Army 1645-1660*, Barnsley, (2005), p. 252.

offensive. Against, the advice of Henry O'Neill, McMahon, decided to make a stand at Scarriffhollis, on 25th June 1650. Reports indicate that 2,000, of the 6,000, Confederate soldiers, were killed on the battlefield, and afterwards, all the trained officers were executed,[7] along with, Owen Roe's son Henry.[8] McMahon, initially escaped, but was captured shortly afterwards, and taken to Enniskillen, where on Coote's orders, 'he was hanged, quartered, and his head, placed on the gates at Londonderry.'[9]

John O'Beirne, Ranelagh in *A Short History of Ireland,* has asserted that, 'by July 1650, Commonwealth armies were in command of, 'all of Ireland,' except, Connaught.'[10] This assertion, is contradicted by the evidence. In fact, two and a half years after, Cromwell had left Ireland, the New Model Army, was still engaged, in an unrelenting war, against the enemy in all provinces. 'By August 1650, two thousand four hundred Irish soldiers, were reported to be, within six miles of Dublin itself.' At the same time in Ulster, and Connaught, at least five thousand Irish troops, were fighting against Coote and Venables. Similar numbers in Munster, commanded by Lord Muskerry, fought against Ludlow's forces. In Leinster, Colonel Grace, led three thousand Parliamentary troops, against Irish forces, commanded, by Colonels Ingoldsworthy, and Abbott. Parliamentary reports, show that at all times, there were numerous minor military encounters. Even after an almost continuous run of parliamentary victories, the Irish refused to capitulate and for every detachment defeated, another sprang up in its place. Although by now bubonic plague was raging throughout Ireland and 'neither side was spared its devastation'.[11]

The three major fortressed towns, Limerick, Galway, and Athlone, were still holding out against the Parliamentary forces. Moreover, the division between Ormond and the Irish Catholics,

---

[7] Gardiner, *op.cit.*, Vol., II, pp. 106-107.
[8] Martyn Bennett, *The Civil Wars in Britain and Ireland 1638-1651*, Oxford, (1997), p. 352.
[9] Gentles, *op.cit.*, p. 376.
[10] John O'Beirne Ranelagh, *A Short History of Ireland,* Cambridge, (1983), p. 64.
[11] Gentles, *op.cit.*, pp. 379-81.

had also finally come to a head. In June, Limerick had refused admission to a garrison selected for its defence by Ormond; and it was not until 15th July that he agreed to appoint Hugh O'Neill, (the Irish Commander at Clonmel), as the Governor of the City, at the same time permitting him to deploy the regiments of his own choice. However, the majority of the Roman Catholic prelates, like the Limerick inhabitants, suspected Ormond, the Protestant Lord-Lieutenant, of complicity with the enemy, and on 12th August they met at Jamestown to discuss the matter. Meanwhile of course, Charles II had made an agreement with the Presbyterian Scots. Consequently, the Roman Catholic prelates all agreed, it was time for Ormond to return to England, and instructed Catholics, not to obey his orders, revoking the authority he had received from Charles II.[12]

The defeat of the Army of Ulster, and the subsequent collapse of Royalist garrisons in Leinster and Munster, destroyed Ormond's credibility. In addition, his own troops, had become mutinous, and were stricken with plague.[13] On 31st August Ormond announced that he would not stand in the way of the Confederate war effort and asked Charles II for his permission to leave Ireland.[14] Having appointed Clanricarde, as Lord Deputy in Ireland, Ormond, then sailed to France, accompanied by Lord Inchiquin, and other Royalist notables.[15] I agree with Ian Gentles, who believes that; 'Apart from his mediocrity as a military leader, most of Ormond's problems, stemmed from the fact, that he, was trying to hold together, an uneasy coalition, of Protestant Royalists, Old English Catholics, and Gaelic Irish, who fundamentally, distrusted one another.'[16] After Ormond's departure the Irish clergy, and Clanricarde, now Lord Deputy, who was also a Catholic, took control of the defence of Ireland, against the English Parliament.[17]

---

[12] Gardiner, *op.cit*. Vol., II, pp. 99-110.
[13] John Kenyon and Jane H Ohlmeyer, (eds.), *The Civil Wars-A Military History of England, Scotland and Ireland 1638-1660*, Oxford, (1998), p. 160.
[14] Gardiner, *op.cit*., Vol., II, p. 112.
[15] Kenyon, *op.cit*., p. 220.
[16] Gentles, *op.cit.,* p. 362.
[17] Maurice Ashley, *The Greatness of Oliver Cromwell*, London, (1957), p. 238.

Athlone, was under the command, of Sir James Dillon. Ireton, at this stage felt confident enough to divide his army. He sent, Sir Hardress Waller, to continue the siege of Limerick, before making his way to Athlone to join Sir Charles Coote.[18] On reaching Athlone, Ireton instructed Coote to blockade the town, then led his forces through Kings County and Tipperary, capturing several fortified towns.[19]

After scattering Clanricarde's forces, in County Clare, Ireton, turned his attention back to Limerick. He was aware, of divisions within the city, which he hoped to use to his advantage.[20] On 14th June Ireton attempted to take Limerick by storm but was driven back by the inhabitants, who also rejected his proposals for them to surrender.[21] Therefore, Limerick; proved to be Ireton's greatest challenge. Largely due, to the 'modern fortifications, built from the 1590s to the 1640s, which made the town almost impregnable, being surrounded with a triple wall and three walls in turn being protected by water.'[22] Because Limerick, was impossible to take by storm, Ireton, built an extensive 'circumvallation,' including two forts; (Cromwell, and Ireton), then surrounded the town with artillery, which included, mortars, and two demi-cannon.[23] Between the spring, and summer, of 1651, the English Parliament, sent, over 9,000, soldiers, to reinforce their armies, in Ireland. However, over 2,000 of, these new recruits, were killed at Limerick.[24]

Meanwhile, on 18th June 1651, the Catholic commander, Sir James Dillon, surrendered Athlone, to Coote. Throughout the siege of Limerick, Ireton, was forced, to contend, with sustained attacks,

---

[18] Gardiner, *op.cit.*, Vol., II, p. 110.
[19] *Ibid*, p. 111.
[20] Gentles, *op.cit*. p. 378.
[21] Gardiner. *op.cit.*, Vol., II, p. 120.
[22] Ronald Hutton and Wylie Reeves, *Sieges and Fortifications* in Kenyon and Ohlmeyer *(eds), op.cit.*, p. 221.
[23] Rolf Loeber and Geoffrey Parker, 'The Military Revolution in Seventeenth-Century Ireland,' in Jane H. Ohlmeyer, (ed), *Ireland from Independence to Occupation 1641-1660*, Cambridge, (1995), p. 81.
[24] Gentles, *op.cit*, p. 379.

to relieve the town, by enemy forces, under the command of Lord Muskerry, and Colonel David Roche.[25] For example in July, Muskerry, attempted to relieve Limerick with an army of 3,000 men. However he was cut off by Lord Broghill's forces, which resulted in a pitched battle. Broghill reported in a letter from Ireland:

> We fired into each others faces and mingled. I had the happiness to kill the officer which led the division I charged, and after round dispute, though we were much outnumbered and winged, that they charged us in flank and rear, and their pikes too galled us exceedingly, yet after a second charge on one of their rallying divisions, we gave them total rout, and carried all that wing of horse and foot before us.[26]

Ireton's, siege of Limerick, dragged on miserably; until October 1651.[27] However, a defector betrayed the garrison, and informed Ireton, about a vulnerable section of wall. Almost at once, Ireton blasted a hole in this wall with his cannon, forcing the garrison to capitulate soon afterwards.[28] On 27th October, when the garrison marched out, 'two of its soldiers dropped dead from plague.'[29] There seems little doubt, that if Cromwell had been in command of the siege, it may have concluded sooner. Cromwell, would have, tried to exploit the desire, of two thirds of the town, to negotiate terms, considering the plague raging within its wall. Ireton however, lacked Cromwell's political acumen.[30] Ireton, of course, did not live to see the conquest completed. He died of plague, in November 1651, leaving his successors, Ludlow, Fleetwood, Coote, and Broghill, to bring, conquest to a close.[31]

---

[25] *Ibid.*

[26] James Scott Wheeler, *Cromwell in Ireland,* Dublin, (1999), p. 217.

[27] John Buchan, *Oliver Cromwell*, London, (1934), p. 297.

[28] Hutton and Reeves, *op.cit.*, p. 221. *The Civil Wars.*

[29] Buchan, *op.cit.*, p. 297. ; Gardiner, *op.cit.*, Vol., II, p. 120.

[30] Gentles, *op.cit.*, p. 379.

[31] Howell, *op.cit.*, pp. 145-6.

Following Ireton's death, Edmund Ludlow, was appointed Commander-in-Chief, of parliamentary forces, in Ireland.[32] Prior to this, on 5th November, Ludlow, had captured Clare Castle. After the fall of Limerick, the parliamentary forces, marched to Galway.[33] However, they were unable to storm; the 'extensive modern stone-faced walls', which, the inhabitants had constructed, during the 1640s. Instead, they blockaded the town, over a period of nine months.[34] In the mean time on 7th April 1652, Colonel John Kelly, surrendered, Jamestown, to Commissary General Reynolds.[35] Finally; on 12th May 1652, Major-General Preston, surrendered the garrison at Galway, to Sir Charles Coote.[36]

After the signing of the Kilkenny articles, on the 12th May 1652, Parliament, offered generous terms, to surrendering garrisons.[37] Ludlow, was reported to be receiving, weekly surrenders, of Irish Commanders, that were, for the most part allowed, to travel to foreign states, along with their men, who were not at war, with the Parliament of England.[38] On 26th May 1652, Major Bryn O'Rouke surrendered the Ballyshannon garrison, in County Donegal.[39] Lord Muskerry, Commander-in-Chief of His Majesty's Forces, in the province of Munster, signed articles agreeing to surrender 22nd June 1652, with Parliamentary Commander, Major General Sir Hardress Waller.[40] On 28th June 1652, Major General Lucas Taaff, and Sir Ullicke Burke, Lord of Clanricarde, the Kings Lord Deputy of Ireland surrendered to Commissary-General John Reynolds.[41] The Lord of Slane, surrendered to Colonel John Fowke, on behalf, of the soldiers of the garrison of Mullagh.[42]

---

[32] Buchan, *op.cit.*, p. 297.
[33] Gentles, *op.cit.*, p. 380.
[34] Hutton and Reeves, *op.cit.*, p. 221. *The Civil Wars.*
[35] John T. Gilbert, (eds), *A Contemporary History of Affairs in Ireland from 1641-1652*, Vol. III, Part II, pp. 320-321.
[36] Barnard, *op.cit.*, p. 182.
[37] Gilbert, *op.cit.*, Vol. III, Part II, pp. 315-316.
[38] Buchan, *op.cit.*, p. 297.
[39] Gilbert, *op.cit.*, Vol. III, Part II, pp. 320-321.
[40] *Ibid*, pp. 324-327.
[41] *Ibid,* pp. 331-333.
[42] *Ibid*, pp. 333-334.

Nevertheless, even by the end of December 1652, a joint report, from *The Commissioners, and Officers of the Army, to the Council of State,* read as follows:

> Since the death of the Lord Deputy we have made a more particular inquiry into the condition of the enemy, whose numbers now in arms within the several parts of this dominion, according to our best information, we do not judge to be less than 30,000, besides the people generally ready to join with them upon any occasion, yet many of them incline to come in and accept conditions, to which purposes several of their considerable officers have made overtures unto yours, for the most part insisting upon licence to go beyond sea.[43]

The Commissioners, also reported, that many of the Irish commanders, could see the futility of their position, and were prepared to withdraw from Ireland, if they were granted, permission to enlist in service of the King of Spain. As many as 30,000 Irish soldiers left Ireland, to serve in continental armies by the end of the year.[44]

To counter the popular belief, that Cromwell, accomplished the final re-conquest of Ireland, during his military campaign, it must be noted, by the end of August 1652, in a fuller joint report, from *The Commissioners and Officers of the Army to the Council of* State, estimated:

> The total number of the forces within the dominion of Ireland, according to the musters taken in June and July 1652, are as followeth: Ninety-nine troops, consisting of 6742 private soldiers and 623 non-

---

[43] Robert Dunlop, (ed.), *Ireland Under the Commonwealth: Being a Selection of Documents Relating to the Government of Ireland, 1651-1659*, 2 Vols., Manchester, (1913), Vol. 1, p. 113.

[44] Gardiner, *op.cit.*, Vol., II, p. 126.

commission officers, amounts to 7365 men. Twenty-
two troops of dragoons, consisting of 1293 private
soldiers and 154 non-commission officers amounts to
1447 men. Two hundred and seventy-four companies
of foot consisting of 22,850 private soldiers and 2466
non-commission officers amounts to 25,316 men. Total
34,128.[45]

This was almost three times the number, which Cromwell, had
landed with in 1649.[46] In September 1652, Fleetwood, who had
recently married Ireton's widow, Cromwell's Daughter, and
succeeded Ludlow, as Commander-in-chief in Ireland.[47]

Although the majority of the three, to four hundred fortressed
towns, and castles, were held by Parliamentary forces, armed
bands, known as; Tories continually attacked their garrisons and
patrols throughout Ireland. They then disappeared into the
mountains, bogs, or forest, making it impossible, for cavalry to follow
them, adopting, guerrilla tactics, suited to themselves, and, their
environment. In the final, stage of the war, some, parliamentary
officers, copied the tactics of the enemies. For example; in, County
Wicklow, Colonel Hewson, in an attempt, to prevent local Tories,
from surviving the winter, destroyed cattle, and burned crops. At
the same time, 'Sir Hardress Waller, wasted the whole barony of
Burren.'[48]

To counter, the popular belief, that Cromwell accomplished, the
final re-conquest of Ireland, during his military campaign, it should
be highlighted, that he, had served in Ireland, for only nine months
and fourteen days.[49] At the time of his departure, most of Ireland,
was still unsubdued.[50] The final, formal surrender of Irish forces,

---

[45] Dunlop, *op.cit.*, Vol. 1, pp. 248-9.
[46] Gentles, *op.cit.*, p. 381.
[47] Buchan, *op.cit.*, p. 297.
[48] Gentles, *op.cit.*, p. 381.
[49] Antonia Fraser, *Cromwell Our Chief of Men*, London, (1973), Paperback
edition, (2004), p. 444.
[50] Barnard, *op.cit.*, p. 181.

did not occur, until 27th April 1653 almost two and a half years later.[51]

Throughout his military campaign in Ireland, Cromwell's engagement with enemies had been dominated by a series of protracted sieges and storms on fortressed towns and castles.[52] He had 'restricted this campaign to only those areas where English rule had been previously well established and where deserters from Royalist armies eased his work,'[53] largely around the east and south coast of Ireland. 'The results were mixed with hard won victories at Drogheda and Wexford and further successes at Kilkenny and Clonmel, though only at high cost of parliamentary dead.'[54] Furthermore, Cromwell never fought an open field engagement, unlike Michael Jones, before Cromwell arrived in Ireland.[55] The other major field engagements, occurred after Cromwell had returned to England, under the commands of Sir Charles Coote, Lord Broghill, Henry Ireton, Edmund Ludlow and Charles Fleetwood.[56]

In conclusion, the popular belief, that Cromwell, completed the final re-conquest of Ireland, is demonstrably false. Even by the middle of 1652, parliamentary commanders, reported they were clashing, with armies much bigger, than their own, although by this time, as many as 34,000 Irish soldiers had left Ireland to serve in continental armies.[57] By August 1652, the strength, of the New Model Army in Ireland, had grown to a total of 34,128 men.[58] This was almost three times the number, of which Cromwell, had landed with in 1649.[59]

---

[51] Gilbert, (eds), *op.cit.*, Vol. III, Part, II, pp. 374-375.; Articles of Agreements regarding the various surrender of both Royalist and Confederate forces, in Ireland, have been reprinted in Gilbert, pp. 296-375.
[52] Gaunt, *op.cit.*, p. 229.
[53] Barnard, *op.cit.*, p. 181.
[54] Gaunt, *op.cit.*, p. 229.
[55] Gentles, *op.cit.*, p. 381.
[56] Barnard, *op.cit.*, p. 182.
[57] Gentles, op.cit., p. 381. Gardiner, *op.cit.*, Vol. II, p. 126.
[58] Dunlop, *op.cit.*, Vol. 1, p. 113.
[59] Gentles, *op.cit.*, p. 381.

In fact, organised, Irish resistance continued until 27th April 1653, when Colonel Phillip O'Reilly, finally surrendered, with his regiments of both horse and foot, to Parliamentary Commanders Colonel Jones, and Lord General Fleetwood, at the Castle of Cloughwater.[60] Almost two and a half years after Cromwell, had left Ireland. In contrast, it was shown that the final re-conquest of Ireland, was accomplished, by other parliamentary commanders, like Henry Ireton, Edmund Ludlow, Lord Broghill, Sir Charles Coote, and Charles Fleetwood. This fact, has also been, quietly passed over by, Cromwell's enemies.[61]

---

[60] Gilbert, *op.cit.*, Vol. III, Part II, pp. 374-375.
[61] Barnard, *op.cit.*, p. 182; Buchan, *op.cit.*, p. 297.

Thomas Wentworth, First Earl of Strafford.
(National Portrait Gallery)

Conclusion

Throughout this Book, I have used the relevant historiography, and selected contemporary sources, much of it contained in the conflicting explanations and assessments, to illustrate; the diversity of opinion, on Cromwell's actions in Ireland, and to suggest, that many of the myths, associated with this, are not based on fact or documentary evidence, and are of questionable historical validity or, at least, there are other more plausible, less anti-Cromwellian, well documented interpretations, that warrant equal consideration.

The historiography of Oliver Cromwell is of great importance, as it reveals why, common perceptions are prejudiced, based upon the origin of the opinion. It has been demonstrated, that during the seventeenth and eighteenth centuries; history was mostly written in the form of chronicles, which were understood to be records of actual events. When in fact, following the Restoration in 1660, 'Royalist propaganda swept the board.'[1] This began with Royalist propagandist; James Heath's *Flagellum: The Life and Death of O. Cromwell the Late Usurper*, (1663), which Carlyle calls, 'the chief fountain of lies about Cromwell.' Heath's book achieved six editions under Charles II followed by a host of similar works,[2] which formed the basis of all subsequent education of people about Cromwell in English History. Although, finally, 'Cromwell emerges

---

[1] Maurice Ashley, *The Greatness of Oliver Cromwell*, London, (1957), p. 21.
[2] D. H. Pennington, 'Cromwell and the Historians,' *History Today*, Vol. 8. No. 9, September, (1958), p. 598.

in the nineteenth century, either heroic or vile, according to the party or religion of the constructor.'[3]

The Irish demonisation of Cromwell, began soon after the conquest of Ireland, when the Irish Clergy returned to France, Spain, and Italy, where they wrote martyrologies to reflect the losses caused, to the Catholic Church and its congregation, which severely curtailed the hegemony of the Catholic Church in Ireland. Most of the histories mainly written by Jesuits, 'spiked with vitriol, found their way into print later, some of the most important emerging in the nineteenth century.'[4]

This demonisation of Cromwell, was further developed by Prendergast, in *The Cromwellian Settlement of Ireland, (1865)*, in which he diverted attention away from the Irish insurrection of 1641 to Cromwellian Ireland.[5] When Murphy published his *Cromwell in Ireland, (1883)*, he explained, 'with Prendergast a New Era of Irish history had began.'[6] This was soon followed by Patrick Moran's *Historical Sketch of the Persecutions Suffered by the Catholics of Ireland under the Rule of Cromwell and the Puritans, (1885)*. It was largely these three works, which were influential in creating and developing, the original myths, which were highly sectarian and anti Cromwellian. Since then and to large extent Irish writers, have continued to divert attention away from the Irish uprising of 1641. Whilst, in the words of, Nicholas Canny 'looking to the later Cromwellian atrocities at Drogheda, and Wexford, as the source of their own martyrology.'[7]

---

[3] Toby Barnard, 'Irish Images of Cromwell,' in R.C. Richardson, (ed.), *Images of Cromwell*: Essays *for and by Roger Howell, Jnr*. Manchester, (1993), p.182.
[4] *Ibid*, p.193.
[5] *Ibid*, p.183.
[6] Denis Murphy, S.J. *Cromwell in Ireland. A History of Cromwell's Irish Campaign*, Dublin, (1883), p.vi.
[7] Nichola Canny, '*What Really happened in 1641?*' in Jane H. Ohlmeyer, (ed), *Ireland from Independence to Occupation 1641-1660*. Cambridge, (1995). p. 26.

At the time of Cromwell's arrival in Ireland, Ormond had rallied all the parties in Ireland against the new republic. These English Royalists and the Scottish Presbyterians in Ulster, who, while they all had their own agenda, were united in their attempt to get Charles II on the throne.[8]

Only two Irish towns, Dublin and Derry, remained strong for the Commonwealth at the time of Cromwell's arrival. Cromwell went to Ireland on the instructions of the Council of State of England, bearing with him the Acts of Parliament, to empower him to perform his duties.[9] Cromwell's speech in Dublin, clearly outlined his purpose in being in Ireland, and offered 'peace and protection' from the Parliament of England to the Irish people, should they help him in his endeavours. Cromwell's real purpose was plain – the assertion of English parliamentary control in Ireland.

At Drogheda, Cromwell offered terms to the garrison, warning the Governor of the consequences should he refuse. His summons was refused, and the storm began. After this initial rejection, Cromwell refused subsequent quarter to the garrison, in accordance with the contemporary rules of war. In dismissing as myths, the claims made in biased historical accounts, the following points have been made. Firstly, the majority of the inhabitants of Drogheda, in September 1649, were New English settlers, who were Protestants, although there is little doubt that a small number of the inhabitants would have been Irish Catholics.

It has been demonstrated that the majority of the soldiers defending Drogheda, like the inhabitants, were also mostly English. Whilst there is no doubt that the officers were English, many were Catholics, like its governor, Arthur Aston. On the other hand Colonel Byrne, commanded a whole regiment of Protestant Englishmen. In addition 'Ormond's soldiers, consisted of not only many recent English settlers, but also Royalist refugees, from England, who had no claim to be Irish in any sense.'[10] Primary historical

---

[8] Thomas Carlyle, *Oliver Cromwell's Letters and Speeches, with Elucidations*, (3 Vols in one), London, (1849), p. 290.
[9] *Ibid*. p. 292.
[10] Ronald Hutton, *The British Republic 1649-1660*, London, (1990), p. 46.

documents show, that at Drogheda, Cromwell and the New Model Army, were fighting mostly Englishmen, many of whom were Protestants, and not all Catholic Irishmen, contrary to the often asserted popular historical opinions.

Whilst there is some evidence, that some Royalist officers and soldiers, were put to the sword, on the Mill Mount, after quarter had been given, there is no proof that this occurred with Cromwell's knowledge. It has been demonstrated that in fact the remainder of the garrison, did not surrender and were not put to the sword unarmed but died fighting. In addition to Cromwell's own letters, the two authentic documents I have presented in Chapter Three, one of them from a Royalist officer seem to disprove conclusively the story of a general massacre. There is also sufficient, conflicting, evidence to strongly challenge the myth, that the whole garrison was slaughtered after they had surrendered.

Cromwell's orders at Drogheda, were quite specific, he forbade his men to spare any, that were in arms in the town. This would have included Ormond's soldiers and any armed citizens, involved in the defence of the town. 'Although it is possible, that some unarmed citizens were accidentally killed, there is simply no evidence of this from an eye-witness, and only rumours and reports at second hand.'[11] One such report, was the fictional account, of a massacre of women and children, made by Thomas-a-Wood to his brother Anthony.[12]

There was, no documented evidence of any killings in the North Town, other than Cromwell's own account, and no documented, eye witness accounts, by either side in existence, for the killing of town citizens to date. Cromwell, could not have been responsible for the near 1000 people being put to the sword, in the North Town, in or around St. Peter's Church, as he did not, enter into the North Town, until 10/11th September 1649. Any killings, in Drogheda, prior to that date, would have to have been under the jurisdiction

---

[11] James Anthony Froude, *Ireland in the Eighteenth Century*, London, (1901), p. 125.
[12] Hutton, *op.cit.*, p. 47.; Martyn Bennett, *The Civil Wars in Britain and Ireland 1638-1651*, Oxford, (1997), p. 330.

and authority, of Aston as Governor of Drogheda. Remembering of course, the vast majority of the soldiers defending the North Town, were all spared, and shipped to the 'Barbadoes' as slaves.

In fact, on 14th September 1649 Cromwell issued a pass of safety, offering protection to the inhabitants, and the peaceful behaviour of troops. It must be remembered if New Model soldiers, had killed any unarmed inhabitants at Drogheda, they would have disobeyed Cromwell's orders. He forbade his men to spare any bearing arms. The popular belief that none of the garrison's soldiers escaped, except for one lieutenant, is also a myth. Lord Inchiquin reported to Ormond, 'many men, and some officers, have made their escapes out of Drogheda, some of every regiment have come unto me...Garret Dungan, is one, and is at Tecraghan... Lieutenant Collonell Cavenagh, is escaped to Mark Trevor, who is at Carrickmacross.'[13]

'Cromwell's alleged massacre of Drogheda, is invariably cited, as an example of Cromwell's brutality to the Irish; but as a matter of fact, the vast majority of the victims, were English. Practically all the officers and by far the greater part of the garrison were English. As to this point there is absolutely no room for doubt.'[14] Patrick Corish agrees, 'How many of them were English and how many of them were Irish, seems beyond establishing, but the serving officers, were chiefly English, as was the Commander Sir Arthur Aston, a Catholic Royalist.' The myth, that the soldiers and the greater part of the garrison, were Irish Catholics, was created, then developed, in the nineteenth century, for propaganda and partisan purposes and is not supported by the evidence I have produced.

At Wexford, Cromwell summoned and offered terms, not once but twice, over a period of six days, during which time he continued to receive offers to negotiate, from the enemy. Only when he found the enemy, were considering taking on reinforcements, during this

---

[13] J.T. Gilbert, (ed.), *A Contemporary History of Affairs in Ireland from A.D. 1641 to 1652*, (3 Vols), Dublin, (1879-80), Vol.II, p. xxiii.
[14] Ernest Hamilton, Lord, *The Irish Rebellion of 1641*, London, (1920), p. 367.

waiting period, did Cromwell revoke his offer. In the meantime, Sinnot's men, quit the walls of Wexford and Cromwell's men, took advantage of this fact, entering the town, where they then acted without orders from Cromwell. The strongest reason, to dismiss the myths, relating to Cromwell's behaviour at Wexford, is that they have never been supported by eye-witness accounts. They were later interpolations from afar.

Cromwell, did not devastate, every town he captured. At New Ross, Cromwell granted generous terms to the surrendering garrison, after which five hundred English soldiers, went over to Cromwell and the New Model. On the other hand, those of the garrison, still loyal to the Royalist cause, were allowed to march out with their arms, baggage, drums beating, and colours flying. The civilian inhabitants of New Ross, were also protected from plunder and violence, as Cromwell had promised.

Once Cork, had declared for Parliament, lots of other towns in the Province of Munster, followed their example. These towns included Bandon, Kinsale and Youghal.[15] Similarly Arklow, Limbrick, Ferns and Enniscorthy surrendered to the New Model Army. Thereby avoiding violent confrontations.

Roghill, Fethard, Cashel, Callan and Cahir were also taken by Cromwell and the New Model and, again, there is no evidence that these places, were the subject of brutal, or inhumane tactics, Like the other towns that submitted, the inhabitants either surrendered, left, or burnt and destroyed the towns, before Cromwell arrived.

It should also be remembered that many towns enjoyed the same terms of surrender as at Kilkenny, namely that the civilian population be permitted to remain unmolested, and, that the clergy be allowed to depart with their goods, along with the officers and soldiers of the city and castle.

There were two towns, which did not capitulate to Cromwell: Waterford and Clonmel. At Waterford, Cromwell summoned the town unsuccessfully, but did not pursue the refusal with a storm.

[15] Ian Gentles, *The New Model Army in England, Ireland, and Scotland, 1645-1653*, Oxford, (1992), p. 368.

Nevertheless taking the Fort Passage gave Cromwell access to the sea and continued supplies while its loss, for Waterford and other towns along the coast, meant that they no longer had access to sea routes for supplies or reinforcements of men and artillery.[16] At no time and, in no records available, is there any evidence to show that Cromwell even attempted to take Waterford by force.

The popular belief that Cromwell's military campaign in Ireland was fought on the basis of English Protestant against Irish Catholic was critically examined in Chapter Five and found wanting.

In examining, the popular belief, that Cromwell was responsible, for ordering wholesale and indiscriminate massacre of ordinary unarmed Catholic civilians, in the towns that he besieged, there was no evidence to support this myth. It is clear, that in all cases, Cromwell's enemies were given the opportunity to surrender in order to save bloodshed on both sides. In marked contrast to this myth the articles of capitulation at the various towns, which included New Ross, Fethard, Cashel, Cahir, Gowran, Kilkenny, and Clonmel, display Cromwell's humanity. Surrendering garrisons were given generous terms and treated with mercy and honour.

In dismissing the myth, related to Cromwell at Clonmel, that he conspired with Major Fennell, to admit New Model soldiers into the garrison for five hundred pounds, it was found that it was not supported by eye-witness accounts. It was also demonstrated in Chapter Six, that there are more believable and historically documented, explanations and assessments, than those manifested in the myths.

It should, also be remembered, that during the night Hugh O'Neill and his men, slipped out of Clonmel un-noticed, retreating towards Waterford. Subsequently Cromwell, received a deputation, to which he readily granted, the lives and estates of the inhabitants, on condition, of the surrender of the 'town and garrison'. Furthermore, even though he had been deceived, Cromwell nevertheless, stood by his word and when the soldiery entered Clonmel, they offered no damage to life or property. Furthermore, it was also established that Parliamentary losses at Clonmel, were

---

[16] Ashley, *op.cit.*, p. 238.

similar to Royalist losses, at Drogheda and Wexford. In marked contrast however, while the events at 'Drogheda and Wexford, have been magnified and well publicized, Clonmel has been quietly passed over by Cromwell's enemies.'[17]

Some historians argue, that the Royalist forces in Ireland, had been beaten before Cromwell arrived, when Michael Jones defeated Ormond, at the battle of Rathmines. I would argue, however that it was in his role as Commander in Chief, that Cromwell was responsible for the Parliamentary victory in Ireland. Cromwell's deployment of New Model Army, along with his use of political warfare, firstly divided the Protestant Royalists, from the Catholic Irish leaders; and, in addition, his achievement of co-operation between the army and the fleet, the organisation of supplies, along with effective movement and use, of his siege artillery, all proved he was an experienced military Commander. When Cromwell first arrived in Dublin there were still large Royalist forces in the field against him, and at first the Irish were universally hostile. Despite this, Cromwell maintained discipline, preserving as far as possible the health and morale of his men. Furthermore, he manoeuvred his various columns with skill, even with heavy casualties and shortages of pay, about which he constantly complained to the English Parliament.[18]

Cromwell had good reason for bringing the Irish campaign to a conclusion, as soon as possible. Given an opportunity, Ormond would have undoubtedly tried to force the New Model into a series of protracted sieges. If he had allowed this to happen, the Irish weather would have accomplished, by sickness, what Ormond could never hope to do with the force of arms.

The popular belief, that Cromwell, completed the final re-conquest of Ireland is demonstrably false. Even by the middle of 1652, parliamentary commanders, reported they were still clashing with armies much bigger than their own, although by this time as many as 34,000 Irish soldiers had left Ireland to serve in continental

---

[17] Barnard, *op.cit.*, p. 182.
[18] Ashley, *op.cit.*, p. 238.

armies.[19] Remembering of course, by August 1652, the strength of the New Model Army in Ireland, had grown to a total of 34,128 [20] men, almost three times the number of which Cromwell had landed with in 1649.[21] In fact organised Irish resistance, continued until 27th April 1653, when Colonel Phillip O'Reilly, finally surrendered, with his regiments of both horse and foot, to Parliamentary Commanders Colonel Jones, and Lord General Fleetwood, at the Castle of Cloughwater.[22] Almost two and a half years after Cromwell had left Ireland.[23] This fact has been quietly passed over by Cromwell's enemies. Wheeler believes, 'A failure of Irish leadership, not 'Cromwell's Curse,' dashed Catholic hopes, for religious toleration, and political autonomy.'[24] Whilst on the other hand, Loeber and Parker conclude, 'Ireland's eventual defeat, and subjugation, by England, stemmed essentially; from political, not military, factors.'[25] However, there seems little doubt that it was a combination of both these factors.

There seems little doubt that 'the reporting of events during the 1640s and 1650s have been characterised by myth, denial, or exaggeration. This created a form of sectarian and religious bigotry, which has survived in parts of Ireland, until today.' In reality, 'the 1641 Ulster massacres mean as much to the Protestant tradition, as Cromwell's 'atrocities' at Drogheda, in 1649, do to Catholic popular culture.' [26] In the words of Herbert Rowen, 'the massacre

---

[19] Gentles, *op. cit.,* p. 381. Gardiner, *op. cit.,* Vol. II, p. 126.

[20] Robert Dunlop, (ed), *Ireland under the Commonwealth: Being a selection of Documents Relating to the Government of Ireland, 1651-1659*, 2 Vols., Manchester, (1913), Vol.1, p. 113.

[21] Gentles, *op. cit.,* p. 381.

[22] Gilbert, *op.cit.,* pp. 374-375.

[23] John Morrill, 'Between War and Peace 1651-1652, in John Kenyon and Jane H. Ohlmeyer (eds), *The Civil Wars, A Military History of England, Scotland and Ireland 1638-1660*, Oxford, (1998), *op.cit.* p. 306.

[24] James Scott Wheeler, 'Four Armies in Ireland,' in Jane H Ohlmeyer, (ed), *Ireland from Independence to Occupation 1641-1660.* Cambridge, (1995), p. 65.

[25] Rolf Loeber and Geoffrey Parker, 'The Military Revolution in Seventeenth-Century Ireland,' in Jane H. Ohlmeyer, (ed), *Ireland from Independence to Occupation, 1641-1660*, Cambridge, (1995), p. 88.

of Drogheda became fixed in Irish memories, as proof of English savagery, an "Irish Guy Fawkes Day," as it were, which embittered them against their conquerors for centuries.'[27]

On the one hand Cromwell, became an Irish Guy Fawkes, while on the other hand 'William III, not Cromwell, would be celebrated, as the architect of the Irish Protestant ascendancy.'[28]

Ronald Hutton summarises that:

> The 'Curse of Cromwell' is still today supposed to be a common Irish malediction. To citizens of the Republic of Eire it signifies subjugation by the English, accompanied by massacres of a quite abnormal ferocity. Is either association correct? The first has much justification, for as we shall see the island became subject to direct rule by the English Parliament for the first time, and much of it passed into the hands of English newcomers. But in another sense the war of 1649-53 was, like all Ireland's conflicts, a civil strife. Both Ormond's forces and those of the Commonwealth were Anglo-Irish. Among the Catholics were most of the descendants of the Norman and English settlers who had seized half of Ireland in the Middle Ages. One of the greatest Gaelic chiefs, Muireadhach Ò Brien, Lord Inchiquin, was a Protestant who had fought for Parliament until thwarted ambition led him to change sides in 1648. Ormond's soldiers included not only many recent English settlers but also royalist refugees from England who had no claim to be Irish in any sense. The whole

---

[26] Jane H. Ohlmeyer, (ed), *Ireland from Independence to Occupation*, Cambridge, (1995), *op.cit.*, p.23.

[27] Herbert H. Rowen, *A History of early Modern Europe 1500-1815*, Indianapolis, (1977), p. 260.

[28] T.C. Barnard, 'Settling and unsettling Ireland: the Cromwellian and Williamite Revolutions,' in Jane H. Ohlmeyer, (ed.), *op.cit.*, Chapter 13, pp. 265-91, especially p. 266.

royalist-Catholic coalition owed loyalty to a King who intended to reside in England as before. The Commonwealth's garrison at Derry consisted of Protestants resident in Ireland before the wars. The same sort of people were included in the force which Cromwell led out of Dublin and many more joined it as it advanced. Cromwell couched his appeals in religious, rather than nationalist terms. His avowed aim was to succour the Protestants of Ireland and to defeat the Catholic 'rebellion' which had begun in 1641.[29]

It is also clear that Oliver Cromwell has been used as a scapegoat, whereas more ruthless English commanders in Ireland, like 'Grey, Sidney, Essex, Mountjoy, Schomberg, Ginkel, Duff or Humbert,' had their reputations untainted.[30]

During the reign of Elizabeth I, Sir Francis Drake landed at Rathlin Island, located off the coast of Ulster, and slaughtered the families of the MacDonnells, who had sought safety there. Drake and his Commander, the Earl of Essex revelled in this glorious victory. 'The Irish uprising of 1641, began with the greatest massacre of civilians, recorded in the history of the British Isles.' In 1645, the storming of Sligo, by Sir Charles Coote, was accompanied by the massacre of the whole garrison, together with many of its inhabitants. In 1647 Lord Inchiquin, sacked Cashel committing a similar atrocity.[31] Following Cromwell's departure, both parliamentary Commanders, Lord Broghill and Sir Charles Coote, committed atrocities against Catholic forces in Ireland, but they are rarely singled out for treatment, unlike Cromwell.[32]

In conclusion, an examination of the myths regarding Cromwell in Ireland in the light of broader historiographical evidence, reveals,

---

[29] Hutton, *op.cit.*, p. 46.
[30] Barnard, *op.cit.*, p. 181.
[31] Hutton, *op.cit.*, p. 47.
[32] James Scott Wheeler, *Cromwell in Ireland*, Dublin, (1999), p. 5.

a systematic blackening of Cromwell's character.[33] In the final analysis, this evidence suggests, that most of the allegations against Cromwell are at best dubious, and in most part not supported by documented historical evidence. I agree with Ashley that, 'the blame for the historical failure of England's policy in Ireland' does not 'lie at the door of any one man.'[34] Sadly it suited both nations to magnify the actions of Cromwell in Ireland,[35] in ways that prostituted history, to political and religious, propaganda.

---

[33] Robert S. Paul, *The Lord Protector: Religion and Politics in the Life of Oliver Cromwell*, London, (1955), p. 382.
[34] Ashley, *op.cit.*, p. 239.
[35] Hutton, *op.cit.*, p. 48.

Appendix

MILITARY LISTS, MUSTER-ROLLS, ETC.[1]

I. GARRISON IN THE TOWN OF DROGHEDA, PRIOR TO SIEGE BY OLIVER CROMWELL IN 1649.

A list of the severall troopes of horse in the garrison within the towne of Droghadah, 30th August, 1649, with their intertainment.

Maior Buttler :

				£	s.	d.
Maior	...	...	...	03	00	00
Lieftenant...	...	...		01	04	00
Q[u]art[ermaster] ...		...		00	12	00
Chaplaine ...	...	...		01	01	00
Cornet	...	...		00	18	00
Trumpet	...	...		00	09	00
Marshell	...	...	...	00	16	00
2 Corp[or]alls, 9s. a peece				00	18	00
27 Troopers, 6s, a peece			...	08	02	00
				£17	00	00

Captaine Harpall :		£	s.	d.		Sir James Preston :		£	s.	d.
Captaine	...	02	10	00		Captain	...	02	10	00
Leiftenant ...	...	01	04	00		Lieftenant ...	...	01	04	00
Cornet	...	00	18	00		Cornet	...	00	18	00
Quarterm[astor]	...	00	12	00		Quartermaster	...	00	12	00
Chaplaine ...	...	01	01	00		2 Corp[or]alls	...	00	18	00
2 Corp[or]alls	...	00	18	00		Trumpeter	...	00	09	00
A trumpeter	...	00	09	00		34 Troopers	...	10	04	00
21 Troopers	...	06	06	00				£16	15	00
		£13	18	00						

Sir John Dongan :		£	s.	d.		Liftenant-Collonel Dungan :		£	s.	d.
Captain	...	02	10	00		Captain	...	02	10	00
Lieftenant ...	...	01	04	00		Lieftenant ...	...	01	04	00
Cornet	...	00	18	00		Cornet	...	00	18	00
Quart[ermaster]	...	00	12	00		Quarter[master]	...	00	12	00
2 Corp[or]alls	...	00	18	00		2 Corp[or]alls	...	00	18	00
A Trumpeter	...	00	09	00		Trumpeter ...	...	00	09	00
23 Troopers	...	06	18	00		22 Troopers	...	06	12	00
		£13	09	00				£13	03	00

1. Ormonde Archives, Kilkenny Castle, Irěland.

[1]J.T. Gilbert, (ed), *A Contemporary History of Affairs in Ireland, (1641-52)*, containing the narrative entitled, *An Amphorismal discovery of a treasonable faction*, 3 vols. Irish Archaelogical Society, Dublin, (1879-80) Vol. II, pp. 496-499.

Captain Plunckit's Troope:

		£	s.	d.
Captain ...	...	02	10	00
Lieftenant ...	...	01	04	00
Cornet ...	...	00	18	00
Quart[master]	...	00	12	00
2 Corp[or]alls	...	00	18	00
A trumpeter	...	00	09	00
22 Troopers	...	09	00	00
		£15	11	00

Captaine Fleming's troope:

		£	s.	d.
Captaine ...	...	02	10	00
Lieftenant ...	...	01	04	00
Cornet ...	...	00	18	00
Quartermaster	...	00	12	00
Chaplaine ...	...	01	01	00
2 Corp[or]alls	...	00	18	00
A Trumpeter	...	00	09	00
Marchell	...	00	16	00
60 Troopers	...	18	00	00
		£26	08	00

Captaine Finglas troop:

		£	s.	d.
Captaine ...	...	02	10	00
Lieftenant ...	...	01	04	00
Cornet ...	...	00	18	00
Quarter[master]	...	00	12	00
Chaplane ...	...	01	01	00
2 Corporalls	...	00	18	00
Trumpet ...	...	00	09	00
Marshell ...	...	00	16	00
48 Troopers	...	14	08	00
		£22	16	00

Sume totall of the weekly pay to the 8 troops amount to £139.

The number of the horse is 256

The number of the commanders and officers belonging to the horse ... 63

319

Colonell Byrne:

				£	s.	d.
Colonell	...	04	10	00
Leiftenant-Colonell ...	...	...	03	00	00
Maior	...	...	02	05	00
7 Captaines	...	...	10	10	00
9 Leiftenants, 15s. a peice ...	...	06	15	00
9 Ensignes, 10s. a peice ...	...	04	10	00
19 Sargeants, 3s. 6d. a peice	...	03	06	6
41 Corporals and Drum ...	...	06	03	0
385 Private souldiers, 3s. 6d. a peice	67	07	0
2 Chaplins, 17s. 6d. a peice ...	...	01	15	0
Quartermaster ...	...	...	00	15	0
Marshall	...	...	00	12	0
Chirurgion and his Mate ...	...	00	18	0
Cariage Master	...	00	10	0
				£112	16	06

	£	s.	d.
Of my Lord of Inchequin's armie :			
Ensigne	oo	10	o
69 Souldiers	8	12	6
	£9	2	6
Colonell Wale :			
Colonell	04	10	o
Maior	02	05	o
7 Captains, 30s. a peice	10	10	o
12 Leitenants, 15s. a peice	09	00	o
12 Ensignes, 10s. a peice	06	00	o
21 Sargeants, 3s. 6d. a peice ...	03	13	6
36 Corporalls, 3s. a peice	05	08	o
7 Drums, 3s. a peice	01	01	o
391 Souldiers	68	08	6
2 Chaplins, 17s. 6d. a peice ...	01	15	o
Quartermaster	00	15	o
Marshall	00	12	o
Chirurgeon and his Mate	00	18	o
Cariage Master	00	10	o
	£115	o	o
His Excellencie's Regiment :*			
Collonell	04	10	o
Maior	03	00	oo
9 Captaines	13	10	oo
11 Leiftenants	08	05	oo
9 Ensignes	04	10	oo
22 Seriants	07	14	oo
13 Drums	01	19	oo
423 Private souldiers	74	00	06
7 Reformades	02	02	oo
A Preacher and a Chaplin	01	08	oo
Chirurgion and his Mate	00	18	oo
Quarter-Master	00	15	oo
Cariage-Master	00	10	oo
3 Reformades	00	18	oo
6 Souldiers	01	01	oo
Marshall	00	12	oo
27 Corporalls...	04	01	oo
	£129	13	06

* The Marquis of Ormonde's regiment : Sir Edmund Verney, Lieutenant-Colonel. See *ante*, p. 269.

				£	s.	d.
Colonell Warren:						
Colonel	...	...	...	4	10	00
Maior	...	...	...	2	05	00
9 Captaines, 30s. a peice	...	...	13	10	00
11 Leftenants, 15s. a peice	...	...	08	05	00
11 Ensignes, 10s. a peice	...	...	05	10	00
22 Sargeants, 3s. 6d. a peice	...	...	3	17	00
14 Drums, 3s. a peice	...	...	02	02	0
33 Corporalls, 3s. a peice	...	...	04	19	0
528 Private souldiers, 3s. 6d. a peice	92	08	0
2 Chaplins, 17s. 6d. a peice	...	...	1	15	00
Quartermaster	...	...	...	00	15	00
Marshall	...	...	...	00	12	00
Chirurgeon and his Mate	...	...	00	18	0
Cariage Master	...	...	...	00	10	0
				£141	**16**	**0**

				£	s.	d.
Trayne of Artillery:						
The towne Maior	...	...	...	00	15	00
His Man	...	...	...	00	05	00
Clarke of the store	...	...	...	00	07	06
William Pearson, Master gunner	...	00	10	00
William Wade, gunner	...	...	00	08	00
Georg Calluert, gunner	...	...	00	08	00
Phebus Begnall, gonner's mate	...	00	05	00
Thomas Paine, gunner's mate	...	00	05	00
Thomas Bankes, gunner's mate	...	00	05	00
Robert Euers, Carpenter	...	...	00	08	00
John Keane, his mate	...	...	00	05	00
William Purchas, smyth	...	...	00	06	08
				£04	**08**	**02**

					£	s.	d.
Sume of the weekly paye to the foote is	...	...	...	...	512	17	0
Sume of the weekly pay to the horse	...	...	...	...	139	0	0
To Captaine White	...	...	...	...	...	02	05	0
To Chubbe, a wounded souldier, by his Exelencie's order	...	...	00	05	0

Number of the commanders, officers, and troope	319
Number of the commanders, officers, and foote belonging to the redgments	2221
The wounded souldiers of My Lord of Inchequeene's, being numbered 69 theirin reckoned belonging to the train of Artillerie	0012
In the whole	2552

Bibliography

Printed Primary Sources

Abbott, W.C., *Writings and Speeches of Oliver Cromwell*, (4 Vols.), Cambridge, Mass., (1937-47).

Carlyle, Thomas, *Oliver Cromwell's, Letters and Speeches with Elucidations*, 2ⁿᵈ edition, Ward Lock and Co., London, (1846).

Carlyle, Thomas, *Oliver Cromwell's, Letters and Speeches with Elucidations*, 2ⁿᵈ revised edition, (3 Vols. in one), Ward Lock and Co., London, (1846).

Clarendon, Edward Hyde, Earl of, *The History of the Rebellion and Civil Wars in England*, (ed.), W.D. Macray, 6 Vols., Oxford, (1888).

Dunlop, Robert (ed.), *Ireland Under the Commonwealth: Being a Selection of Documents Relating to the Government of Ireland, 1651-1659,* (2 Vols., Manchester, 1913).

Firth, C.H. and Rait, R.S., (eds.), *Acts and Ordinances of the Interregnum, 1641-1660*, 3 Vols., London, (1911).

Gilbert, J.T. (ed.), *A Contemporary History of Affairs in Ireland from AD 1641 to 1652 containing the...narrative an 'Amphorismal discovery of treasonable faction,'* 3 Vols., Dublin, (1879-80).

Hogan, E.D. (ed.), *The History of the War of Ireland from 1641-1653, by a British Officer of the Regiment of Sir John Clotsworthy*, McGlashan and Gill, Dublin, (1873).

Petty, Sir William, *The Political Anatomy of Ireland*, Brown, London, (1691).

Stainer, Charles (ed.), *Speeches of Oliver Cromwell 1644-1658,* Henry Frowde, London, (1901).

Secondary Sources

Adair, John,   *By the Sword Divided - Eyewitnesses of the English Civil War*, Century Publishing Co. Ltd., London, (1983). Paperback edition, Sutton Publishing, (1998).

Ardagh, John,   *Ireland and the Irish, Portrait of a Changing Society*, Hamish Hamilton, London, (1994).

Ashley, Maurice,   *The Greatness of Oliver Cromwell*, Hodder and Stoughton, London, (1957).

Ashley, Maurice,   *Oliver Cromwell and the Puritan Revolution*, The English Universities Press Ltd., London, (1958).

Ashley, Maurice,   *England in the Seventeenth Century,* Penguin Books, Harmondsworth, (1970).

Ashley, Maurice,   *Oliver Cromwell and His World*, Thames and Hudson, London, (1972).

Ashley, Maurice,   *The English Civil War–A Concise History*, Thames and Hudson, London, (1974). Paperback edition, Sutton Publishing, (1998).

Ashton, Robert,   *The English Civil War – Conservatism and Revolution 1603-1649*, Weidenfeld and Nicholson, London, (1978).

Aylmer, G.E. (ed.), *The Interregnum: The Quest for Settlement 1646-1660,* Macmillan Press Ltd., London, (1972).

Aylmer, G.E. (ed.), *The Levellers in the English Revolution,* Thames and Hudson, London, (1975).

Aylmer, G.E. (ed.), *The Struggle for the Constitution 1603-1689, England in the Seventeenth Century,* (second edition), Blandford Press, London, (1986).

Baldock, T.S.,   *Cromwell as a Soldier*, Kegan, Paul, French, Trubner and Co., London, (1899).

Bardon, Jonathon, *A History of Ulster,* Black Staff Press, Belfast, (1992).

Barnard, T.C., *Cromwellian Ireland, English Government and Reform in Ireland*, Oxford University Press, Oxford, (1975).

Bartlett, Thomas and *A Military History of Ireland*, Cambridge Jeffrey, Keith (eds.), University Press, Cambridge, (1996).

Beckett, J.C., *A Short History of Ireland,* Hutchinson University Library, London, 5th edition, (1973).

Belloc, Hillaire, *Cromwell*, Cassell and Company Ltd., 2nd edition, London, (1936).

Bennett, Martyn, *The Civil War in Britain and Ireland 1638-1651,* Blackwell Publishers, Oxford, (1997).

Bennett, Martyn, *The Civil Wars 1637-1653,* Sutton Publishing Limited, Stroud, Gloucester, (1998).

Bottigheimer, K.S.,*English Money and Irish Land. The 'Adventurers' in the Cromwellian settlement of Ireland*, Oxford, (1971).

Boyce, George *The Making of Modern Irish History*, and O'Day, Alan, Routledge, London, (1996)

Brady, Ciaran, (ed.), *Interpreting Irish History, The Debate on Historical Revisionism 1938-1994*, Irish Academic Press, Dublin, (1994).

Buchan, John, *Oliver Cromwell*, Hodder and Stoughton Ltd., London, (1934).

Canny, Nicholas, P., *Kingdom and Colony: Ireland in the Atlantic World, 1560-1800*, Baltimore, (1988).

Canny, Nicholas, P., *From Reformation to Restoration: Ireland, 1534-1660*, Dublin, (1987).

Canny, Nicholas, P., *The Elizabethan Conquest of Ireland: A Pattern Established 1565-76.* The Harvester Press, Hassocks, Sussex, (1976).

Capp, Bernard, *Cromwell's Navy: The Fleet and the English Revolution, 1645-1660,* Oxford, (1989).

Churchill, Winston, *The Island Race*, Cassell, London, (1964).

Churchill, Winston, *A History of the English Speaking Peoples, The New World,* Cassell, London, (1974).

Clarke, Aiden,   *The Old English in Ireland 1625-1642,* London, (1966).

Coonan, Thomas, *The Irish Catholic Confederacy and the Puritan Revolution,* Clonmore and Reynolds Ltd, Dublin, (1954).

Coward, Barry,   *Cromwell,* Longman, London, (1991).

Curtis, Edmund, *A History of Medieval Ireland from 1086-1513,* Methuen, London, (1923), Re-issued, (1978).

Dalton, John,   *The History of Drogheda – With its Environs: and an Introductory Memoir of the Dublin to Drogheda Railway,* Dublin, (1844).

Davis, J.C.,   *Oliver Cromwell,* Arnold, London, (2001).

Dow, F.D.,   *Cromwellian Scotland 1651-1660,* John Donald Publishers Ltd., Edinburgh, (1979).

Esson, D.M.R.,   *The Curse of Cromwell: A History of the Ironside Conquest of Ireland, 1649-53,* Leo Cooper, Totowa, New Jersey, (1971).

Firth, C.H.,   *Oliver Cromwell and the Rule of the Puritans in England,* Oxford University Press, London, (1900).

Firth, C.H.,   *The Regimental History of Cromwell's Army,* 2 Vols, Oxford, (1940), re-issued (1991)

Firth, C.H.,   *Cromwell's Army: A History of the English Soldier during the Civil Wars, the Commonwealth and Protectorate,* London (1902); re-issued, (1992).

Foster, R.F., (ed.), *The Oxford History of Ireland,* Oxford University Press, Oxford, (1989).

Foster, R.F.,   *Modern Ireland 1600-1972,* London, (1988).

Foster, R.F., (ed.), *The Oxford Illustrated History of Ireland,* Paperback, Oxford University Press, Oxford, (1989).

Fraser, Antonia, *Cromwell – Our Chief of Men,* Weidenfeld & Nicolson, London, (1973), Paperback edition, Orion Books, Ltd, London, (2004)

Froude, James, A., *The English in Ireland in the Eighteenth Century*, 3 Vols., Longmans, Green and Co., London, (1887)

Gardiner, S.R., *Oliver Cromwell,* Longmans, Green and Co., London, (1909).

Gardiner, S.R., *History of the Commonwealth and Protectorate 1649-1656,* 4 Vols. Longmans, Green and Co., London, (1903).

Gardiner, S.R., *History of the great civil war, 1642-1649* (new edn., 4 vols., London, 1893; Paperback edition, Orion Publishing Group Ltd, London, (1987).

Gaunt, Peter, *Oliver Cromwell*, Blackwell, Oxford, (1996).

Gaunt, Peter *Oliver Cromwell*, Historic Lives Series, British Library, London, (2004).

Gentles, Ian, *The New Model Army in England, Ireland and Scotland 1645-1653,* Blackwell, Oxford, (1992).

Gibson, Michael, *Cavaliers and Roundheads*, Wayland Publ., London, (1973).

Gillingham, John, *Cromwell-Portrait of a Soldier*, Wiedenfeld and Nicholson, London, (1976).

Gregg, Pauline, *Oliver Cromwell*, J.M. Dent and Sons Ltd., London, (1988).

Hamilton, Ernest, *The Irish Rebellion of 1641*, London, (1920).

Hardacre, Paul H., *The Royalists During the Puritan Revolution*, Martinus Nijhoff, The Hague, (1956).

Harrison, Frederick, *Twelve English Statesmen – Oliver Cromwell,* Macmillan and Co. Ltd., London, (1888).

Harrison, Frederick, *Oliver Cromwell*, Macmillan and Co. Ltd., London, (1922).

Hayes-McCoy, G.A., *Irish Battles, A Military History of Ireland*, Belfast, (1989).

Hunt, Tristram, *The English Civil War-At First Hand*, Weidenfeld & Nicolson, London, (2002), Paperback edition, Orion Books Ltd, London, (2003).

197

Hutton, Ronald, *The British Republic 1649-1660*, Macmillan, London, (1990).

Johnson, Paul, *Ireland Land of Trouble: A History from the Twelfth Century to the Present Day*, Eyre Methuen, London, (1980).

Kee, Robert, *Ireland: A History*, Little, Brown and Co., Boston, (1980).

Kearny, Hugh, *Strafford in Ireland 1633-41: A Study in Absolutism,* Cambridge University Press, Cambridge, (1989).

Kelly, Kevin, J., *The Longest War*, Zed Books Ltd., London, (1983).

Kenyon, John, *The Civil Wars in England*, London, (1996).

Kenyon, John and *The Civil Wars - A Military History of*
Ohlmeyer, Jane H. (eds.), *England, Scotland and Ireland 1638-1660,* Oxford University Press, Oxford, (1998).

Kerrigan, Paul, M.,*Castles and Fortifications in Ireland 1485-1945*, The Collins Press, Cork, (1995).

Lamont, William and *Politics, Religion and Literature in the*
Oldfield, Sybill, *Seventeenth Century,* Dent, London, (1975).

Lecky, William E.H., *A History of Ireland in the Eighteenth Century*, 5, Vols., Longmans, Green and Co., (1913), originally published between 1878 and 1890.

Lydon, James, *The Making of Ireland – From Ancient Times to Present,* Routledge, London, (1998).

Macaulay, Lord, *History of England – To the Death of William III,* Vol.1, Heron Books, London, (1976).

MacCuarta, Brian S.J., (ed), *Ulster 1641 – Aspects of the Rising*, Institute of Irish Studies, Belfast, (1993).

Marryat, Frederick, *The Children of the New Forest* J.M. Dent & Sons, London, this edition, (1968), first published (1847).

Moody, T.W., *A New History of Ireland, III: Early Modern*
Martin, F.X., and *Ireland 1534-1691*, Oxford (1976), repr. with
Byrne, F.J. (eds.), corrections (1978).

Moran, Patrick, Francis, *Historical Sketch of the Persecutions*
DD.,   *Suffered by the Catholics of Ireland*
                        Under the Rule of Cromwell and the
                        Puritans, M.H. Gill and Son Ltd., Dublin,
                        (1885).
Morrill, John, (ed.), *The Oxford Illustrated History of Tudor*
                        and Stuart Britain, Oxford University Press,
                        (1996)
Morrill, John,   *Oliver Cromwell and the English Revolution*,
                        Longman, New York, (1990).
Murphy, Denis S.J., *Cromwell in Ireland: a History of*
                        Cromwell's Irish Campaign [with Maps,
                        Plans and Illustrations] M.H. Gill & Son,
                        Dublin, (1883).
Murphy, Denis S.J., *Cromwell in Ireland: a History of*
                        Cromwell's Irish Campaign, (new edition),
                        M.H. Gill and Son, Dublin, (1902).
O'Brien, Maire and *A Concise History of Ireland*, 3rd edition
Cruise, Conor,   revised, Thames and Hudson, London, (1973)
Ohlmeyer, Jane, H., *Civil War and Restoration in Three*
                        Stuart Kingdoms: *the Career of Randal*
                        MacDonnell, Marquis of Antrim 1609-1683,
                        Cambridge University Press, Cambridge,
                        (1993).
Ohlmeyer, Jane, H. (ed), *Ireland from Independence to*
                        Occupation 1641-1660, Cambridge
                        University Press, Cambridge, (1995).
Paul, Robert S.,   *The Lord Protector, Religion and Politics in*
                        the Life of Oliver Cromwell, Lutterworth
                        Press, London, (1955).
Prendergast, J.P., *The Cromwellian Settlement of Ireland*,
                        Dublin, (1865).
Ranelagh, John, O'Beirne, *A Short History of Ireland*, 2nd
                        edition, Cambridge University Press,
                        Cambridge, (1983).
Ranelagh, John, O'Beirne, *Ireland: An Illustrated History*,
                        Collins, London, (1981).

Bibliography

Reilly, Tom,   *Cromwell - An Honourable Enemy. The
                      Untold Story of the Cromwellian Invasion
                      of Ireland*, Brandon, Ireland, (1998),
                      Paperback edition, Orion Books Ltd. London,
                      (1999).

Richardson, R.C. (ed.),   *Images of Oliver Cromwell – Essays
                      for and by Roger Howell, Jnr.*, Manchester
                      University Press, Manchester, (1993).

Roberts, Keith,   *Cromwell's War Machine, The New Model
                      Army 1645-1660*, Pen & Sword Books Ltd,
                      Barnsley, (2005).

Roots, Ivan,   *Cromwell-A Profile*, Macmillan, London,
                      (1973).

Royle, Trevor,   *Civil War – The Wars of the Three Kingdoms
                      1638-1660,* Little, Brown, (2004), Paperback
                      edition, Abacus, London, (2005).

Rowen, Herbert, H.,   *A History of Early Modern Europe
                      1500-1815*, Bobbs Merrill Educational
                      Publishing, Indianapolis, (1977).

Schama, Simon,   *A History of Britain, The British Wars 1603-
                      1776*, BBC Worldwide Ltd., London, (2001).

Smith, David L.,   *Oliver Cromwell, Politics and Religion in the
                      -English Revolution, 1640-1658,* (documents
                      and commentary)*,* Cambridge University Press,
                      (1991).

Somerset-Fry, Peter   *A History of Ireland*, Routledge,
and Fiona,   London, (1988), (paperback edition), (1991).

Taylor, Philip, A.M. (ed.), *The Origins of the English Civil War,
                      Conspiracy, Crusade or Class Conflict?,*
                      D.C. Heath and Co., Boston, (1960).

Underdown, David,   *Royalist Conspiracy in England*, Yale,
                      (1971).

Wedgewood, C.V., *Oliver Cromwell*, Duckworth, London, (1939).

Wedgewood, C.V., *Thomas Wentworth First Earl of Strafford
                      1593-1641, A Revaluation*, Johnathan Cape,
                      London, (1961), Paperback edition, The Orion
                      Publishing Group Ltd, London, (2000).

Wheeler, James, Scott,   *Cromwell in Ireland,* Gill and
Macmillan, Dublin, (1999).

Woolrych, Austin,   *Battles of the English Civil War*, Macmillan,
London, (1966). Paperback edition, Phoenix,
London, (1991).

Worden, Blair,   *Roundhead Reputations – The English Civil
War and the Passions of Posterity*, Allen
Lane, Penguin Press, London, (2001).

Young, Peter and   *The English Civil War - A Military History
Holmes, Richard,*   *of the Three Civil Wars 1642-1651*, Eyre
Methuen, London, (1974).

Journals and Articles

Barnard, T.C.,   'Planters and policies in Cromwellian Ireland,'
Past and Present, No. 61, (1973), pp. 31-69.

Bryan, D.,   'Colonel Richard Grace, 1651-1652,' *Irish
Sword*, 4, (1959-60).

Burke, James,   'The New Model Army and the problems of
siege Warfare, 1648-51', *Irish Historical
Studies*, Vol. XXVII, No. 105, May, (1990),
pp. 1-29.

Carlin, Norah,   'The Levellers and the conquest of Ireland in
1649,' *The Historical Journal*, 30, 2, (1987),
pp. 269-88.

de Beer, E.S.,   'Some recent works on Oliver Cromwell,'
History, Vol. XXIII, June, (1938) – March,
(1939), pp. 120-34.

Durston, Chris,   'Let Ireland be quiet: opposition in England to
the Cromwellian conquest of Ireland,' *History
Workshop Journal*, No. 21, Spring, (1986).

Freer, Alan,   'Until the age of Nelson, Robert Blake was
England's Greatest Admiral,' *Military History*,
April, (2006).

Gardiner, S.R.,   'The transportation to Connaught,' *English Historical Review,* 14, (1899).

Hardacre, P.H.,   'Writings on Oliver Cromwell since 1929,' *The Journal of Modern History*, Vol. XXXIII, No. 1 (1961), pp. 1-14.

Hazlett, Hugh,   'The financing of the British armies in Ireland, 1641-9,' *Irish Historical Studies*, No. 1, March, (1938).

Lindley, Keith,   'The impact of the 1641 rebellion upon England and Wales 1641-5,' *Irish Historical Studies*, Vol., XVIII, No. 70, September, (1972).

Morrill, John,   'Textualising and contextualising Cromwell,' *The Historical Journal*, September, Vol. 33, No. 3, (1990), pp. 629-639.

Murray, R.H.,   'Cromwell at Drogheda - a reply to J.B. Williams' *The Nineteenth Century*, Vol. LXXII, December, (1912).

Ohlmeyer, Jane, H, 'The 'Antrim Plot' of 1641-A Myth?' *The Historical Journal*, September, Vol. 35, No. 4, (1992), pp. 905-919.

Ohlmeyer, Jane, H 'The Marquis of Antrim: A Stuart turn kilt?' *History Today*, March, (1993), pp. 13-18.

Ohlmeyer, Jane, H, 'The wars of the three kingdoms,' *History Today*, Vol. 48, November, (1998), pp. 16-29.

Pennington, D.H.,   'Cromwell and the historians,' *History Today*, Vol. 8, No. 9, September, (1958), pp. 598-605.

Russell, Conrad,   'The British background to the Irish Rebellion of 1641,' *Historical Research*, No. 61, (1988).

Simms, J.G.,   'Cromwell's siege of Waterford 1649,' *The Irish Sword*, 4, (1959-60).

Simms, J.G.,   'Cromwell at Drogheda 1649,' *The Irish Sword*, XI, (1973-1974).

Taylor, Barry M.,   'Siege and slaughter at Drogheda,' *Military History*, Vol. 16, Issue 4, (1999), p. 62.

Williams, J.B.,	'Fresh Light on Cromwell at Drogheda,' *The Nineteenth Century*, Vol. LXXII, September, (1912).
Williams, J.B.,	'Cromwell's massacre at Wexford,' *Irish Ecclesiastical Record*, Series 5, Vol. l, June, (1913).
Williams, J.B.,	'The truth concerning the massacre at Drogheda' *Dublin Review*, Vol. CXLVI.

Collection of Essays

Barnard, Toby,	'Irish images of Cromwell', in R.C. Richardson (ed.), *Images of Oliver Cromwell: Essays for and by Roger Howell, Jnr.*, Manchester University Press, Manchester, (1993).
Capp, Bernard,	'Naval operations,' in John Kenyon and Jane

H. Ohlmeyer, (eds.), *The Civil Wars, A Military History of England, Scotland and Ireland 1638-1660,* Oxford, (1998).

Corish, Patrick, J., 'The Cromwellian Conquest 1649-53,' in T.W. Moody, F.X. Martin and F.J Byrne, (eds.), *History of Ireland, III, Early Modern Ireland 1534-1691*, Chapter XIII, Oxford, (1976).

Corish, Patrick, J., 'The Cromwellian Regime 1650-1660,' in T.W. Moody, F.X. Martin & F.J. Byrne, (eds.), *History of Ireland, III, Early Modern Ireland 1534-1691*, Oxford University Press, Oxford, (1976).

Edwards, Peter, 'Logistics and supply,' in John Kenyon and Jane Ohlmeyer, (eds.), *The Civil Wars, A Military History of England, Scotland and Ireland 1638-1660*, Oxford, (1998).

Furgol, Edward, 'The civil wars in Scotland,' in John Kenyon and Jane Ohlmeyer, (eds.), *The Civil Wars, A Military History of England, Scotland and Ireland 1638-1660,* Oxford, (1998).

Gentles, Ian,   'The civil wars in England,' in John Kenyon
and Jane Ohlmeyer, (eds.), *The Civil Wars, A
Military History of England, Scotland and
Ireland 1638-1660,* Oxford, (1998).

Gillespie, Raymond, 'The Irish economy at War, 1641-1652,' in
Jane. H. Ohlmeyer, (ed.), *Ireland from
Independence to Occupation 1641-1660,*
Cambridge University Press, Cambridge,
(1995).

Howell, Roger, Jnr, 'Images of Oliver Cromwell,' R.C. Richardson,
(ed.), *Images of Oliver Cromwell: Essays for
and by Roger Howell, Jnr.,* Manchester
University Press, Manchester, (1993).

Howell, Roger, Jnr, 'That imp of Satan,' the Restoration image of
Cromwell,' in R.C. Richardson, (ed.), *Images
of Oliver Cromwell: Essays for and by
Roger Howell, Jnr.* Manchester University
Press, Manchester, (1993).

Howell, Roger, Jnr, 'Cromwell the English Revolution and Political
Symbolism in Eighteenth century England,' in
R.C. Richardson (ed*.), Images of Oliver
Cromwell: Essays for and by Roger Howell,
Jnr.,* Manchester University Press,
Manchester, (1993).

Howell, Roger, Jnr, 'Who needs another Cromwell? The nineteenth
century image of Oliver Cromwell,' in R.C.
Richardson, (ed.), *Images of Oliver Cromwell:
Essays for and by Roger Howell, Jnr.,*
Manchester University Press, Manchester,
(1993).

Howell, Roger Jnr, 'Cromwell and his Parliaments: the Trevor
Roper Thesis revisited,' in R.C. Richardson,
(ed.), *Images of Oliver Cromwell: Essays for
and by Roger Howell, Jnr.,* Manchester
University Press, Manchester, (1993).

Howell, Roger Jnr, 'Cromwell's personality: the problems and
promises of a pyschohistorical approach,' in

R.C. Richardson, (ed.), *Images of Oliver Cromwell: Essays for and by Roger Howell, Jnr.*, Manchester University Press, Manchester, (1993).

Hutton, Ronald   'Sieges and Fortifications,' in John Kenyon and Jane and Reeves, Wylie, Ohlmeyer, (eds.), *The Civil Wars, A Military History of England, Scotland and Ireland 1638-1660*, Oxford, (1998).

Kenyon, John and   'The background to the civil wars in the Stuart
Ohlmeyer, Jane, H.,   Kingdoms,' in John Kenyon and Jane H. Ohlmeyer, (eds.), *The Civil Wars, A Military History of England, Scotland and Ireland 1638-1660*, Oxford, (1998).

Karsten, Peter,   'Cromwell in America,' in R.C. Richardson, (ed.), *Images of Cromwell: Essays for and by Roger Howell, Jnr.*, Manchester University Press, Manchester, (1993).

Lamont, William,   'Oliver Cromwell and English Calvinism,' in Peter Gaunt, (ed.), *Cromwell 400*, Essex, (1999).

Loeber, Rolf and   The military revolution in seventeen century
Parker, Geoffrey,   Ireland,' in Jane H, Ohlmeyer, (ed.), *Ireland from Independence to Occupation 1641-1660*, Cambridge University Press, (1995).

McKenny, Kevin,   'The seventeenth-century land settlement in Ireland: towards a statistical interpretation,' in Jane H. Ohlmeyer, (ed.), *Ireland from Independence to Occupation 1641-1660*, Cambridge University Press, Cambridge, (1995).

Ohlmeyer, Jane, H.,   'The wars of religion, 1603-1660,' in Thomas Bartlett and Keith Jeffrey, (eds.), *A Military History of Ireland*, Cambridge University Press, Cambridge, (1996).

205

Richardson, R.C., 'Cromwell and the inter-war European dictators,' in R.C. Richardson, (ed.), *Images of Cromwell: Essays for and by Roger Howell, Jnr.*, Manchester University Press, Manchester, (1993).

Roots, Ivan, 'Carlyle's Cromwell,' in R.C. Richardson, (ed.), *Images of Cromwell: Essays for and by Roger Howell, Jnr.,* Manchester University Press, Manchester, (1993).

Speck, W.A., 'Cromwell and the Glorious Revolution,' in R.C. Richardson, (ed.), *Images of Cromwell: Essays for and by Roger Howell, Jn*r., Manchester University Press, Manchester, (1993).

Stevenson, David, 'Cromwell, Scotland and Ireland,' in John Morrill, (ed.), *Oliver Cromwell and the English Revolution*, New York, (1990).

Wheeler, Scott, 'Four armies in Ireland,' in Jane H. Ohlmeyer, (ed.), *Ireland from Independence to Occupation 1641-1660*, Cambridge University Press, Cambridge, (1995).

Woolrych, Austin, 'Cromwell as a Soldier,' in John Morrill, (ed.), *Oliver Cromwell and the English Revolution*, New York, (1990).

Newspapers

The Times, 'Should Cromwell Have a Statue,' Friday, 29th August, (1845), p. 5.

The Times, 'Cromwell's Statue,' Wednesday, 3rd September, (1845), p. 5.

The Times, 'Letter,' Friday, 5th September, (1845), p. 8.

The Times, 'Should Cromwell Have a Statue,' Tuesday, 9th September, (1845), p. 8.

The Times, 'Cromwell in Ireland,' 10th September, (1888), p. 3.

The Times, 'Cromwell in Ireland,' 19th September, (1888), p. 6.
The Times, 'Cromwell in Ireland,' 22nd September, (1888), p. 10.
The Times, 'Tercentenary of Cromwell's Birth,' 17th April, (1899), p. 6.
The Times, 'Tercentenary of Oliver Cromwell,' 27th April, (1899), p. 7.
The Times, 'The Cromwell Tercentenary,' 28th April, (1899), p. 8.
The Times, 'Sir William Butler on Cromwell,' 26th March, (1902), p. 4.

Theses

Dunn, Kerrie, 'Cromwell: The Soldier – An Assessment of his strategy and Tactics,' (Unpublished B.A. Hons. Thesis), University of New England, NSW, Australia, (1980).

Lindley, Keith, J., 'The Part Played by the Catholics in the English Civil War,' (Unpublished Ph.D. Thesis), University of Manchester, (1968).

McKenny, Kevin, 'A Seventeenth-century "real estate company." The 1649 Officers and the Irish Land Settlements, 1641-1681,' (Unpublished M.A. Thesis), National University of Ireland, Maynooth, (1989).

Mc Keiver, Philip, G., 'Cromwell in Ireland : Myths and Reality,' (Unpublished M.A. Hons Thesis), University of New England, NSW, Australia, (2004).

George Monck, 1st Duke of Albermarle
(National Portrait Gallery)

Select Bibliography

The principal, and most reliable sources, for a history of biography of Cromwell; are his own writings and speeches. The first published collection was by Thomas Carlyle, *The Letters and Speeches of Oliver Cromwell* (2, Vols., London, 1845). A second edition was to appear in 1846. However the best and most reliable copy, particularly regarding Cromwell in Ireland, is *Oliver Cromwell's Letters and Speeches with Elucidations,* by Carlyle 2nd Revised edition, (3 Vols, in one), London, (1846). This edition, contains; a large number of additional letters, and many notes and observations, not included in the First Edition and, it is designated by Carlyle as 'The Final One.' Although a further copy appeared in 1849. A copy of Carlyle's work, was also edited by S.C. Lomas and published in three volumes in 1904. Whilst Mrs. Lomas' copy, is well laid out and more easily read it is selective. As a result, the reader, cannot maintain a chronology of Cromwell's Irish campaign using this source. W.C. Abbott accumulated a much larger set, *The Writings and Speeches of Oliver Cromwell,* (4 Vols., Cambridge, Mass, (1937-47). Many of the letters transcribed by Carlyle, are reproduced in this work. However, it contains many other documents about, rather than by Cromwell, and with Abbott's own commentary, sympathetic to the Royalist cause. The most comprehensive, and reliable collection of Cromwell's state speeches, is one that was compiled by C.L. Stainer, (ed.), *Speeches of Oliver Cromwell, 1644-58,* Oxford, (1901). Ivan Roots (ed.), *Speeches of Oliver Cromwell,* London, (1989), also draws on Stainer, reproducing his major speeches.

'The general rule,' wrote Carlyle, about biographies of Cromwell, is that 'you can find as many inaccuracies as you like; dig where you please, water will come'. That rule, seems to apply to many of the biographies since Carlyle's day. Nevertheless, despite their age, S.R. Gardiner, *Oliver Cromwell*, London, (1899) and T.S. Baldock, *Cromwell as a Soldier*, London, (1899), are still valuable. In the twentieth century C. Firth, *Oliver Cromwell and the Rule of the Puritans in England*, London, (1900), was followed by J. Morley, *Oliver Cromwell*, London (1900), F. Harrison *Oliver Cromwell*, London, (1922), C.V. Wedgewood, *Oliver Cromwell*, London, (1939), are masterpieces of compression. J. Buchan, *Oliver Cromwell*, London (1934), H. Belloc, *Cromwell*, London, (1936), are irredeemably biased. Whilst R.S. Paul, *The Lord Protector, Religion and Politics in the Life of Oliver Cromwell* London, (1955) is strong on Cromwell's religious thought. Followed by M. Ashley, *The Greatness of Oliver Cromwell*, London, (1957), C. Hill, *God's Englishman*, Harmondsworth, (1970). In addition M. Ashley, *Oliver Cromwell and His World*, London, (1972) is well illustrated. I. Roots, *Cromwell – A Profile* contains a collection of now dated essays on Cromwell and his policies. This is followed by A. Fraser, *Cromwell – Our Chief of Men,* probably one of the best known biographies outside academic circles. J. Gillingham, *Cromwell – Portrait of a Soldier*, London, (1976), as the title suggests, focuses on Cromwell's military career. R. Howell, *Cromwell*, Boston, (1977), P. Gregg *Oliver Cromwell*, London, (1988), more or less follow the traditional approach. More recent studies include J. Morrill, (ed.), *Oliver Cromwell and the English Revolution*, Harlow, (1990), is good to gain an understanding of various aspects of Cromwell, his life and policies, B. Coward, *Oliver Cromwell*, Harlow, (1991), is a study of Cromwell, as a political figure, and the historical problems associated with his exercise of power. R.C. Richardson, (ed.), *Images of Oliver Cromwell: Essays for and by Roger Howell, Jnr.,* Manchester, (1993), is a collection of essays written by, and for, the late Roger Howell. At the time of his death, Howell was close to completing a project on the historiography of Cromwell and the way his reputation has been made, and re-made, in succeeding generations. This concise volume contains essays by Howell himself, who writes on Cromwell's reputation in the seventeenth, eighteenth and nineteenth centuries. W. Speck writes on *Cromwell and the Glorious Revolution*, Ivan Roots discusses *Carlyle's Cromwell,*

R.C. Richardson, *Cromwell in America*, and finally T.C. Barnard, *Irish Images of Cromwell*, challenges the mythologies in which Cromwell has been portrayed by Irish historians. P. Gaunt, *Oliver Cromwell*, Oxford, (1996), is another masterpiece of compression, followed by J.C. Davis, *Oliver Cromwell*, (Reputations Series), London, (2001). The vast majority of the biographies, devote at least one chapter to Cromwell in Ireland. Blair Worden, in *Roundhead Reputations - The English Civil Wars and The Passions of Posterity*, London, (2001), tells the Parliamentarian side of the story. He devotes three chapters to Cromwell, namely, Oliver Cromwell: from Villain to Hero, Victorian Cromwell, and Carlyle's Cromwell.

Cromwell's Irish Campaign

The best general introduction to Cromwell's campaigns in Ireland is to be found in S.R. Gardiner, *History of the Commonwealth and Protectorate 1649-1656*, 4 Vols., London, (1903), completed after Gardiner's death by C.H. Firth. More recent studies include Ian Gentles, *The New Model Army in England, Ireland and Scotland 1645-1653*, Oxford, (1992). Tom Reilly, *Cromwell, An Honourable Enemy*, Brandon, (1998), is a revisionist re-examination of Cromwell's Irish campaign of 1649-1650, as seen from an Irish perspective. James Scott Wheeler, *Cromwell in Ireland*, New York, (1999), takes the traditional approach to Cromwell. Most recently, Keith Roberts, in *Cromwell's War Machine, The New Model Army 1645-1660*, Barnsley, (2005), includes a brief account of Cromwell's Irish Campaign.

The Civil War In Ireland

Many of the primary documents relating to the Irish Civil War, have been reprinted in J.T. Gilbert (ed.), *A Contemporary History of Affairs in Ireland (1641-1652), containing the narrative entitled An Amphorismal discovery of treasonable faction,'*

3 Vols., Irish Archaeological and Celtic Society, Dublin, (1879-1880); and Robert Dunlop, (ed), *Ireland under the Commonwealth: being, a selection of documents relating to the government of Ireland, 1651-9* (2 Vols, Manchester 1913), C.H. Firth and R.S. Rait, (ed), *Acts and ordinances of the Interregnum, 1642-1660*, (3 Vols. London 1911), For a general background, and integrated account of the, 'Wars of the Three Kingdoms,' which also focus on the Civil War in Ireland, refer to S.R. Gardiner, *History of the Great Civil War, 1642-1649*, 4 Vols. London, (1888), reprinted (1987), and S.R. Gardiner, *History of the Commonwealth and Protectorate, 1649-1660*, (4. Vols. 1903), Conrad Russell, *The Fall of the British Monarchies,* Oxford, (1991), M. Bennett, *The Civil Wars in Britain and Ireland, 1638-1651,* Oxford, (1997); John Kenyon and Jane Ohlmeyer (ed.). *The Civil Wars – A Military History of England, Scotland, and Ireland, 1638-1660*, Oxford, (1998), J.R. Young, (ed.), *Celtic Dimensions of the British Civil Wars,* Edinburgh, (1997), In addition, the close interconnections, between the Three Stuart Kingdoms, are discussed in J.H. Ohlmeyer, *Civil War, and Restoration, in Three Stuart Kingdoms: The Career of Randal MacDonnell, Marquis of Antrim, 1609-1683*, Cambridge, (1993). D. Stevenson, *Scottish Covenanters and Irish Confederates: Scottish-Irish Relations in the Mid-seventeenth Century*, Belfast, (1981). However, all those seeking to deepen their understanding, of this period in Irish history, will need to consult the collection of essays, in J.H. Ohlmeyer (ed.), *Ireland from Independence to Occupation 1641-1660*, Cambridge, (1995), which include J.H. Ohlmeyer, Introduction, 'A failed revolution?'; N. Canny, 'What really happened in Ireland in 1641?' covers aspects, of the rising of that year, S. Wheeler; 'Four armies in Ireland,' the rival armies, fighting in Ireland, during the 1640's; R. Loeber and G. Parker, 'The military revolution in seventeenth century Ireland'; J.H. Ohlmeyer, 'Ireland independent: confederate foreign policy and international relations, during the mid-seventeenth century.' M. O'Riordan, 'Political' poems, in the mid-seventeenth century crisis.' J. Adamson, 'Strafford,s ghost: the British context of Viscount Lisle's lieutenancy of Ireland.' R. Gillespie, 'The British

economy at war, 1641-1652.' K. McKenny, 'The seventeenth century land settlement in Ireland: towards a statistical interpretation,' in which, he publishes the results of his computerised based research, into changing land ownership in Ireland, as a result, of the so called Cromwellian land settlements. His detailed work on West Ulster, reveals that, dispossession and survival, was not, as previously believed, solely determined by ethnicity; and religion, but was also affected, by 'the survival strategies and complex politicking,' by individual land owners. P. Kilroy, 'Radical religion in Ireland, 1641-1660,' discusses the spread of radical Protestantism in Ireland. A. Clarke, '1659, The Road to Restoration,' T.C. Barnard's conclusion: 'Settling and unsettling Ireland: the Cromwellian and Williamite revolutions.' Whilst, T.C. Barnard's, *Cromwellian Ireland, English Government and Reform in Ireland,* Oxford, (1975), demonstrates, that Cromwellian policy in Ireland, was much more, than a chronicle of barbarism.

Lieutenant General Fleetwood
(National Portrait Gallery)

INDEX

Index